Geography of Extreme Environments

DESERTS

POLAR REGIONS

THE TROPICS

Extreme Climates

Desert

Ice Covered

Tundra

Wet tropics

Deserts

Charles F. Gritzner
South Dakota State University

CHELSEA HOUSE
PUBLISHERS
An imprint of Infobase Publishing

This book is dedicated to the memory of the author's parents,
Charles F. and Laura E. Gritzner, who instilled in their children
a love of and understanding of the desert lands and peoples.

FRONTIS The Polar Regions, Wet Tropics, and Deserts are highlighted on this map of the world's extreme climates.

Deserts

Copyright © 2007 by Infobase Publishing

Chelsea House
An imprint of Infobase Publishing
132 West 31st Street
New York, NY 10001

Library of Congress Cataloging-in-Publication Data

Gritzner, Charles F.
  Deserts / Charles F. Gritzner.
      p. cm. — (Geography of extreme environments)
  Includes bibliographical references and index.
  ISBN 0-7910-9234-8 (hardcover)
1. Deserts—Juvenile literature. I. Title. II. Series
  GB612.G76 2006
  910.915'4—dc22   2006025584

Chelsea House books are available at special discounts when purchased in bulk quantities for businesses, associations, institutions, or sales promotions. Please call our Special Sales Department in New York at (212) 967-8800 or (800) 322-8755.

You can find Chelsea House on the World Wide Web at http://www.chelseahouse.com

Cover design by Ben Peterson
Series design by Keith Trego

Printed in the United States of America

Bang KT 10 9 8 7 6 5 4 3 2 1

This book is printed on acid-free paper.

All links and Web addresses were checked and verified to be correct at the time of publication. Because of the dynamic nature of the Web, some addresses and links may have changed since publication and may no longer be valid.

Contents

Introducing the Desert Realm

About 20 percent of Earth's surface is classified as "desert." When you think of these arid lands, what images come to mind? Most typically, perhaps, one might see this: a string of camels trudging their way across an endless sea of sand dunes. The caravan's small group of pastoral nomads constantly gaze toward the distant horizon for any sign of a break in the monotonous landscape. Suddenly, an excited cry rings out! After days of plodding across the bleak, barren, almost lifeless terrain, the travelers see a speck of green looming far ahead. Could it be a mirage, one of nature's cruel tricks that is common to desert lands? The weary travelers pick up their pace, beckoned by the sight of an oasis. There, they know that fresh, life-giving water will quench the thirst of man and beast alike.

On reaching the oasis, the featureless desert landscape changes abruptly. Towering date palms, their fronds swaying gently in the breeze, cast shadows that create a welcome mat of cooling shade. A bright carpet of green spreads across the valley, where rich soil and irrigation combine to support fields of grains and other crops. Buildings made of sun-dried mud bricks seem to blend right into the very earth from which they were built.

Throughout the rain-starved region, life is scant, limited to those few areas such as this oasis, where moisture is available. Frequent blinding dust storms pose an omnipresent threat to humans and animals alike. Venomous insects and deadly reptiles abound, and a lack of water and scorching temperatures constantly test the limits of human endurance. Few people are able to manage a living in this harsh natural setting. Those who do call the desert home are somehow able to survive despite nature's tiny yield and frequent wrath. Their way of life is largely molded by nature, which allows few comforts, luxuries, or material possessions. Their worldview is largely limited to the desert lands they call home. In the desert, after all, nature is the dominant force, one that overwhelms all else.

Does most, if not all, of the foregoing image fit your stereotype of desert lands and peoples? If it does, you are not alone! The features and conditions described in the brief introduction do, of course, exist in some locations. But for the most part, they are mere fantasy—little more than mythical exaggerations imprinted in our minds by Hollywood, television, popular literature, and other sources. Geographers refer to these perceptions as "mental maps." Have you ever visited a new location and found it to be much different than you had imagined? Our mental images are often far removed from the geographic reality of the places they portray. And generally speaking, as environments become increasingly extreme in their conditions—such as polar, wet tropical, or desert lands—the more distorted will be our mental maps of these regions.

Certainly this is true of desert regions—those areas of Earth's surface in which moisture is insufficient to support abundant plant and animal life under natural conditions. Throughout this book, an attempt is made to separate fact from fiction. Deserts are discussed in terms of their varied conditions, distinctive landscapes, and diverse patterns of human adaptation and ways of living. Viewed geographically, deserts may assume a much more positive image as you gain a better understanding of this fascinating realm.

A HOME IN THE DESERT

Humans have inhabited the desert environment for much of history—perhaps a million or more years. As we began the long journey northward from our ancestral homeland, believed by scientists to have been equatorial eastern Africa, our ancient ancestors eventually wandered into desert lands. Perhaps their travels followed the long natural pathway formed by the vast oasis of the Nile River. Whether it was this or some other route that was followed, it is important to realize that culture (learned human behavior) is what helped humans adapt to their changing conditions. Early human culture included expanding knowledge, a better arsenal of tools (including control of fire), and improved skills; all of this made possible an expansion of the human habitat. Through time, humans were finally able to slip from the bonds of nature's grip and move into lands that were environmentally more challenging.

In reality, deserts have long been one of Earth's most productive environments. Much early plant and animal domestication occurred in desert regions ranging from the Nile Valley to the Middle East and across the Atlantic in coastal Peru. These developments contributed to the growth of many great early civilizations—including those that emerged in the Middle East and ultimately became "Western civilization." The desert region of the American Southwest was home to a number of early high cultures. They include the Pueblo peoples and central Arizona's Hohokam Indians, who practiced what at the time may have been the world's most advanced form of irrigation. Rather than being "primitive" and "captives of the environment," some desert peoples were for thousands of years among the world's most advanced populations. Through time, they learned many different ways to live comfortably and

With approximately 75 million residents, Egypt is one of the most populated countries within the desert region. Pictured here is the Nile River, which flows through downtown Cairo—the world's sixteenth-largest city.

productively in lands that may seem barren to many observers.

Although some desert regions support very low populations, arid lands are also home to some of the world's densest and most rapidly growing populations. Egypt, for example, has a population of roughly 75 million people, nearly all of whom are squeezed into the narrow Nile Valley. The valley is about the size of South Carolina, which has a population of just over 4 million.

Desert populations are growing elsewhere in the world, too. During the past half century, the fastest growing section of the United States has been the desert Southwest. The population of Arizona has more than tripled since 1970 and Phoenix, the state's capital city, has experienced explosive growth, nearly 3,000 percent since 1950. Today, the fastest-growing city and state in the United States are also the driest: Las Vegas and Nevada, respectively. In fact, the population of Las Vegas has more than doubled since 1990.

People hold many different perceptions of deserts. Those who are unfamiliar with this extreme environment often believe in images of desert lands and inhabitants that are exaggerated or simply incorrect. Other ideas are valid (for instance, yes, many deserts are extremely hot and dry); yet the great diversity of physical landscapes and cultures living in arid environments makes it very difficult to generalize about the region. The life of the Aborigines in Australia's remote desert outback region differs vastly from that enjoyed by people living in modern cities with booming populations, such as Phoenix, Las Vegas, or other U.S. cities in the desert Southwest. Throughout this book, attention is focused on explaining contrasting conditions such as these, whether natural or human in nature.

Location, distribution, pattern, and interaction are key concepts that geographers use to explain variations, whether local or global in scale. Answers to geographical questions can often be found in the location and conditions of a place's natural environment. Or, in other instances, explanations are found in the culture (way of life) and history of the places and their human inhabitants. In this geographical study of deserts, let us begin by defining this extreme environment. As you will see, it is not as easy a task as one might think.

WHAT IS A DESERT?

How would *you* define a desert? Would it surprise you to know that scientists do not agree on a definition? Everyone agrees that deserts are defined by their low amounts of precipitation. Scant moisture, in turn, contributes to other geographic elements, such as vegetation, animal life habitat, soils, landforms, and water features. In this book, deserts are limited to those areas of the world that experience most if not all of the following conditions:

1. **Regions that receive less than 10 inches (25 centimeters) of precipitation annually.** Whereas most deserts receive less than 10 inches of precipitation each year, there are several problems associated with the use of this cut-off. Most deserts, of course, receive considerably less moisture each year. But so, too, do many of the world's polar lands.

   In fact, much of the areas of Greenland and Antarctica are among the driest places in the world—although their cover of glacial ice may reach several miles in depth. These "polar deserts" are not discussed in this book. (The interested reader is referred to *Polar Regions*, a companion to this book in the Chelsea House series Geography of Extreme Environments.)

2. **Water loss through evaporation exceeds moisture gained by precipitation.** By this definition, more moisture is lost than is gained, leaving a deficit. Evaporation, of course, requires heat—and no place else on Earth can match the tropical and subtropical deserts for their scorching temperature extremes. This definition also helps to explain why polar lands, despite very low amounts of precipitation, really do not qualify as deserts. Because of their relatively low temperatures year-round, very little surface moisture is lost through evaporation. In some desert lands, though, the moisture deficit amounts to several hundred inches.

3. **Water bodies, with few exceptions, are scarce.** In desert lands, most basins do not fill to the point that they overflow with water. After periods of precipitation, a lake may form briefly, only to vanish as conditions dry out, leaving a residue of salt and other minerals accumulated on the ground. Most streams, too, are "here today, gone tomorrow." After a period of rainfall, a normally dry streambed can become a rushing torrent. As the storm passes, however, the flow vanishes just as rapidly as it appeared. One major exception is found in "exotic streams." These rivers

have their sources, or headwaters, in humid lands, making it possible for them to flow through a desert landscape throughout the year. These rivers, or oases, rank among the world's oldest and most significant centers of civilization. The Tigris, Euphrates, Nile, and Indus rivers are important Old World examples.

4. **Landforms clearly show the impact of arid land weathering and erosion.** As you will learn in a subsequent chapter, desert landforms are unique. Surprisingly, perhaps, the work of moving water is the chief agent involved in sculpting arid land features.

5. **Plant life is scant in response to the lack of available moisture.** Plants are few, generally small, and widely scattered. In order to survive under conditions of aridity, these *xerophytes* (drought-resistant plants) have developed a variety of survival mechanisms. Agricultural crops cannot be grown without irrigation. Nomads, who travel the deserts with their flocks of animals, including camels, depend upon the availability of drought-resistant plants upon which their animals can graze.

6. **Humans have culturally adapted to conditions of aridity.** Through time, different cultures have adapted in many different ways to desert conditions.

Cultural ecology—how people culturally adapt to, use, and change the lands in which they live—has long been a major focus of geographic research. Understanding these critical relationships is one of the geographer's most important tasks. In this context, it is essential that the reader recognize that it is *culture*, rather than the physical environment, that is the active agent in establishing such patterns of living. In terms of day-to-day living, adaptations are evident in such features or conditions as housing materials and design, clothing, means of obtaining and storing water, diet, and daily schedule of activities.

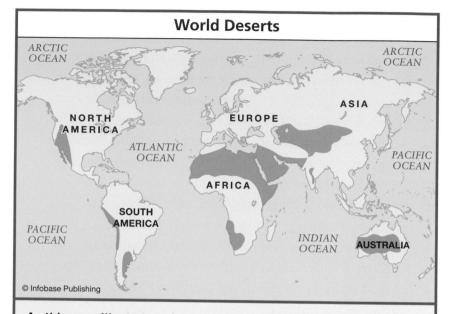

World Deserts

As this map illustrates, desert regions are located on five of the earth's seven continents. The continent of Africa contains the world's largest desert, the Sahara, which covers an area of more than 3.5 million square miles (9 million square kilometers).

THE WORLD'S DESERT LANDS

Where are the lands that, according to the above criteria, constitute the world's deserts and cover about 20 percent of Earth's surface? Surprisingly, perhaps, they are found on all continents except Europe and Antarctica. Most desert land lies in a subtropical belt extending between 20 and 30 degrees latitude on both sides of the equator. Under certain conditions, deserts also form outside of this general boundary.

Each desert is further divided into many subregions. By continent, they include:

- North America: Colorado-Sonara; Great Basin; Mohave; Chihuahuan
- South America: Peru-Atacama (world's driest desert); Patagonian

- Africa: Sahara (world's largest desert), also with regional names such as Egypt's Nubian Desert; Kalahari (also known as the Namib Desert, along the Atlantic coast)
- Asia: Southwest Asia (including the Arabian, Dasht-E-Kavir, Thar, and Great Indian deserts); Central Asia (Gobi, Taklamakan, Ordos, Kara Kum, and Kyzyl Kum)
- Australia: Australian (Gibson, Great Sandy, Great Victoria, and Simpson deserts)

WHY ARE DESERT LANDS IMPORTANT?

To geographers, all places are important simply because they are there. About places and their conditions, geographers also generally ask, "*What* is *where, why there*, and *why care*?" This is a definition that you will want to keep in mind as you learn about the world's desert lands and peoples. The "what," of course, refers to deserts and their varied physical and cultural features and conditions. Answering the "why there" and "why care" questions is the subject to which most of this book is devoted.

Historically, arid lands have been the cradles of many highly developed cultures, including those that contributed to our own Western civilization. Today, a substantial portion of the world's petroleum comes from desert lands in Southwest Asia. American and allied military forces, of course, are actively involved in this turbulent region that is of vital importance to the global community. Between the distant past and today, we find many traits that we consider our own, but are traced to desert origins. They include the idea of monotheism (one God) that dominates Western religions, our use of Arabic numerals (can you imagine doing long division using Roman numerals?), and many of our agricultural plants.

VISITING THE WORLD'S DESERTS

In the pages of this book, you will visit the world's deserts and learn about the conditions that make desert lands so unique. Our journey will begin with the study of weather and climate, those conditions that in one way or another influence nearly every other geographic condition within deserts. Climate, of course, is the primary influence on ecosystems. We will then move on to other aspects of the physical environment. In desert lands, the ecosystem is characterized by the relative lack of natural vegetation. Limited plant life, in turn, contributes to meager animal habitats, resulting in limited diversity among animal life, too. Landforms, soils, and ample water resources also show the marked effects of aridity.

After visiting the natural wonders of desert lands, we will wander through the corridors of time, visiting ancient peoples and civilizations. You will be surprised at how advanced many of these civilizations were, even though they flourished thousands of years ago. Here and there, we will also meet very traditional present-day cultures and briefly glimpse at the world through the eyes of their people. Today, of course, so many unique cultures call the desert home that it is impossible to speak of "desert people" in any meaningful way.

European influences on desert peoples are relatively recent. Earliest contact extends back only about 500 years, and much more recently in some areas. European people simply were not accustomed to what they perceived to be very harsh desert conditions; hence, they avoided arid lands. When contact did occur between European peoples and desert dwellers, it often led to conflict. Problems often arose from marked differences in such traits as values, religious beliefs, patterns of social behavior, levels of technology, and economic interests. By and large, the European influences have always revolved around economic exploitation, particularly in activities that involve extracting natural resources from the land.

Following this brief glimpse into the region's historical geography, our attention will turn to contemporary patterns. We will look in depth at the most important aspects of the region's cultural patterns, including its social, economic, and political geography. Finally, we will take a brief tour of the world's various deserts and peek into the region's future.

Are you ready for an exciting journey? If so, you had better fill several canteens, pack away some sunscreen, and put on some comfortable clothing and shoes. And don't forget your sunglasses! Let's begin your geographical trip to and through the extreme environment of deserts.

2

Weather and Climate of Arid Lands

More than a century ago, the following statement of unknown origin was written about the desert region of the southwestern United States: "The land is not worth a cent . . . [it] is a region of . . . wild beasts, shifting sands, whirlwinds of dust, cactus and prairie dogs." The author was referring to the desert near present-day Phoenix, Arizona, one of the fastest-growing areas of the United States during the past 50 years. Our perceptions—the way we feel about places—change through time. Certainly this is true of arid lands. Aridity, of course, is the main condition that is common to all desert lands. It has a profound impact on all other elements of the physical environment. It also provides challenges to which cultures must adapt if they are to survive and thrive. Water, of course, is the key to life in deserts. In this chapter, you will learn about the conditions of weather (day to day) and climate (long-term average) that make arid lands unique.

In Chapter 1, you were introduced to a number of stereotypical images of arid lands. Myths such as these convey false impressions of deserts (and many of Earth's other environments). Some common yet mistaken beliefs include: Rain has never fallen in some deserts; all deserts are scorching hot; when rain does fall in a desert, it is a downpour; dust storms are a major cause of accidental death in deserts; and the Sahara is the world's driest region. In this chapter, you will learn why each of these statements is false.

CHARACTERISTICS OF PRECIPITATION

As was stated previously, precipitation in arid lands is scant, less than 10 inches (25 centimeters) per year. As you have learned, however, this definition also includes several other regions, including much of the Arctic and Antarctic realms. Most scientists define a desert as a region in which a moisture deficit exists; that is, more moisture is lost by evaporation than is received through precipitation. In much of the world's tropical and midlatitude desert regions, temperatures are capable of evaporating several hundred inches of moisture annually. Reservoirs in tropical deserts can lose about three feet (one meter) of water a month through evaporation.

In addition to scarcity, several other conditions are typical of precipitation in arid lands. First, total amounts of annual precipitation may occur within a very short period of time—an hour, a day, or during several short storms spread over a period of several weeks. Months may pass without a cloud in the sky. Second, rainfall is very unreliable, making annual average precipitation figures all but meaningless. In Cairo, Egypt, for example, only about half of all years receive measurable rainfall. Several communities in northern Chile's Atacama Desert, the world's driest spot, average .01 inch (.03 centimeters) of rainfall per year. But they may go 15 to 20 years without a drop of rain! There is no place on Earth, however, that has never received a drop of precipitation.

Northern Chile's Atacama Desert, which stretches 600 to 700 miles (966 to 1,127 kilometers) north to south, is the world's driest place. The region's extreme aridity is caused by several factors, including the fact that the desert lies within a belt of high pressure and the Andes Mountains block precipitation.

A third condition, counter to widespread belief, is that rainfall in desert regions is not a torrential downpour when it does occur. In fact, no type of storm is peculiar to desert regions. The impression that deluges are common stems from the fact that small amounts of rainfall can cause tremendous damage in parched desert landscapes. In humid regions, vegetation slows runoff, and drainage systems are well developed and able to accommodate that runoff. In deserts, however, there is little plant life to slow down the flow of water that gathers rapidly in streams. Steep slopes and nonporous ground may further speed the flow of runoff. Stream channels, where they exist, may be clogged with sand and other debris. These conditions contribute to the number one environmental hazard in most desert regions: flash flooding.

Flash Floods

Flash floods can be awesome to witness and devastating in their effect. Imagine a streambed that is bone dry. The sun is shining overhead, but dark thunderstorm clouds on the horizon indicate that rain has been falling for some time over the distant mountains. Suddenly, you hear a thunderous roar. Looking up the dry streambed, you see a wall of water—as high as a rooftop—surging toward you! You barely make it to high ground as the growling, churning, angry floodwater begins to eat away the very ground upon which you were standing just moments ago. Downstream, everything in the way will feel the wrath of the floodwater and know its destructive force.

Even an inch (2.5 centimeters) of rain can result in flash flooding that causes massive destruction. Entire villages, farm fields, and roads can be swept away. Nearly a century ago, two inches of rain (five centimeters) in Cairo, Egypt, resulted in a flash flood that sent water surging as high as the windows of streetcars. In Tucson, Arizona, in 1961, about three-quarters of an inch (1.9 centimeters) of rain fell over nearby mountains. Flash flooding in the city resulted in three deaths in separate accidents as vehicles passing through normally dry streambeds were swept away when struck by a torrent of water. It may seem strange that drowning, not dust storms, is far and away the most common cause of environmentally related accidental death in desert regions. To avoid this hazard, travelers should never camp in a dry streambed and always be extremely cautious when crossing dry streambeds when rain is falling in the area.

Low Relative Humidity

As you might expect, the relative humidity (the amount of moisture in the atmosphere) is very low in most desert regions. When humidity is high, the processes by which nature creates precipitation are easily achieved. Humid regions generally receive ample precipitation. When humidity is low; however, it is much more difficult to "squeeze" the small amount of moisture from the atmosphere, and thus cause rain. Regions with low relative humidity, therefore, tend to be dry. Additionally, if humidity is low, the air can easily accept more moisture. This is why water evaporates so rapidly in arid lands. All air contains some moisture. In 1963, Tucson, Arizona, established a world record low of 1 percent relative humidity.

If you have never experienced extremely dry atmospheric conditions, some of the things that occur in the desert might come as a surprise. Can you imagine being in a temperature exceeding 100°F (40°C) and not noticing any sweating? You are, of course, sweating, but the moisture evaporates immediately and leaves your skin dry. Clothing hung on a line often dries in minutes. If you get out of water, as from a pool, your body will be completely dry in a very short period of time.

Dry air can serve another purpose. Put a drop of moisture on the back of your hand and blow on it for several seconds. Does it feel cool? Unless it is very humid, it should. Blowing caused some of the moisture to evaporate. As liquid turns to vapor, heat energy is lost, hence the cooling effect that you notice. This principle is used in some rather ingenious ways. For example, many homes in arid lands are cooled by "swamp coolers." The device is little more than a large box on a roof through which a fan pulls dry air in through wet pads. As moisture from the pads is evaporated, heat energy is lost and the air is cooled before it passes into the building. Years ago, when driving across the desert, one could not help but notice that nearly all vehicles had a "bag" of water hanging from the bumper. The bags would "sweat" and as the moisture evaporated from their surface, the water within would be cooled. And before air-conditioning was invented for vehicles, nearly all car seats had "cool cushions." These simple and inexpensive cushions allowed air to circulate between the body and car seat, thereby allowing perspiration to evaporate and the body to be cooled.

Aridity does more than just keep you dry and cool. Areas with low humidity are also ideal for the preservation of some ancient artifacts. For example, wood may remain preserved for centuries in desert regions. In fact, in the desert Southwest of the United States, dendrochronologists (scientists who calculate the ages of trees using growth rings) have been able to date archaeological sites back some 2,000 years using tree rings in preserved roof beams.

WHAT CAUSES ARIDITY?

When one first looks at a map of the world's deserts, their distribution may appear to be quite random. But look closely. Do you see any common patterns? For example, notice that many of them are located roughly between 20 and 30 degrees latitude north and south of the equator. And with a few exceptions, they are in the central and western, rather than eastern, margins of continents. There is also a relationship between deserts and the downwind side of high mountain ranges, as well as with coastal areas that are bordered by cold water currents. In order to understand the global distribution of desert lands, one must know the causes of aridity. With this in mind, let us spend a moment reviewing some basic principles of *meteorology*, the science of weather.

Let's begin with some basic physics: How is liquid turned into vapor (evaporation) and, conversely, how is vapor turned into liquid (precipitation)? Perhaps you already know the answers: Heat the liquid (such as by boiling water on a stove) to evaporate it, and cool the vapor to condense it. Air must be cooled to condense (the conversion from vapor to liquid) and turn into precipitation (any form of falling moisture). Conversely, the warmer air is, the more moisture it is able to hold; in this way, the air on a hot summer day can become thick with humidity without any rainfall occurring. Air itself circulates in the atmosphere: Rising air becomes cooler, and descending air warms. This warming effect on descending air is characteristic of the world's desert regions.

In nature, four primary conditions are responsible for arid conditions: high atmospheric pressure, the orographic rain shadow effect, cold water currents, and a combination of prevailing wind direction and distance from a source of moisture. Let's briefly consider each of these conditions.

First, we will discuss atmospheric pressure. Have you ever seen the face of a barometer? Rising pressure on a barometer is a signal that weather should improve, whereas a drop in pressure is a sign that conditions may deteriorate. High pressure usually is associated with clear, dry, calm weather. In equatorial areas, air rises into the upper atmosphere (thereby cooling and precipitating). Eventually, however, the rising air must descend, which it does in a broad band located roughly between 20 and 30 degrees north and south of the equator. As the air descends, it warms. In turn, its relative humidity is lowered and its ability to hold moisture increases. Aridity is the result.

This condition explains the deserts in the southwestern United States and in northwestern Mexico, the Sahara and Arabian deserts, the Kalahari Desert, and the arid lands of Australia.

Now, let's explore another cause of aridity: orographic rain shadow effect. In many locations throughout the world, very wet and very dry conditions occur in close proximity to one another on opposite sides of a mountain range. In fact, cacti and desert scrub grow just miles from the world's wettest spot on the mountainous Hawaiian island of Kauai. The term *orographic rain shadow effect* sounds complicated, but is fairly simple to explain. *Oro* refers to "mountain." When prevailing winds blow up a mountain slope, the air is cooled. Moisture condenses, and precipitation occurs on the side of the mountain from which the prevailing winds came. The air passes over the mountain barrier and descends and warms, creating what is called a "rain shadow." In the United States, prevailing winds blow across the Sierra Nevada and Cascade mountain ranges, creating rain shadow desert conditions on the eastern side of the ranges. In South America, winds blow over the southern Andes to create the arid conditions of Argentina's Patagonia region.

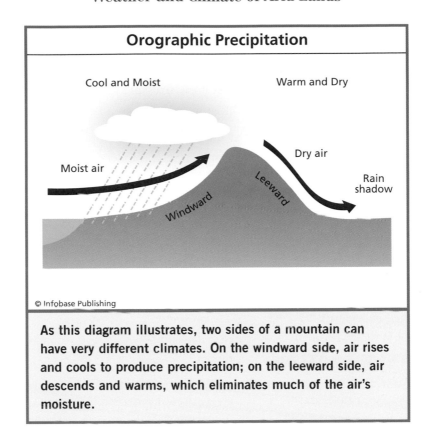

Orographic Precipitation

Cool and Moist

Warm and Dry

Moist air

Dry air

Rain shadow

Windward

Leeward

© Infobase Publishing

As this diagram illustrates, two sides of a mountain can have very different climates. On the windward side, air rises and cools to produce precipitation; on the leeward side, air descends and warms, which eliminates much of the air's moisture.

On the western edge of continents, where land faces cold-water ocean currents, desert conditions intensify. The driest portion of southwestern Africa's Kalahari Desert, for example, is the desert coast of Namibia that faces the cold Benguela Current. This occurs because wind warms as it blows across cold water and onto warmer land surfaces.

The direction of the wind and how far away a place is from a source of moisture (such as a lake or ocean) can also cause aridity. In some locations, winds have crossed thousands of miles of land and have been drained of their moisture before they arrive at a particular spot. This condition explains much of the aridity in Central Asia and in portions of the Sahara.

Finally, some deserts result from a combination of two or more of the factors discussed here. The driest location in the

United States, for example, is Death Valley, California, which during an average year receives about 2 inches (5 centimeters) of precipitation. Not only does the valley lie in a semipermanent belt of high pressure, but also it is on the rain shadow side of the Sierra Nevada Mountains.

Nowhere in the world is the effect of combined controls more evident than in the coastal deserts of Peru and Chile, along the Pacific Coast of South America. Here, the Atacama Desert is the world's driest by a considerable margin. It lies within the belt of high pressure; the coast lies in the rain shadow of the southeast trade winds as they descend over the Andes Mountains; the coast is hugged by the cold waters of the Peru (Humboldt) Current; and because of distance and wind direction, moisture-bearing winds from the Atlantic are blocked by the towering Andes.

TEMPERATURE

Scorching temperatures certainly come to mind when one thinks of deserts. Indeed, the world's highest temperatures have occurred in arid lands. In 1922, the temperature reached a sizzling 136°F (58°C) at Al Aziziyah, a city in northwestern Libya. California's Death Valley is close behind with a reading of 134°F (57°C). Not all deserts are hot, though. Some arid regions of interior Asia are cool because they lie at high elevations. The same is true of cooler mountain "islands" that bring relief to upland regions in the southwestern United States and other desert highland regions. In fact, it is not unusual for the nation's highest and lowest temperatures to be recorded within a short distance of one another in Arizona or California. South America's Atacama Desert, as well as others that border cold water currents, is quite cool. Lima, Peru, is located at 17 degrees south latitude, a position that one might expect to be quite tropical. Yet the city, a few miles inland from the cold Peru Current, experiences an annual temperature average of about 68°F (20°C). And although it is one of the

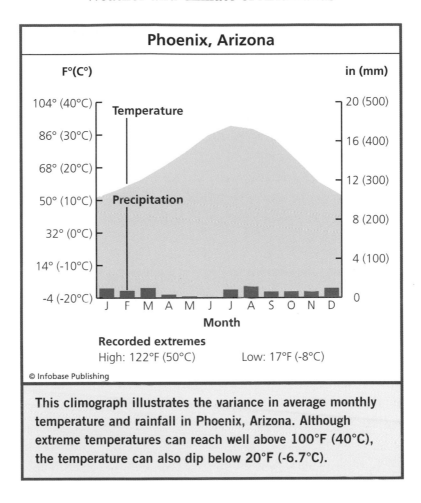

Phoenix, Arizona

| F°(C°) | | in (mm) |

Temperature

Precipitation

Month

Recorded extremes
High: 122°F (50°C)   Low: 17°F (-8°C)

© Infobase Publishing

This climograph illustrates the variance in average monthly temperature and rainfall in Phoenix, Arizona. Although extreme temperatures can reach well above 100°F (40°C), the temperature can also dip below 20°F (-6.7°C).

driest cities in the world, Lima's record high temperature is a "cool" 93°F (34°C).

Understanding Desert Temperatures

Desert temperature extremes are not only the world's highest, but they also feature some conditions that are unique. One might wonder, for example, why the world's hottest conditions are recorded in the low-middle latitudes rather than somewhere along the equator. The answer lies in atmospheric moisture and cloud cover. In the wet tropics, a moist atmosphere and clouds serve as a "shield" absorbing and reflecting incoming solar radiation. At night, the same shield or blanket holds heat close to the surface. Whereas the wet tropics do experience the world's highest *annual average* temperature conditions, they fall far short of desert lands in recording high extremes. In fact, temperatures rarely reach 100°F (38°C) anyplace near the equator.

Because of the relatively dry atmosphere and lack of cloud cover, daily temperature ranges are also extreme in arid lands. Solar energy can easily reach the surface to create heat, but

It's *How* Hot?

Temperatures can be quite misleading. Accounts may read: "Service personnel swelter as temperatures soar to 150 degrees in Iraq," and, "The temperature soared to a scorching 173 degrees this afternoon in Phoenix." Such reports, of course, are grossly incorrect in regard to *official* temperatures. The official world record high temperature is 136°F (58°C). But this figure is all but meaningless. How hot it is depends upon a number of things: "official" temperatures, temperatures in the sun versus shade, and the temperature you actually feel as a result of combined temperature, humidity, and air circulation.

Official temperatures must be recorded at a weather station that is part of the National Oceanic and Atmospheric Administration (NOAA) network. Many stations, therefore, simply are not "official." This is why state extremes can be many degrees higher (or in the winter, lower) than the nation's official high (or low). Under official conditions, a thermometer must be contained within a white, open-sided box located several feet above the ground surface. This means that official temperatures are taken in the shade. The *actual* temperature, the one you are experiencing if exposed to the sun, can be many the heat also easily escapes back into the atmosphere once the sun sets. Imagine a sweltering midafternoon temperature in the mid-120s°F (about 51°C) dropping to a teeth-chattering mid-20s°F (–4°C) that night. This world record, a 100°F (55°C) range in a single day, actually happened in Al Aziziyah, Libya.

WINDS

Imagine water flowing down an incline—from higher ground to lower ground. Although it is less visible, air functions in the same way: It moves from areas of higher atmospheric

degrees higher. You can easily check this difference yourself. On a hot day, determine what the official afternoon temperature is and then place a thermometer in the sun several feet above the ground for several minutes. After you get that recording, place it on the ground on a dark-colored surface. Now you know why it can feel incredibly hot when you are in the sun working or playing. Under extreme conditions, surface temperatures above a dark surface can soar as high as 200°F (93°C).

Finally, there is the temperature your body actually feels. The *sensible temperature* (or *heat index*) is influenced by humidity and wind. At high temperatures, it is much more comfortable when conditions are dry and air is moving. Under extremely humid conditions, temperatures in the upper 80s or lower 90s°F (30° to 35°C) can be quite uncomfortable. In the dry desert atmosphere, however, a temperature of 100°F (55°C), or even a few degrees higher, is hardly noticed. These high temperatures will be even more comfortable if the wind is blowing.

So, as you have read, the thermometer and your body do not always agree. "How hot is it?" depends upon a number of factors.

The Harmattan, a hot, dry wind, blows from the northeast and east from the southern Sahara Desert during the winter. The wind typically carries large amounts of dust, which is pictured here where a woman in the village of Youdiou, Mali, draws water from a well.

pressure to areas of lower pressure. The moving air, or wind, can be affected by both large-scale and local pressure differences. As the air flows, it is also influenced by surface configuration, such as mountains or the presence (or lack) of vegetation. As you read previously, most deserts are areas of high pressure. On a global scale, wind blows out of the lower midlatitude high-pressure system toward areas of lower pressure. Winds blowing toward the poles create the prevailing westerlies in both hemispheres; those blowing toward the equator form the northeast trade winds in the Northern Hemisphere and southeast trade winds in the Southern Hemisphere. The *Sirocco* is a hot, dry wind that blows from the Sahara northward into southern Europe. The *Harmattan,* hot, dry winds blowing northeast or east from the Sahara Desert, bring similar conditions to the west coast of Africa. *Burans* are cold, dry winds that blow from interior Asia during winter months. They can cause rapid and severe drops in temperature in warmer areas of the Black Sea and eastern Mediterranean.

Most local winds blow in response to one or more of three conditions. To understand the origin of wind, two factors must be kept in mind. First, it is important to identify conditions that contribute to sharp differences in local temperatures and atmospheric pressure. Second, you must know that, at a local scale, high temperatures create low pressure and low temperatures create high pressure. To understand local winds, then, all one needs to do is look for environmental conditions that create marked differences in temperature and pressure on a regular basis.

Anyone who has spent time along the seashore or in a mountain valley is certainly aware of the almost constant breezes that blow in these environments, particularly during the summer months. Respectively, these winds are known as *land-sea* breezes and *mountain-valley* breezes. Along a coast, the land becomes much warmer than the adjacent water during the daytime. Low pressure, therefore, forms over land and high pressure over water, resulting in refreshing sea breezes blowing onshore. During nighttime, the pattern reverses: Land cools and water temperature remains constant, resulting in low pressure over the water and high pressure over land. This results in a land breeze. In mountains, cooler air at high elevation "flows" down slopes into the valley during the nighttime, creating mountain breezes. During the heat of the day, the valley floor heats, overlying air expands, and expanding air rises, creating an upslope flow of air, or valley breezes. Both wind conditions are, of course, confined to those areas in which large water bodies or mountains are present. A third wind is the "dust devil," those small, dancing, and harmless tornado-like winds that are common to even midlatitude areas. They result from microthermal conditions and generally occur only during summer days.

INFLUENCE OF THE WIND

Much of the wind's so-called influence on the conditions in a desert is overrated. Desert dust storms are not directly responsible for deaths; they can and do, however, kill indirectly. In the desert Southwest of the United States, there have been numerous accidents—including massive highway pileups resulting in many deaths—when people drive too fast into a blinding dust storm. But dust storms are actually much more common and severe in overgrazed steppe grasslands that border some deserts, than in the deserts themselves. The "sandblasting" effect of sand storms also is exaggerated. Vehicles driving into a sand storm can be severely pitted, with both glass and paint damaged. But the destruction is caused by the speed of the vehicle, rather than the movement of the sand itself. Although popular literature often attributes the origin of natural bridges and rock windows to the work of sand, this belief is without scientific basis. In fact, in a number of desert regions, petroglyphs (drawings done by humans on rock) have withstood thousands of years of exposure to windblown sand.

This is not to say, however, that the wind does not greatly affect the conditions in a desert environment. Perhaps the most important aspect of desert winds is the role they play in evaporating moisture. It is extremely easy, for example, to become dehydrated when temperatures are high and the wind is blowing. The body perspires, but sweat does not accumulate because it evaporates immediately. On a dry, windy day, skin dries and flakes, and eyes dry out and burn, lips dry and crack, hair crackles with electricity, and body liquid is lost rapidly through dehydration. The use of body oil was very important to ancient peoples for this reason, as lotions are to desert peoples today.

3

Geography of Land and Water

Throughout the desert world, nature's imprint dominates the landscape. Strange as it may seem, water is the primary force at work sculpting landforms in arid lands. To the keen eye of the geomorphologist (scientists who study landforms), telltale signs of water's work appear almost everywhere. Water is also the single most important factor in human settlement and land use in desert regions. For thousands of years, oasis sites have served as magnets to human settlement. For reasons to be discussed in Chapter 5, many early civilizations also emerged in desert oasis sites. Because they are so closely linked, land and water are the combined focus of this chapter.

LANDFORM FEATURES

Landform features and surface conditions of the land can combine to present obstacles, or offer potentials for human use. Throughout much of the world's desert realm, plains, valleys, and plateaus dominate the landscape. But there are also towering mountain ranges that rise like islands above the surrounding plains. In some respects, each of these landforms plays a more prominent role in arid lands than elsewhere. River valleys and their fertile floodplains, in particular, play a very important role in the settlement and economy of desert regions.

Mountains and Plateaus

Highlands occur in most, although not all, desert regions. The Colorado Plateau sprawls across much of the desert Southwest of the United States, and numerous mountain ranges dot the deserts of northwestern Mexico and the western United States. In South America, the high and rugged Andes back the Atacama Desert, where in some places only a few miles of desert lie sandwiched between the Pacific Ocean and the towering mountains. In southern Argentina, the desert region of Patagonia lies on a plateau surface backed by the Andes to the west. The Atlas Mountain range rises more than 2 miles (3.2 kilometers) above the Sahara Desert in northwestern Africa. Deep within the Sahara, the Ahaggar, Tibisti, and Aïr mountains provide visual, temperature, and moisture relief to an otherwise hot, dry, desert plains landscape. Many mountains and plateaus create a complex pattern of relief in Southwest Asia. The deserts of inner Asia are ringed by mountains, some of which are among the world's highest. Much of the Australian Desert is an uplifted plateau, broken in places by low mountains. The Kalahari Desert is also a relatively flat plateau with scattered hills in Namibia.

High elevations are of particular importance in desert regions for two primary reasons. First, temperatures cool (about 3.5°F per 1,000 feet increase in elevation, or 1°C per 300 meters) with increasing elevation. In hot desert regions, mountains and upland plateaus therefore provide relief from the blistering heat of surrounding desert lowlands. For millennia, pastoral nomads have driven their flocks into highland areas during summer months. Today, many mountain communities in the desert Southwest of the United States, such as Flagstaff, Arizona, and Santa Fe, New Mexico, are booming. Of even greater importance is the role mountains serve as the "faucets" that provide water for desert lands. Because of the orographic effect (explained in Chapter 2), mountains create conditions that allow them to be considerably moister than surrounding deserts. This water, in turn, eventually flows into the parched valleys below, creating oasis sites. Nearly all rivers flowing across desert landscapes have their origin in surrounding highlands. Some rivers, like the Nile and Indus, begin far beyond the deserts across which they flow.

Because of marked differences in both temperature and moisture, mountains offer a variety of environments for plants and animals. These varied habitats, in turn, shelter and sustain a considerable diversity of flora and fauna. Mountains, in fact, generally have a much greater variety of plants and animals than are found on adjacent plains and plateaus. Mountains and rugged plateaus can also serve as areas of safety and refuge for human populations. Throughout history, powerful civilizations or governments have sometimes forced smaller, weaker groups to abandon their customs and become part of the larger group. Occasionally those smaller groups have instead sought shelter in rugged lands, choosing to live in locations quite remote from other peoples. Living in near isolation from others allows these groups to retain much of their traditional culture, including language, religion, and customs. The Kurds, an ethnic group scattered across the rugged terrain of the Middle East and Southwest Asia, are one such group that chose isolation to preserve its identity.

Historically, mountains have been held sacred by many if not most desert cultures. Judaism, Christianity, and Islam each contain many references to important events occurring in mountainous locations. Some cultures even built their own "mountains." For example, the ancient Egyptians built pyramids, and the members of several cultures in Central and South America built ziggurats, which are similar in shape to the Egyptian pyramids, but have large steps climbing up the sides. In the modern world, many mountainous areas still hold on to their importance by being important centers of mining activity, recreation, and tourism.

Plains and Desert Surfaces

Most desert-dwellers, as is true for settlers in other environments, live on lowland plains. In fact, plains dominate desert surfaces throughout much of the world. Some plains are extremely fertile and highly productive agriculturally. Others are sterile, their soils rendered useless by extensive deposits of salts. A vast "sea of sand" is the stereotypical image of the desert surface held by many people. This, too, is yet another desert myth.

Desert floors are composed of three types of surface: *reg*, *hammada*, and *erg*. These terms originally described different desert conditions in the Sahara, but today they are used in reference to surface conditions throughout the world's deserts. Reg is the most common surface, covering perhaps two-thirds to three-fourths of all desert landscapes. This is a gravel surface, formed by small stones that settle tightly together as sand and dust are blown or washed away. Through time, minerals drawn to the surface by evaporation form cement that binds the stones together. As sand blows across the desert floor, it acts like sandpaper, smoothing and polishing the gravel surface. When soil moisture evaporates, a dark, shiny mineral stain called "desert varnish" forms on the weathered rock pebbles. The smooth, solid sheet of dark-colored gravel can easily be driven across, hence the name for this surface in the United States—"desert pavement."

Hammadas are desert surfaces covered by large rocks or bare bedrock. This type of surface is particularly common in mountains, on plateaus, and at the base of uplands. Perhaps 15 to 20 percent of the world's desert surface is hammada. Because of its ruggedness, a hammada surface makes travel very difficult whether by animal or motor vehicle.

Great Sand Dunes National Park in south-central Colorado is one of two large erg, or sandy, deserts in the United States. Pictured here is a hiker walking toward a massive sand dune near Alamosa, Colorado, shortly after Sand Dunes became a national park in September 2004.

Ergs are sandy deserts. Although this desert surface has captured the popular imagination, their area is actually quite small, covering about 10 percent of the world's desert landscape.

The figure is much smaller in the American deserts, where sand covers no more than a scant 1 percent of the surface. Erg surfaces assume many forms, including sand dunes, sand sheets, and rippling sand seas. These features occur in locations where windblown sand is deposited. Dunes take many forms, from the crescent-shaped *barkhans* to massive sand seas characterized by a variety of complex dune forms. Some dunes in the Sahara Desert reach a height of nearly 500 feet (150 meters) and mountain-like ergs have ridges that can reach a height of 1,000 feet (300 meters). The southern interior of the Arabian Peninsula—an area known as the "Empty Quarter"—has the world's largest concentration of erg surface. In the United States, two areas of erg desert stand out: the dune fields located just to the west of the Colorado River in southeastern California, and the Great Sand Dunes National Park in Colorado's San Luis Valley.

Erosion in Arid Lands

Nowhere in the world is the work of moving water as an erosional agent more evident than in desert landscapes. Canyons, natural bridges, rock windows, and countless other shapes attest to nature's artistic ability. Certainly Arizona's Grand Canyon, scoured over millions of years by the Colorado River, is one of the world's most spectacular erosional features. In size, however, this magnificent feature is dwarfed by Mexico's Cañon del Cobre (Copper Canyon), a huge trench scoured into the Sierra Madre Occidental.

A typical desert landscape might be one of highlands bordering a large basin. At the foot of the mountain (the piedmont), *alluvial fans* are formed where streams flowing from the highlands deposit debris in the shape of a fan. When joined together, the fans form a *bajada slope*, a gentle slope often covered with fertile soil and occasional freshwater springs. Because of these favorable conditions, many desert cities are located at the foot of mountain ranges. At its lowest elevation, the basin (*bolson*) itself will often have interior drainage. In the absence of outflow, a salt accumulation builds up such as on the floor of the Great Basin and Bonneville Salt Flats in Utah and Nevada.

DESERT SOILS

Soils may not seem interesting at first, but our lives depend upon them. Increasingly, much of our citrus fruit and winter vegetables come from the Colorado-Sonora Desert region and huge farms in Southern California, Arizona, and northwestern Mexico. As you have seen, the great majority of desert surfaces are covered by gravel, large rocks, or sand. Fertile soils only occur in limited areas such as the lower reaches of bajada slopes and in river valleys. In both locations, the soils are of alluvial origin, that is, silt deposited by moving water. Desert soil is rich in soluble minerals. In humid climates, much of the mineral content is drawn out of the soil. Because of aridity, this is not the case in deserts. Some scientists believe that the world's first farmers planted crops in the fertile soils of the Nile Valley and in the region known as Mesopotamia, the land between the Tigris and Euphrates rivers in Iraq. Fortunately, because so much desert soil is the result of stream deposits, many areas of alluvial soils also have a reliable water source. These two elements, with the added benefits of long, hot growing seasons, combine to form some of the world's most productive agricultural landscapes.

WATER FEATURES

Nowhere in the world is water more scarce, and hence more precious, than in desert lands. Where land lays parched, plant and animal life (including human life) is scant to nonexistent. On the other hand, where ample freshwater is present—by either natural or artificial means—the desert blooms with productivity and human habitation. For thousands of years, the valleys of the Nile, Tigris, Euphrates, and Indus rivers have supported some of the world's highest population densities. Population growth and the dawn of early civilizations were supported by very productive alluvial soils and thriving irrigated farming. In the Americas, development came much later. But early native cultures in the Southwest boasted excellent farmers and today the Colorado and Rio Grande rivers are lifelines that support both agriculture and millions of people.

An oasis is a location in an arid land where good water is available. Some oases are natural, such as river valleys, springs, or groundwater that can be brought to the surface by wells. Others are artificial, in the sense that they exist only because water is diverted from some distant source. Increasingly, desert cities such as Las Vegas, Phoenix, and Tucson are able to grow

Water from the Sahara Desert?

While drilling for oil in the desert of southern Libya in the 1950s, drillers made an amazing discovery: A huge freshwater aquifer lies deep beneath the surface of the Sahara Desert. As yet, this discovery has not led to a rush into the desert interior. It has, however, contributed to what some observers claim to be the world's largest and most costly engineering venture, Libya's Great Man-Made River Project. Built by the Libyan government at a cost equivalent to $25 billion in U.S. currency, the aqueduct brings groundwater from the heart of the Sahara Desert in the southern part of the country northward to the heavily populated coastal region. No wonder that Libya's president, Muammar al-Qaddafi, calls the project the "Eighth Wonder of the World."

Begun in 1984, the project draws water from 1,300 wells, most of which are more than 1,600 feet (500 meters) deep. The aqueduct is made from a concrete pipe that is 13 feet (4 meters) in diameter, which runs underground for about 2,500 miles (4,000 kilometers), including its branches. Each day, the huge pipeline transports enough water to thirsty coastal farms and cities to cover one square mile of land to a depth of one foot.

only because of water being diverted from a distant source—the Colorado River.

The water resources of desert lands include a surprisingly large number of seas and gulfs, rivers and streams, lakes, and groundwater supplies. Where they occur, they are of great importance. Large water bodies influence climate, moderating temperatures and increasing atmospheric moisture (including humidity that make hot weather seem even hotter). Surface water bodies also are important economically. Fish and other aquatic resources have long been important to many coastal peoples. For thousands of years, the Nile River, Red and Arabian seas, Persian Gulf, and other water bodies have been important shipping lanes. The Nile River and the Red Sea were linked by a canal in about 1900 B.C., nearly four millennia before the opening of the Suez Canal.

Seas and Gulfs

Historically, the Mediterranean Sea, Red Sea, Gulf of Aden, Persian Gulf, and Arabian Sea were the focal points of world transportation, trade and commerce, and cultural exchange. Phoenician and Arab navigators were legendary in their bravery, skill, and accomplishments. To early Spaniards, the Sea of Cortéz (Gulf of California) was of early interest, too.

Four inland seas are of particular interest, each for a different reason. The basin of the Caspian Sea may contain one of the world's greatest untapped stores of petroleum. Some other water bodies, particularly those in the Middle East, also lie over some of the world's major petroleum deposits.

East of the Caspian, in the Kyzyl-Kum Desert, lies one of the world's most environmentally degraded water bodies, the Sea of Aral. Water from the Amu Darya and Syr Darya rivers, which flow into the Aral, was diverted for agricultural use in the middle years of the twentieth century. A flourishing agricultural economy based upon irrigated cotton thrived, but the Sea of Aral withered almost entirely away.

The Dead Sea occupies a deep trench located on the border between Israel and Jordan. Its shoreline, at 1,339 feet (408

Located between the countries of Kazakhstan and Uzbekistan in Central Asia, the Aral Sea was once the world's fourth-largest lake. Today, the lake is more than half its original size, largely due to the diversion of the Amu Darya and Syr Darya rivers. Pictured here is a Kazakh villager, in 2005, collecting water from a well in an area that once formed the bed of the Aral Sea.

meters) below sea level, is the lowest point of dry land on Earth's surface. Water from the Jordan River, which flows into the Dead Sea, is increasingly used for agricultural and domestic purposes. As a result, the salty water body continues to drop in level—nearly 40 feet (12 meters) in the past 50 years.

Finally, few Americans know that we have our own inland sea—the Salton Sea. In 1905, the Colorado River jumped its banks and flowed to the northwest into Southern California's Imperial and Coachella valleys, which lie more than 200 feet below sea level in places. The water of the Salton Sea (as its name suggests) is salty. It is also heavily polluted by agricultural runoff that finds its way to the sea. As a result, this water body in the desert has not attracted much in the way of settlement or successful economic development.

Southern California's Salton Sea was formed during the first decade of the twentieth century, when the Colorado River jumped its banks and flowed westward into the Imperial Valley. The floor of the inland water body lies about 270 feet (82 meters) below sea level and occupies a basin of interior drainage.

Rivers

Rivers, where they flow reliably, are the lifelines of desert regions. The most important are exotic streams, which are rivers that originate in wetter areas and flow into and across the arid lands. For thousands of years, they have played an extremely important role in the economy, settlement, population, and trade within arid regions. The Nile, Tigris and Euphrates, and Indus rivers all begin their journeys outside of the deserts through which they flow. And each river-formed, ribbon-like oasis has long been an important hearth of civilization.

The Nile holds the distinction of being the world's longest river, stretching 4,249 miles (6,825 kilometers) from its source in equatorial Africa to its mouth in the Mediterranean Sea. Although much smaller than the Nile, the Jordan River is extremely important to the millions of people living in its drainage basin. The river drains portions of Lebanon, Syria, Israel, and Jordan before it flows into the Dead Sea. Waters of the Jordan are not only hotly contested by the countries through which the river flows, but they are becoming increasingly polluted and of diminishing flow. Farther east, major sources of the Indus River lie in Kashmir, an area fought over by India and Pakistan. Were India to gain control of the region and divert the headwaters of the Indus into its own desert region, it would spell disaster for Pakistan.

The Nile is the only river that crosses a part of the Sahara Desert. The Great Bend of the Niger does stretch northward into the southern Sahara, though. Elsewhere, most streams—as is characteristic of local watercourses throughout the desert realm—are intermittent. They flow seasonally, or in many cases, only briefly after periods of rain. Such streams go by various names, including *dry wash* (English), *arroyo* (Spanish), and *wadi* (Arabic). These are the seemingly harmless channels in which flash floods occur. In 1922, for example, a flash flood surging down a wadi flowing from the Ahaggar highlands in the central Sahara swept away the Algerian oasis settlement of Tamanrasset.

Rivers have played a negligible role in historical settlement and economic development in the desert lands of southern Africa, Australia, and the U.S. Southwest. In coastal Peru, however, small streams across the Atacama Desert en route from their Andean headwaters to the Pacific Ocean have played a very important historical role. Here, agricultural civilizations have thrived for at least five thousand years.

Lakes

An estimated 90 percent of the world's lakes were created by glaciation, but very little of the desert world was glaciated. As a result, there are relatively few natural freshwater bodies of any size or importance in the world's desert lands. No permanent natural lakes of importance occupy the desert lands

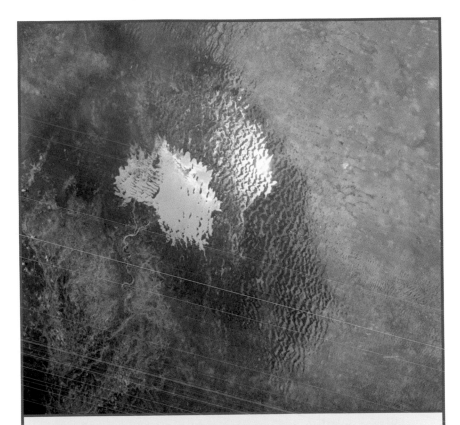

Lake Chad, located on the southern margin of the Sahara Desert and bordered by the countries of Cameroon, Chad, Niger, and Nigeria, is thought to be the remnant of an inland sea. This image from space was taken by the space shuttle *Discovery* in 1988 and shows the shrinking water level of the lake.

of Australia, or the Americas, but there are a few elsewhere. Among the most prominent lakes of Southwest Asia are the Sea of Galilee, the aforementioned Caspian Sea (technically a lake), the lakes and marshes of Mesopotamia, and a number of small water bodies in eastern Turkey, Iran, and Afghanistan. The small Sea of Galilee holds historical and religious significance because of its association with Jesus Christ's teachings. Today, it is a key link in Israel's national water program.

Africa is home to two of the world's strangest lakes: Lake Chad, located on the southern margin of the Sahara Desert, and the Okavango Delta in the Kalahari Desert. Although both lakes occupy basins of interior drainage—hence, should be saline—they are freshwater bodies. This seemingly impossible condition long puzzled scientists. Now, however, it is known that water does, indeed, flow outward from the lakes, but it flows underground into vast aquifers, or water deposits. Neither lake supports much in the way of settlement or economic development.

All of the world's desert lands have temporary or intermittent lakes. Regionally, they are identified by many local terms such as *shott* (Arabic) and *playa* (Spanish). Some are quite large. In humid lands, basins tend to fill with water to become lakes. In arid lands, however, most basins do not fill with water, at least not permanently. After periods of precipitation, water may accumulate in a basin, but it is soon lost to evaporation or seeps into the ground. Australia, for example, has dozens of "here today, gone tomorrow" lakes, some that occupy hundreds of square miles after rains fall, only to soon disappear. Salt deposits accumulate on the floor of these basins. Therefore, they are of little value in terms of recreation or farming. Some do, however, yield valuable deposits of various salts and borax, as well as potassium, an important metal.

During the ice age, many of the world's basins did contain large freshwater lakes. Much of the Great Basin in the United States, for example, was covered by Lake Bonneville, whose largest remnant is today's Great Salt Lake. When the lakes dried out, they left deep deposits of salt, as on the Bonneville Salt Flats that stretch between Utah and Nevada west of Salt Lake City.

Certainly one of the most interesting of all desert lakes is Lop Nor, the "Wandering Lake" in western China's Takla Makan Desert. Early travelers along the trade routes that linked China and the eastern Mediterranean referred to a lake that would vanish. Centuries later, even Marco Polo commented on the strange appearance and disappearance of Lop Nor. It was not until the 1930s that Swedish explorer Sven Hedin found the answer to the 2,000-year-old mystery. As happens with many rivers, including the Hwang He in China and both the lower Colorado and Mississippi rivers in the United States, they often change their course. The river that fed the lake in one basin would eventually shift its course, only to flow into another basin and create another water body.

Groundwater

Groundwater also sustains desert oases and therefore settlement and economic development in many locations. In the ground, water occurs in two types of aquifers. Some are shallow, located just beneath the surface of river valleys, basins, and alluvial fans at the foot of mountains. These aquifers fluctuate rapidly in response to local precipitation and water withdrawal. In some locations, huge aquifers exist, often at a depth of a thousand or more feet (300 meters). Water in these deposits may be thousands of years old, having been stored during more humid periods of the ancient ice age. In some locations, water reaches the surface naturally as springs. Elsewhere, it is accessible only by digging or drilling wells. In North Africa and the Middle East, subterranean aqueducts called *qanats*, have carried water to oasis communities and fields for several thousand years.

As populations, farming, and other consumers of water expand, pressure on all arid land water supplies increases. Much of the American Southwest would wither away were it not for aquifers and massive water storage and projects involving dams, reservoirs, aqueducts, and canals. In many parts of the desert realm, water supplies are experiencing rapid decline. When this occurs, oases are no longer able to support their populations, or the agricultural activity upon which people often depend. Clearly, water is the key to survival in arid lands. In the following chapter, you will learn how plants and animals are able to survive in harsh desert conditions.

4

The Desert Ecosystem

M any people hold an image of a desert landscape empty of plant and animal life. Yet for the vast majority of arid lands, this, too, is a myth. Most deserts are alive with flora and fauna. Unlike more humid environments, however, most organisms are quite small. A full-grown vine may spread only inches, and flowers of a plant in bloom may reach no higher than your ankle. Many animals are nocturnal, which allows them to avoid the scorching temperatures in the daytime. One thing all desert plants and animals share in common is the ability to survive conditions of extreme heat and aridity.

RUNNING AN ENVIRONMENTAL OBSTACLE COURSE

Ecology is the study of interrelationships that exist in how organisms adapt to the environments in which they live. Each life-form has a habitat, the natural environment to which it is adapted. Very few life-forms are able to survive in all of Earth's ecosystems. Life abounds in areas such as the wet tropics, where conditions remain hot and humid throughout the year. With so few environmental challenges, it is little wonder that tropical lands are home to perhaps 80 percent of all plant and animal species. Polar and desert regions, on the other hand, put severe limits on flora and fauna alike. In deserts, plants and animals that are not adapted to the region's lack of moisture, extreme temperatures, and other challenging environmental conditions simply cannot survive. As is true in polar lands, too, the number of desert species is somewhat limited.

Plants and animals do not arrive in a harsh environment and then adapt to its extreme conditions. Rather, they already possess traits that make survival possible before they even reach a new and more demanding environment. Think of it as an obstacle course in which each new station or activity is increasingly difficult. Very few people are able to get past all the challenges to reach the finish line. The ones who do finish were already athletic at the beginning—they didn't become more skilled as the course went on. So it is with plants and animals and their natural habitats.

In the region around the equator, nature's obstacles offer few challenges that are very easily overcome. Moving away from the wet tropics, however, plants and animals begin to encounter environmental barriers to which they are not adapted. As conditions become increasingly difficult, fewer and fewer plants and animals possess the traits needed to survive. In essence, they "drop out" of the journey through Earth's environmental obstacle course. By the time the end of the course is reached—the desert, in this example—very few species are able to successfully meet the challenges imposed by nature. For arid environments, these conditions include temperature extremes, a shorter growing season, a sharp decrease in and reliability of moisture, as well as other limiting factors. Those species who complete the course (reach the desert) are those plants and animals that already possessed one or more traits that make it possible for them to survive under harsh desert conditions.

DESERT PLANTS

When you think of "typical" desert vegetation, what comes to mind? Typically, many different kinds of cactus pop into view. If this is your image, it may come as a surprise to learn that cacti are both indigenous (native to) and endemic (restricted to, at least under natural conditions) to the North American deserts. And the best-known cactus of all, the saguaro (sah-war-o), only grows in a very small area of southern Arizona and adjacent Sonora, Mexico.

All desert plants possess one or more properties that allow them to survive under conditions of limited and unreliable moisture. Some of the more common traits include the following:

- **Root systems:** Many desert plants have root systems that reach deep into the earth to seek moisture, some to depths of more than 200 feet (60 meters). In order to take advantage of surface moisture after a light shower, however, they also have roots that stretch sideways very near the surface.
- **Annuals with very short life cycles:** Many non-woody (without bark), seed-bearing plants have a very short life cycle. After a shower, some seeds can begin to grow into new plants within a matter of days. Some plants grow, blossom, and sow their seeds within several weeks. A beautiful carpet of flowers can turn into a barren landscape in a matter of days.
- **Seeds can hold onto their growing power for long periods of time:** In the Atacama Desert, many years can pass without a drop of rain. Yet when rain does fall, sleeping seeds burst into life. Seeds taken from ancient Egyptian tombs, thousands of years old, have germinated when placed in moist soil! This ability to last allows plants to survive extremely long periods of drought.
- **Plant size and structure:** Most desert plants are small and grow close to the ground. Small plants require little

The large tree-sized saguaro cactus is native to only a small portion of southern Arizona and northern Mexico. Saguaros can live up to 200 years, but because they grow and propagate very slowly, they are considered endangered.

moisture to survive. Growing close to the ground protects them from the drying effects of the wind, thereby reducing water loss.

- **Spacing:** In order to reduce competition for scant moisture supplies, plants tend to be scattered. Actually, this characteristic is a "survival of the fittest" competition. Once a plant becomes established, its root system is able to deny water to newly sprouted plants. Some plants also discharge toxins that limit competing plant life.
- **Retain moisture:** Some species are able to hold moisture in pulpy branches, stems, or trunks. After a period of precipitation, a saguaro cactus can store up to 2 tons, or 470 gallons (1,800 liters), of water! These giants of the desert

Southwest also can lose up to 80 percent of their weight through dehydration and still survive. Most cacti, including the barrel cactus, have some means of storing water.

- **Leaves:** Most desert plants have small, thick, "waxy," furry leaves, and some have leaves that fold up or turn their backside toward the sun during the heat of the day. Each of these characteristics reduces water loss.
- **Protective traits:** In order to avoid damage or destruction by grazing animals, many desert plants have disagreeable traits that make them either bad-tasting or difficult to eat. Some are bitter, or even poisonous. Others are tough, have rough or sharp leaves, and are well armed with thorns.

Plant Ecology

Visitors to desert lands may be surprised by the great differences in vegetation that covers the ground from place to place, often within short distances. Desert flora are keenly adapted to those environmental conditions in which they are best able to survive. Minor and seemingly insignificant differences in habitat make a huge difference in where certain plants are found. Plants respond to such environmental conditions as slope, exposure to the sun, elevation, the courses of dry streams, and even large rocks that provide shade. No matter where it is located, each species has found a home based on such factors as moisture, temperature, soil, or some other environmental condition.

On the desert floor, a narrow ribbon of bright green may wind across the landscape, nourished by the invisible moisture in the earth beneath a dry streambed. Nearby, the north- and south-facing slopes of a small hill have quite different forms of plant life. Salt-tolerant species such as tamarisks encircle the salt-encrusted floor of the dry lake occupying the lowest portion of the basin. Elsewhere on the desert floor, various species of arid land trees thrive. In the American Southwest, mesquite, palo verde, and ironwood dominate the wooded landscape, but there are other species as well. Upslope, where conditions are a little wetter, grasslands replace the typical desert flora. A short trip into the mountains reveals a thriving forest of pine and aspen trees, and other species. (Arizona in fact is home to the world's largest ponderosa pine forest.)

THE HUMAN IMPRINT ON DESERT LANDSCAPES

No landscape remains forever unchanged, and desert lands are particularly fragile. In New Mexico, 150-year-old wagon tracks from pioneers traveling the Santa Fe Trail are still clearly etched into the land. Modern recreational vehicles are taking a tremendous toll on vegetation in the southwestern United States, turning plant-covered terrain into sandy desert surfaces. Surprisingly, a period of ample rainfall can be a desert's worst enemy. In previous chapters, you read about the destruction of flash floods and erosion in arid lands. Unusually wet conditions can cause a seemingly barren desert to burst into life with a carpet of grass and other plant life. Once the vegetation dries out, however, it is in danger of burning. Desert fires have altered the vegetation in many desert locations, including those in the United States.

Closely related to naturally occurring desert conditions is a process called *desertification*, which is the creation of deserts through human action. The process is most common to desert fringe areas, those areas that receive 10 to perhaps 15 or even 20 inches (25 to 50 centimeters) of precipitation a year. Here, conditions are moist enough to allow grassland vegetation, grazing, and even dry-land farming. During wet years, human populations prosper. When the inevitable drought period returns, however, grasses wither, crops die in the field, and water holes dry out. What once was productive land can turn into a barren desert landscape. This happened in the interior of the United States during the Dust Bowl era of the 1930s. During the 1970s, desertification brought disaster to the Sahel, a belt of land immediately south of Africa's Sahara Desert that

(continues on page 56)

Camels
Ships of the Desert

For thousands of years, camels were immensely important to desert life. Imagine the nineteenth-century American West without horses; to desert dwellers in Asia, and later in North Africa, the camel was of equal if not greater importance. Few animals are better adapted to arid conditions. Camels are well known for their ability to go long stretches of time without water. They are able to "load up" with 20 to 25 gallons (about 75 to 95 liters) of water at a time and to dehydrate up to 30 percent of their body weight and still function. During the cool season and with good grazing conditions, these amazing animals can go up to two weeks without taking a drink. If working during the hot season of the year and if grazing conditions are poor, the time is cut in half, to about one week.

The camel has other features that make it ideally suited to the desert. Its hump stores fat that provides energy during prolonged periods when little food is available. Its feet are padded, for walking across sand or loose dirt. The camel's eye has a transparent membrane to protect against windblown sand. Its lips are very tough, so it can eat coarse vegetation.

Camels are native to Asia. They did not enter North Africa until sometime during the first millennium B.C. There are two types of camels: the single hump dromedary of Arabia and Africa and the double hump Bactrian, common to the deserts of southern and Central Asia. How can one ever remember which is which? It is simple if you remember this: Turn D and B on their backs, and you get one hump and two humps! Here is a hint to remember which region they each come from: Only the double hump Bactrian has the letter "c" in the name, and China has more camels than any other country.

Camels were introduced into the deserts of the American Southwest by Jefferson Davis in the mid-1850s. He thought that they would be an ideal replacement for horses in the desert that stretched from western Texas to the California gold fields. His experiment was short-lived. The animals' padded feet were well suited to sand, but not to sharp rock. Many of the animals were simply turned loose. Wild camels were seen roaming the deserts of western Texas and southwestern Arizona until at least the end of the nineteenth century. The hardy beasts also were introduced into the Australian desert during the last half of the nineteenth century. At one time, their population reached 300,000 and today perhaps 200,000 remain wandering around the country's desert landscape.

Camels have inhabited Africa since the first millennium B.C. and are well adapted to arid conditions. Thanks largely to their ability to store fat in their humps and up to 20 to 25 gallons of water within their body, they can go long periods without eating or drinking.

(continued from page 53)

stretches across almost the entire continent. Crop and grazing lands turned to dust, millions of people were forced to leave, and animal herding all but died out in the region. Only now, decades later, is the land beginning to be restored to its previous level of productivity.

DESERT FAUNA

Traditionally, animals have been of greater importance to the people of the desert and polar realms than to any other human settlements. Animals provide milk and meat; hides are used for clothing, shelter, containers, and other useful objects; large animals provide mobility; animals are a medium of exchange; and in desert lands where wood is scarce, dried animal "chips" (dung) are used for fuel. Just like plants, though, all desert animals must be well adapted to conditions of extreme aridity and scorching heat. Perhaps the best known of all desert animals is the camel: the famed "Ship of the Desert."

Most desert fauna possess some means of conserving moisture. It may be by getting moisture from eating plants or insects. Some insects have a watertight outer shell that reduces water loss, making them good sources of water for insect-eating animals. Other animals, like the desert snail, can remain dormant for several years before being revived by rainfall. Many larger animals simply take advantage of available shade. A number of desert animals are nocturnal, coming out only at night when conditions are much cooler.

Each of the world's deserts has its own unique population of fauna. All deserts have herbivores (plant-eating animals) and carnivores (meat-eating animals). And no desert is without its share of reptiles, birds, and insects. Flies and mosquitoes (including those that transmit diseases such as malaria) are a nuisance to everyone. Other unwelcome pests include scorpions, centipedes, various spiders, and ticks and lice. Deserts may bring to mind venomous snakes and lizards. They of course do exist, but are no more numerous or threatening than in many other environments.

Domesticated Animals

The desert areas of Southwest Asia and the surrounding steppe grasslands made up perhaps the world's earliest and most important hearth of animal domestication. About 10,000 to 12,000 years ago, humans began one of history's most important experiments—controlling the reproduction of plants and animals. Animals, of course, had been hunted for hundreds of thousands of years. But through the process of domestication—the taming of wild animals—many uses other than meat and hides became possible. Eventually, animals could be milked, ridden, and used to carry loads, pull vehicles, and plow. Smaller animals such as sheep could provide a constant supply of wool. Of the traditional farm and ranch animals, sheep and goats were the first to be domesticated. Horses, camels, oxen, and yaks soon followed. We don't have any record, however, of when dogs were first tamed. The importance of domesticating all of these animals will be discussed in the next chapter.

5

Native Cultures

C ultural geographers are fascinated by the way people live in groups. We are interested in knowing more about different worldviews and belief systems. The tools and techniques employed by a culture as it etches its imprint on the landscape are the building blocks of geographic study. So, too, is gaining an understanding of the ways in which various cultures use natural resources and how they make a living and distribute their wealth. In this chapter, you will learn about the traditional ways of living practiced by desert-dwelling peoples throughout time. Our focus is on the region's historical and cultural geography.

In previous chapters, you learned many of the myths that are associated with arid environments. As you might suspect, there are misconceptions about desert peoples as well. No myth is more widespread than the belief that all desert peoples are either nomads herding animals, or farmers living in oasis settlements. In reality, no more than about 10 percent of desert dwelling people have ever practiced a nomadic lifestyle. In fact, herds of domesticated livestock were initially limited to the deserts of Central and Southwest Asia and much later to the Sahara. This means that five of the world's eight great desert regions didn't even have animals to herd; therefore, there could be no people herding them. The same holds true for farming. The Middle East and coastal Peru were the only arid lands that developed a tradition of oasis farming, although eventually the practice of irrigated farming also spread to some North American desert peoples.

As is true of traditional cultures worldwide, it is impossible to stereotype a distinct "desert culture." People, after all, are not mere putty in the hands of Mother Nature! As is true of people living in all of Earth's other environments, it is their culture—their traditions, aspirations and needs, tools and skills, knowledge, and other traits—that determines how they live. Through time, desert lands have been home to both the world's most advanced cultures and to some of the least technically developed.

When studying traditional societies, geographers often classify peoples by how they survive or earn a living—such as hunting and gathering, or traditional farming or herding. As cultures continued to become more complex, some early peoples also became village dwellers, and villages often grew into cities. Urban life differs greatly from country living, including the demands it places upon members of urban society. These are the basic cultural patterns and practices around which this chapter is organized. As you learn more about these traditional societies and their ways of living, there is one very important thing to keep in mind. "Education," it can be said, "is learning to survive." Imagine yourself suddenly being stranded, alone, in the middle of some remote desert region. No sign of human life is anywhere to be seen. There is no food or water in sight, temperatures are scorching, and you have no modern tools, weapons, or containers. How long do you think you would survive? (Quite probably less than 36 hours.) The traditional cultures discussed in this chapter have lived under these conditions for thousands of years, and by their standards they have lived quite well. All cultures must be judged solely in the context of how well their way of living serves *them*. Words like "primitive" have no place in the vocabulary of a geographer.

TRADITIONAL HUNTING AND GATHERING PEOPLES

At first, of course, all of the world's population was just trying to survive. People practiced an economy based on hunting or gathering (and in some places, fishing). With the dawn of plant and animal domestication that happened some 10,000 to 15,000 or more years ago in several locations, that earlier way of life began to change. Deserts, of course, were challenging environments. People either had cultures adapted to desert life, or they were unable to survive there. Most people avoided the desert environment entirely. Non-desert dwelling peoples tended to shun the desert simply because their culture was poorly equipped to allow their survival in this extreme environment. Some desert peoples, therefore, lived in isolation not only from other humans, but also from new ideas. As a result, many desert cultures held on to very traditional folkways, or practices, until modern times. Several Native American groups of the Colorado-Sonora Desert had not yet developed farming methods when the first Europeans arrived in the region. Neither farming nor herding were practiced by native peoples of South America's Patagonian Desert, Africa's Kalahari Desert, or the desert region of Australia until recent times, either.

Seri Indians

In the North American desert, some tribal groups gathered nuts and other seeds and hunted. One of the most interesting of these traditional peoples is the Seri, a small tribe living along the shores of the Gulf of California in the Mexican state of Sonora. Numbering only a few hundred, as late as the mid-twentieth century, the Seris lived mostly by gathering plant materials and hunting huge sea turtles in the gulf. They lived in simple shelters, had no domestic animals other than dogs, and knew nothing about farming. Seri women had to walk many miles to a source of freshwater. Only a rough desert trail linked these remote people to the outside world. It is little wonder that a half-century ago, some anthropologists suggested that the Seris were the least-advanced culture in the Western Hemisphere (in a material and technological sense).

During the 1950s, things began to change—and change dramatically—for the Seris. Within the short span of several years, outside "helpers" discovered the Seris' many "needs." First, a well was drilled in their settlement that provided a reliable supply of freshwater. Women no longer had to spend much of their day fetching water from miles away. With their newly gained easy access to water, the Seris were taught how to irrigate and raise crops. Then an electrical generator was installed to provide light and refrigeration to preserve turtle meat. To reduce the Seris' isolation from the rest of the world, an improved road was built that linked their settlement to Hermosillo, Sonora's capital city located about 75 miles (121 kilometers) inland. As though a dam had burst, the Seris suddenly found themselves flooded by strange outsiders and their many influences. But this was just the beginning.

Previously isolated, all but unknown, and extremely traditional in their way of life, the Seris found themselves inundated by people and things with which they had no understanding or prior experience. Some outsiders were simply curious, others came as tourists, and sport fishermen from far and wide were drawn by the lure of gulf fishing. The government, which previously had paid little if any attention to the Seris, made it a requirement for their children to attend school. Missionaries came in hope of converting the Seris to Christianity. With refrigeration and improved access to markets, the Seris soon began to make money selling turtle meat to restaurants. Almost overnight, this discovery catapulted the tribe from a folk economy based on bartering and survival to one based on cash (sales, income, and purchases). With the new demand for turtle meat, the Seris realized that their catch could be increased by using motorboats, which, of course, required not only the purchase of the motors, but also new boats and fuel. Outsiders also introduced sexually transmitted diseases, drugs, and alcohol, which soon began to take a terrible toll. The Seris found themselves caught up in a whirlwind of change for which they were not prepared.

Within a decade, the Seri Indians of coastal Sonora, Mexico, found themselves part of the modern era—a cultural leap that many other cultures experience over a span of centuries. In the process, it took less than a generation to all but destroy the Seris' traditional way of life. Each week, more outsiders and outside influences arrived in the area than had previously visited during the span of a decade. And these outsiders were as different as if they had come from another planet. Spanish and English had to be learned. The Seris' folk religion, the very foundation of their belief system, was shattered as it was challenged by Christianity. Centuries of folk wisdom that had made their survival possible began to vanish, replaced by enforced formal education that had little application to the demands of local living. As the young learned "outside" skills, they began to yearn for a new and more exciting way of life in Hermosillo and elsewhere.

Ultimately, Seri culture was lost; it was swept away by a flood of change imposed upon it by well-meaning outsiders. Are the Seris (and many other traditional cultures that have suffered a similar fate) better off now than they were before their traditional way of life was shattered and replaced by "European ways"? That is a very difficult question to answer and it is not one that anyone is really qualified to make.

What happened to the Seris has, in various ways, changed nearly all traditional cultures. Most Bushmen (!Kung) tribesmen of the Kalahari, Aborigines of Australia's desert outback, and hunters of Patagonia also have been drawn into modern life during recent decades. Traditionally, however, their cultures were very finely adapted to the small offerings of the

Bushmen, such as these members of the Khomani tribe, have inhabited southern Africa's Kalahari Desert for millennia. The Khomanis survive by following seasonal migration routes that lead them to food and water sources.

environments they called home. Their ability to seek, stalk, and kill game was absolutely amazing. As trackers, they had no equals. They knew where to find water and what plant foods could be found during various seasons of the year. Their material possessions were meager, and their formal "textbook" knowledge was nonexistent. Nonetheless, they were brilliant in terms of surviving in some of the world's most challenging environmental conditions.

PASTORAL NOMADISM

Many people incorrectly think that nomads are the "typical" inhabitants of arid lands. Pastoral nomads are tribal peoples who go from place to place following their flocks. The kinds of animals that are herded vary by location, but they can include camels, horses, oxen, and donkeys, as well as sheep and goats. Each of these animals was domesticated in the Middle East;

hence, nomadism began in this region and gradually spread elsewhere in Asia and North Africa. There were no domesticated animals other than dogs in the desert regions of southern Africa, Australia, and South America, (though the llama and alpaca are Andean domesticates).

Rather than randomly wandering, nomads know precisely where they are going and when they need to be there. They follow well-established routes that will lead them to water supplies and better grazing conditions for their livestock. There are two types of migrations that pastoral nomads follow. In most locations, migrations follow the seasons. For example, animals might be driven into cooler highlands during summer months and return to lower elevations during the winter. Elsewhere, the migration may be into the middle of the desert during the wet season and into the more humid steppe grasslands nearby during the desert dry season.

There is a danger in herding that the animals will eat all the plant life in the area, turning it into a barren landscape. To avoid this, nomads must always be on the move. As a result, they have very few material possessions. Much of what they need can be obtained from their flocks, including food, clothing, shelter, blankets, containers for water, and other necessities. Other items in their possession may include weapons (today, knives, guns, and ammunition), cotton cloth, and utensils. Everything they own can be assembled and transported by a large animal such as a horse or camel.

The diet of nomads (as is true of most traditional cultures) offers little variety. Other than meat and milk, which are obtained from their animals, most food is obtained from oasis settlements. If there is a good relationship between the nomads and the people who live in the oasis areas, animals will be exchanged for fruit, vegetables, and grain. Sometimes, though, some groups of nomads may raid an oasis village if they don't get along with the people there. This trading or raiding has gone on for thousands of years in some locations. Fresh fruit and vegetables are rare luxuries available only when an irrigated oasis is nearby. Dates, also obtained from oasis settlements, are a major food item. They are very nutritious and can be dried and preserved for many months. Barley meal is used to make both bread and porridge. Occasionally, after a rainfall, barley will be planted in a dry streambed. Several months later, the nomads will return to harvest the crop. As often as not, however, they find that the grain was either swept away by a flash flood, or already harvested by other nomads. Salt is also a very important item in the diet, because it is essential to survival in hot climates. Coffee, originally cultivated in Yemen on the Arabian Peninsula, is important, too, and often consumed in small, but extremely strong, quantities.

Animals produce food and other useful products. In arid lands with no trees, dried animal dung is used as fuel. Livestock are used in trading with oasis dwellers, and also may be used in the purchase of wives among some groups. Milk is taken from goats, camels, horses, and yaks. Because it is highly perishable, milk is either drunk immediately, or consumed as curdled *ghee*, which has a consistency similar to that of cottage cheese. Meat is a rarely eaten delicacy, because it necessitates the slaughter of an animal that could be used for milk or other products that don't require killing it. In some desert regions, such as the desert of northwestern India, religious restrictions prohibit people from eating animal flesh. The religions of Judaism and Islam also have a meat restriction, specifically against eating pork.

Pillaging and robbing were actually considered to be honorable professions among traditional nomads. One group of nomadic peoples—the caravan owners—stood out from others. They were the "nobility" of the desert realm. Caravans transported goods, and their owners were the merchants, news messengers, and often owners of oases, flocks, and natural resources such as salt. They also were the fighting forces. Often, a tribal group would offer protection to an oasis in exchange for trade items mentioned in the paragraphs above. If the oasis resisted, it might be destroyed. If it agreed, the nomads would not attack, and would also defend the oasis against attacks from other nomadic groups. Nomads, in general, tended to be warriors. For example, throughout time, various fierce nomadic groups came out of Central Asia's deserts. Some fought and others settled and eventually blended into their new environment. The best-known nomads were the Mongols. These skilled horsemen and legendary fighters swept both westward and eastward (where the Great Wall of China was built to protect against their onslaught). In time, they carved out a huge empire, the second largest in history after the British Empire.

Today, pastoral nomadism is in rapid decline throughout the world's desert lands. As pastoral nomads learn of other, seemingly easier, more rewarding, and more attractive, options, many are willing and eager to leave behind the harsh and demanding challenges of nomadic life.

SEDENTARY OASIS SETTLEMENT

As you learned in previous chapters, oases are places where good water is available at the surface. River valleys, dry streambeds, springs at the heads of alluvial fans, and underground water basins are among the more common places where oases occur. In such sites, not only is water available, but under most conditions, so are rich soils deposited by water. The Nile Valley is one of the largest and perhaps the most famous river-formed oasis. During the times of the ancient Egyptian civilization, the river's annual flood brought both water and new silt to the adjacent floodplain. As floodwaters retreated, seeds were planted in the moist and fertile soil, and crops thrived. This flood irrigation was practiced for thousands of years and was the foundation of early Egyptian civilization. Some scientists believe that the world's first plant domestication and farming were practiced in the Nile Valley some 18,000 years ago. Elsewhere in the Middle East, early oasis settlements based on farming were found wherever there existed a reliable supply of good water. Such locations

For more than 10,000 years, the Nile River has supported Egyptian settlements. Pictured here are several feluccas, or traditional wooden sailing boats, which have served as a means of transportation for local residents for thousands of years.

included Mesopotamia, the Jordan River Valley, and the Indus Valley. In the New World, similar conditions were found in several locations including coastal Peru and Arizona's Salt and Gila river valleys.

Oasis sites were home to both the poorest and most downtrodden members of desert society at one extreme and very advanced civilizations at the other. In many traditional oasis settings, settlers were the poorest group. They were discriminated against by the nomads and, indeed, their land often was controlled by nomadic tribesmen. Nomads allowed farmers to keep only a small portion (usually about one-fifth) of what they produced. In part, this arrangement was payment for protection—pay or be raided!

Oases have long been known for their filth, insects, disease, and water suitable for irrigation but not for drinking.

(continues on page 70)

The Mysterious Hohokam

When Europeans first arrived in Arizona's Salt River Valley, they were astonished to find an elaborate and lengthy (about 200 miles, or 320 kilometers) system of long-abandoned irrigation canals. These first white settlers busily set about the task of digging their own canal network to carry water from the Salt River to their fields. The ancient canals were so well engineered, however, that many of the "modern" ditches simply followed the old system. Who were the mysterious people who long ago had built North America's only known irrigation canal system and had turned the central Arizona desert into a productive garden?

Sometime during the first millennium A.D., a people of unknown origin suddenly arrived in what is today the metropolitan area of Phoenix, Arizona. Their culture was unique. In fact, they possessed many traits not found elsewhere (at least in combination) in North America. Chief among the traits was their elaborate irrigation system. Among other crops, they raised lima beans. Their pottery was red-on-buff, and unique in other ways, including many designs of marine life. Jewelry was made from seashells. These are just some of many unique traits possessed by the Hohokam.

Some archaeologists (scientists who study ancient cultures) believe that the Hohokam came from Mexico. But there are clues that hint otherwise. For instance, an archaeological museum in Lima, Peru, houses pottery with a very abstract bird design. It is, amazingly, identical in every respect to a design that appears on Hohokam pottery displayed at the University of Arizona. With this hint, a study was conducted to identify other possible culture trait links between Hohokam culture and peoples of coastal Peru. Ultimately, a dozen traits (including those mentioned above) were discovered that strongly suggest a link between early Peruvian cultures and the Hohokam. Could early desert people from coastal South America have traveled northward by coast, found and followed the Colorado River inland, and ultimately settled in Arizona's Salt River Valley? There is a substantial body of evidence to suggest that this may have happened.

Sometime around A.D. 1400, the Hohokam vanished as mysteriously as they had arrived. In fact, their very name is derived from the Pima Indian term for "those who have vanished." Who were these ancient people, where did they come from, why did they leave, and where did they go? There are many theories, but perhaps the full answer will never be known.

The Hohokam people settled in present-day central and southern Arizona between A.D. 300 and 750 and built extensive irrigation canals in the Salt and Gila River valleys to cultivate their crops. Pictured here are the ruins of Casa Grande, or Great House, which is a four-story building that served as a center for managerial and religious power among the Hohokam.

(continued from page 67)

Buildings appear to many outsiders to be crude and "dirty." In reality, most buildings are constructed of *adobe* (a sun-dried mixture of mud and straw) that is very well suited to hot desert conditions. Walls may be a foot (0.3 meters) or more thick, and the dirt in them offers excellent protection against high temperatures. Rare heavy rains, however, can easily erode an earth-built structure.

Oasis farming uses many types of irrigation. The simplest form is natural flood irrigation, in which humans do not do anything to change the course of water. A more advanced technique is the redirecting of water from streams using a system of small dams and canals. In many locations, water had to be lifted from a lower to higher level. Animal-operated wells (*murakkab*), water scoops (*shaduf*), and water wheels of various designs were commonly used devices. One ingenious method of water transfer found throughout the Middle East, North Africa, and Central Asia is the *qanat* (also *foggara*). Built to reduce water loss through evaporation, these aqueducts may snake for miles underground, just beneath the earth's surface. On the landscape, their presence can be noted by a series of "chimneys" rising above ground. These are the openings through which earth was removed as the aqueduct was excavated, and they also allow access for periodic cleaning and repair.

Traditional farming implements were simple, usually limited to the handheld dibble (sharpened digging stick) or hoe. In some areas, animals (usually oxen) were used to pull the *ard*. This ancient plow, first used in Egypt, broke the soil but did not turn it over to reveal the richer soil beneath. (The "moldboard plow," which turns soil, was not developed until the late nineteenth century.) Traditional crops included barley, wheat, and millet, all of which were first domesticated and cultivated in Southwest Asia. Cotton also was first domesticated and grown in this region. In North Africa and the Middle East, dates were the most important oasis crop. It has been said that the palms grow with their "roots in heaven [wet] and crown in hell [sun]." The tree has many uses. Its fruit is a nutritious food staple. Fibers from the trunk are used in making rope. Fronds (palm leaves) are used for making baskets and matting. Trunks provide lumber, and stems and roots can be used for fuel.

Early oasis settlements also occurred in coastal Peru and the American Southwest. The Peruvian desert and adjacent Andean highlands were home to what became one of the world's great early centers of civilization. Arizona's Hohokam people remain one of archaeology's great mysteries. Although changed in many ways during the past century, thousands of traditional oasis settlements still lie scattered about the world's deserts.

EMERGENCE OF HYDRAULIC CIVILIZATIONS

More than a half-century ago, German-American scholar Karl Wittfogel advanced a bold theory of hydraulic civilizations. He reasoned that a strong central authority was needed for the construction and maintenance of a large-scale irrigation project and for a plan to divide water resources among a civilization's inhabitants. Some individual or group had to be in a position to exercise control over large numbers of people. That controlling agency, regardless of its source of power, provided the unifying bond that ultimately formed the foundation of civilizations.

In essence, then, it can be said that irrigation created civilization and civilizations created irrigation. Of course, it did not always work out this way. As you already have learned from the preceding section on sedentary oasis settlements, not all desert people mastered irrigation and became sedentary oasis farmers. Early hydraulic civilizations thrived in the Nile Valley, Mesopotamia, the Indus Valley, and coastal Peru. They are recognized by various names—Egyptians; Sumerians, Babylonians, Assyrians, and others in the area of the Tigris and Euphrates rivers; Harrapa and Mohenjo-daro in the Indus Valley; and the Moche, Chimu, Nazca, and Inca in Peru.

Geographers, historians, and others have long sought to understand the foundations of civilization. It seems probable that several related conditions combined to help along their origin and evolution. "Civilization" can be defined in many ways. For our purpose, it involves a strong central authority and a considerable increase in the number and complexity of culture traits (material and nonmaterial things possessed by humans). It seems likely that the following series of events were the chief contributors to the rise of early civilizations in arid lands.

Farming, which began perhaps 10,000 to 18,000 years ago in the Middle East, provided a reliable food supply. Large domesticated animals were a source of nonhuman energy providing labor and expanded mobility. With a reliable source of food and food surplus, not all people had to work the fields. People were able to settle in communities, some of which in time grew into thriving cities. Cities have long been the centers of innovation and culture change. They first appeared in Southwest Asia about 7,000 years ago. Additionally, an ample food supply made possible an increase in population and life expectancy. For the first time in history, the elderly could be supported after they no longer were able to contribute to the economy. They did, however, contribute greatly by sharing their wisdom with younger generations.

Irrigation requires coordination—canals or aqueducts must be built and maintained and precious supplies of water must be divided among the civilization's inhabitants. Additionally, when large numbers of people live together in a community, some bonding force such as religion or government must hold them together. Someone must make decisions for the community at large. These needs combined to necessitate the emergence of a strong central authority. In antiquity, this usually led to a theocracy—a governing group that based its power on religious grounds.

Under most conditions, urban people became specialized. Some became skilled potters, weavers, or millers. Others made tools and weapons, were builders, or developed some other talent. Rather than being "jacks of all trades," they became increasingly skilled in their respective fields. Specialization resulted in marked improvements in nearly everything humans did and used. There was also the always-present need to protect fields, livestock, and the communities themselves from attack. Soldiers were needed, as were better weapons, which, in turn, often led to developments that benefited all of society. The wheeled chariot, for example, ultimately gave rise to all vehicles with wheels.

Society was now divided among nomadic herders, sedentary oasis farmers, and urban people specializing in some function and who were governed and protected. The latter group involved a number of administrators, priests and other religious figures, and soldiers. These people did not contribute directly to the basic needs of daily life—the provision of food, water, and raw materials—yet they nonetheless played a very important role. And they needed to be supported by those over whom they held some authority, which led to the practice of collecting taxes. Imposing and collecting taxes requires record keeping, a need that contributed to the development of advanced forms of writing and mathematics. Both our alphabetic form of writing and use of Arabic numerals originated in the Middle East.

Communities are bound to have people who challenge authority. So, religious leaders in a society needed something that could instill the "fear of god" in those who posed such challenges. Astronomy (after geography) is the world's oldest science, and it appears to have been associated with most if not all early civilizations. Could the astronomer's primary role have been to forecast eclipses? Imagine the impact of a priest telling a protesting group, "Cooperate or the sun will disappear!"—and then making good on the threat! Understanding the heavens gave priests a tremendous advantage in their attempt to maintain civil order.

Not all hydraulic cultures achieved what historians refer to as a "civilization." It is true, however, that all civilizations that flourished in arid lands did have two things in common: irrigated farming and a strong central authority.

6

Human Geography

It is impossible to stereotype people by the environments in which they live. As you learned in Chapter 5, traditional desert-dwelling cultures have varied from extremely simple to incredibly complex civilizations. Some people were rural, others urban. Among rural populations, some were herders, others farmers. Urban dwellers included people living in small, remote oasis villages and large cities, bustling with trade and bursting with new ideas. With the possible exception of pastoral nomads, each of these scenarios could be found in each of the world's ecosystems. What most sets desert-dwelling people apart from others is not so much their way of life, but the fact that, in order to survive, their culture must be adapted to aridity.

Today, as in the past, the ways of desert living are marked by vast diversity. In the previous chapter, you learned about the Seri Indians, some of the world's least technologically developed people. Yet within a distance of less than 500 miles from the Seris' homeland lie the modern cities of San Diego, Las Vegas, Phoenix, and Tucson. Similar contrasts can be found throughout much of the desert world. Other than being adapted to the desert environment, there is nothing unique that is common to people living in arid lands. Languages vary, as do religions, customs, dietary patterns, and housing. This chapter presents a general topical overview of the human geography of desert peoples. Our attention will focus upon such topics as folk and popular culture, population and settlement, language and religion, government, and economic activities, intertwined with other traditional geographic themes.

FOLK AND POPULAR CULTURE

One of the greatest "gaps" between peoples today is the one that exists between traditional folk societies and fast-paced contemporary culture. Folk cultures are those that are inward looking, bound by tradition, and tied to customs. Change is threatening to them and they cling to the past. In the pure form (which scarcely exists anyplace in the world today), they are self-sufficient but illiterate (unable to read or write). They live outside the cash economy, providing for their own needs or obtaining needed items by barter. Their daily tasks may last 15 hours, but they are not recognized for contributing to the wealth of their nation.

To understand popular culture, simply think of your own life and that of other people in developed countries. We thrive on fads and change. Education is essential if one is to succeed. Most people learn a specialized trade and we turn to others for countless services—things that in a folk culture, people do for themselves. People hold jobs, and goods and services are purchased. Things we in developed countries do affect others across the globe. For example, how many countries were involved in the manufacture of the clothing that you are wearing right now?

As you can see, vast differences exist between folk and popular cultures, whose members live in vastly different worlds.

Frequently, these worlds collide. In the United States, for example, many Native Americans live in the desert Southwest (and elsewhere, of course). These once proud people were torn apart by Europeans. Their lands—at least those deemed to be of value by Europeans—were taken, and many of them were placed on reservations, where they were doomed to poverty. Many attempts were made to strip them of their own cultures. Economically, socially, and politically, Native Americans in many ways continue to struggle in their relationship with the dominant society.

The clash between traditional societies and contemporary cultures is occurring in varying degrees and with various results throughout the desert realm. It began with the arrival of the first Europeans within the past 500 years. Since the arrival of Spaniards in the New World, many native desert peoples of Peru, northern Chile, and Patagonia have lived in the shadow of the Europeans. The same can be said for Australia's Aborigines and the !Kung (Bushmen) of the Kalahari. Tribal peoples in North Africa, the Middle East, and Central Asia also feel a widening gap between their traditional ways of living and those of the growing urban/industrial society in their regions.

Many observers believe that much of the ongoing conflict between Islamic extremists and the West is based on differences in values held by members of traditional versus contemporary cultures. Western ways are considered to be both alien and threatening to many traditional Muslims, who can neither understand nor accept such aspects of our popular culture as liberal social customs, sex-oriented entertainment media, and materialism.

POPULATION AND SETTLEMENT

Deserts occupy about 20 percent of Earth's land surface and are home to approximately 10 percent of the world's population. But such figures really tell us little about actual conditions. Statistically, of course, the data suggest that desert regions are less densely populated than the world as a whole.

Yet some of the world's most densely packed regions are arid lands. Worldwide, the population density is about 125 people per square mile (48 per square kilometer). In Egypt's Nile Valley, the figure is a whopping 2,000 people per square mile (772 per square kilometer) and in Pakistan's Indus Valley, the density soars to more than 5,000 people per square mile (1,930 per square kilometer). Desert lands, of course, also support some of the world's lowest population densities. In some parts of the Australian desert, the Sahara, and the Arabian Peninsula, density drops below 1 person per 100 square miles. The Sahara Desert is almost the size of the continental United States (the area minus Alaska and Hawaii), yet no railroad or improved roadway crosses the region. Huge areas—thousands of square miles—have no people whatsoever other than, perhaps, a passing nomadic band.

Some desert regions also are among the world's fastest growing. For a half-century, the desert region of the American Southwest has experienced the country's most rapid percentage of growth, meaning the percent by which population has increased, not the actual number of people. Similar stories of growth can be told for many communities throughout the region and for portions of Southern California, Arizona, New Mexico, and West Texas as well. For example, during the early 1950s, Mesa, Arizona, had a population of about 15,000. Today, its population is about 450,000. Desert states of northern Mexico also have experienced considerable growth during recent decades. Most of the population gain in the North American desert is the result of recent migration to the area. Refrigerated air-conditioning, which became widely available in the 1960s, made the deserts and their blistering summer temperatures much more livable.

In the Muslim-dominated portions of the desert realm (North Africa, the Middle East, and Central Asia), populations are growing because of high fertility rates. In many Islamic lands, the rate of natural population increase stands well above the world average (1.2 percent per year), more than double in a

Phoenix, Arizona, is one of only about a dozen desert-region cities with a population that exceeds one million people. The capital of Arizona is currently the sixth-largest city in the United States but is the fastest growing among the top 10 and will soon move past Philadelphia into fifth place.

number of countries. In the Palestinian territory and the West African country of Niger, it soars to a record high 3.4 percent per year. Life expectancy throughout the world's desert lands tends to be comparable to the world average, a little lower in portions of Africa, and somewhat above it in economically well-developed areas.

In terms of settlement, the population is highly clustered around available water. Surprisingly, despite being more clustered than in perhaps any other realm, most desert dwellers are rural rather than urban. In fact, only about a dozen desert cities have a population that exceeds one million. Phoenix, Arizona (3.3 million in the metropolitan area), is the largest in North America. Lima, Peru (6.3 million), is the largest in South America. Only two desert cities rank among the world's 25 most populated urban centers: Karachi, Pakistan (11.8 million, at number 13), and Cairo, Egypt (11.2 million, at number 16).

LANGUAGE AND RELIGION

As folk cultures, desert peoples spoke hundreds of native tongues and worshipped in many different ways. The study of language or religion among native North American cultures, for example, discloses a rich diversity of both and illustrates the tremendous complexity of these basic cultural traits. Most maps showing the global distribution of languages or religion reveal a very interesting and significant characteristic. Throughout much of the world, including desert regions, they show imposed, rather than native, patterns. In other words, languages are often spoken in a particular area because they were introduced by outsiders (for example, colonizers or invaders), instead of naturally developing on their own. Yet some very interesting exceptions do occur. For example, on many maps, "Bushmen" (Khoisan) is shown as the dominant language of the Kalahari, and "Aborigine" is shown as the dominant language of Australia's outback. This, too, reveals something about the culture history of the respective regions: They were not extensively settled or culturally influenced by European settlers.

In most parts of the world (including desert regions), however, maps of language and religion serve as historical documents of conquest and the spread of culture. In the Americas, as one would expect, English and Spanish were imposed upon speakers of native languages. So, too, were Christian faiths: Catholicism in Latin America and both Catholicism and Protestantism in Northern (Anglo) America. In North Africa and much of the Middle East, English or French became the colonial tongue. But because the Europeans were reluctant to settle permanently in desert lands, the European languages never caught on with the masses. Rather, the imprint of spreading Arabian culture—the Islamic faith and the Arabic language—is very evident on the cultural landscape of the regions. Islam also spread into much of the desert region in Central Asia, although the languages are Turkic.

Today, many desert people are multilingual. They will speak their own tribal tongue and perhaps the language of one or more nearby tribes. And certainly the educated elite, those who are involved in international economic, political, or other affairs, will speak one or more European language.

It is both ironic and tragic that religious differences are the source of so much hatred and conflict. Along the southern margin of the Sahara Desert (the Sahel zone), the northern and southern areas of many (if not most) countries are in conflict with one another. In the north are desert people, most of whom practice Islam. In the south are people who are animists (those who believe that things in nature have souls) or Christians. Muslims want to impose *Sharia*, or Islamic law. Non-Muslims heatedly resist this attempt. Elsewhere, Muslims and people of the Jewish faith continue to engage in heated conflict over Israel and the Palestinian territory. Within the realm of Islam itself, there is an increasingly strained conflict between those who practice two different branches of the faith (Sunni and Shia).

Both Christianity and Judaism, of course, began more than 2,000 years ago in what is now Israel. Islam was founded on the Arabian Peninsula during the seventh century A.D. The Christian and Jewish faiths rapidly spread northwestward into Europe. Islam, on the other hand, spread widely throughout the desert lands of North Africa, Southwest Asia, and Central Asia.

Much of the ill will that contributed to open conflict between Christians and Muslims grew during the eleventh through thirteenth centuries. During that period, wave after wave of Christian soldier-missionaries, called Crusaders, swept southeastward from Europe into the Holy Land, which the

Europeans hoped to free from Islamic control. Much of the past century has witnessed the turbulent conflict between Jews and Muslims over Israel's right to exist in the former Palestine. Since 1948, when Israel became an independent Jewish state, it has been under constant threat from its Islamic neighbors. The smoldering embers that were lit between the antagonists many centuries ago have recently burst into flames. Israel has been engaged in a number of military conflicts with nearby Muslim groups, both national and nongovernmental.

GOVERNMENT AND POLITICS

A stable government that is responsive of the needs of its people is essential to economic development and human well-being. Unfortunately, most desert countries have long suffered from poor and often repressive leadership. Many have struggled from open warfare, either with neighbors or as civil conflicts within their own territory. Most countries within the region claim to be republics, but in practice they fall far short of reaching this status. Few countries have benefited from a democratic political system. Particularly throughout the Islamic realm, few governments are elected by and responsible to the people they serve. Many countries, such as Saudi Arabia, Jordan, the United Arab Emirates, Bahrain, and Qatar are ruled by a monarchy, or ruling family. Several countries are theocratic states ruled by Islamic leaders, including Iran and formerly Afghanistan (under the former rule of the Taliban). In the "Horn" of East Africa, Somalia has no government at all; it is the world's only country experiencing a chaotic state of anarchy with no institution or individual in control.

In the Americas, the United States, Mexico, and Chile have achieved true democracies. Peru, after several decades of civil conflict and terrorist activity, appears to be stabilizing. In North Africa and the Middle East, Israel and Egypt are among a small number of countries with a democratic tradition. It is too early to predict the political outcome of the former Soviet Socialist Republics that are now recently independent. Currently, none of them appears to be strongly democratic or completely stable. The arid lands within China and Mongolia are under iron-fisted rule that is not apt to change in the foreseeable future.

As this book goes to press, the world watches anxiously as a huge political gamble takes place in the Middle East. The United States and its allies are attempting to introduce democratic governments to Afghanistan and Iraq. It is far too early to judge whether this will be successful. Afghanistan has been and continues to be primarily a tribal society. Regions surrounding the capital city, Kabul, have for centuries been under the control of powerful tribal chieftains (incorrectly called "warlords" by the U.S. media). It will be extremely difficult to break this long-standing tradition. The other segment of this ongoing attempt to spread democracy is, of course, in Iraq. Disposing of dictator Saddam Hussein and his government was just a start. The country's Sunni and Shia Islamic religious factions have a long history of antagonism toward one another. A third group, the 5 million ethnic Kurds, who have long been discriminated against by other Iraqis, add additional fuel to the flames of animosity and conflict.

In addition to the problems listed above, several other factors pose a serious challenge to political stability. One is the wave of religious extremism that is sweeping through much of the Islamic realm. The movement is an attempt by Islamic leaders to gain political power and to impose *Sharia* rule (Islamic law) on the countries they control. The oil industry is another factor that muddies the political waters throughout much of this desert region. Petroleum is a major part of the global economy, and the world's greatest known reserves of this increasingly scarce natural resource are in North Africa and the Middle East. The United States is but one of many countries that is feverishly attempting to gain the cooperation (if not control) of governments in oil-rich nations. In this context, former U.S. President Jimmy Carter clearly stated the United States's petroleum policy during his 1980 State of the Union address. In what has come to be recognized as the

Carter Doctrine, he said, "Any attempt by an outside force to gain control of the Persian Gulf region will be regarded as an assault on the vital interests of the United States of America."

ECONOMIC ACTIVITY

As is true of many other aspects of cultures in arid lands, it is difficult to stereotype what people do economically. Some aspects of economic activity are, of course, similar among different societies, at least in a very general sense. For example, all cultures occupy space, consume natural resources, and have both material and nonmaterial needs. They also create products and provide services of various types and are involved in the distribution and exchange of their goods and services. But from place to place, the ways in which these basic acts are fulfilled vary greatly. Simply stated, people in the United Arab Emirates, residents of the city of Hermosillo in Mexico, villagers in central China, and nomadic herders in the central Sahara do not fulfill their economic needs in the same way. Natural resources vary greatly from country to country. Nature offers many different opportunities and also imposes certain challenges that differ from place to place. And people dress, eat, and house themselves in different ways depending upon their culture. Also, the manner in which different societies view wealth, distribute capital, and approach the need to save for the future also varies greatly on a regional basis.

Arid lands have very few natural resources that are unique to the area. Aridity does help preserve concentrations of certain soluble minerals, such as the Bonneville Salt Flats in the United States and rich nitrate deposits in northern Chile's Atacama Desert. Aridity also preserves Peru's extensive *guano* beds. On the other hand, arid regions obviously lack the abundance and diversity of biotic resources, including forests, which occur in many humid regions. Metals and fossil fuels, however, are not tied to climates or ecosystems. Farming, despite being limited in some locations by environmental factors, is practiced throughout much of the desert realm.

Utah's Bonneville Salt Flats occupy some 160 square miles (414 square kilometers) of what was once the bottom of ancient Lake Bonneville. As Bonneville dried out, up to 6 feet (1.8 meters) of salt was deposited on the former lake floor. Today, the flats are public lands, and many land speed records have been established by high-speed race cars on the hard, flat surface of the salt flats.

Industrial Development

Industries can be classified as primary, secondary, and tertiary. Much of the desert realm has always been dependent upon primary industries. Primary industries include mining, farming, fishing, and logging. Primary industries oftentimes are owned and managed by huge corporations, which as often as not are based in distant lands. Wages are low and jobs require little in the way of formal education or well-honed skills. It was the lust for gold and other precious metals that first attracted Spaniards to deserts of the New World. Mining has long been an extremely important activity in the North and South American desert regions. Elsewhere, the Kalahari has become a major source of diamonds, and Australia's desert is famous for vast mineral wealth. North Africa and the Middle East are the world's leading producers of petroleum and natural gas.

Farming originated in arid and adjacent semiarid lands of the Middle East. Throughout recorded history, oasis farming has supported local populations, but exports have been relatively insignificant. Today, some exceptions are found in large commercial irrigated operations located in the American

Guano
A Fortune in Bird Droppings

For centuries, coastal Peru has been the source of a rather strange natural resource—guano. This rich source of organic fertilizer is actually dried bird droppings, and has brought a fortune to Peruvians since the time of the ancient Inca civilization. Along Peru's coast, prevailing winds blow the ocean's surface water westward across the Pacific Ocean. As offshore water is displaced, it is replaced by an upwelling of nutrient-rich cold water from deep within the ocean. Small marine organisms called plankton thrive in the cold waters of the Peru Current, immediately off the country's desert coast. Plankton provides the food supply for huge schools of fish, including billions of small anchovies. It is mainly the anchovies that are the primary food source for millions of cormorants, pelicans, boobies, and other sea birds that are attracted to the area by the abundance of food.

Thanks to the millions of birds and their rich diet, millions of tons of bird droppings have accumulated over time on the bone-dry "Guano Islands" that lie just off Peru's coast. During the course of thousands of years, the islands became buried beneath huge deposits of guano, often dozens of feet deep. The accumulations were protected by the area's extreme aridity.

Southwest, northern Mexico, and on a smaller scale in several areas of North Africa and the Middle East. Cotton, fruit, and vegetables are important export crops. Fishing is of local importance both as a business and in feeding local populations. Peru occasionally ranks number one in the world in its harvest from the cold waters of the Peru Current immediately off its coast. Logging in desert lands is of course of little importance.

Centuries ago, the Inca began to use guano as fertilizer, becoming the only native people in the Americas to deliberately fertilize their crops. After Europeans arrived in the region, the nitrogen-rich fertilizer began finding markets in Europe and North America and mining activities boomed. But can you imagine what the working conditions were like in the guano mines? From various written accounts, they must have been among the world's absolute worst working environments.

Mortality among the Native Americans who were forced to work the mines was so high that the Europeans sought an alternative source of laborers. To find workers to mine the guano islands, the Spaniards turned to China. Today, nearly 1 percent of Peru's population traces its ancestry to these early Chinese guano miners. Today, Peru has more than 2,000 Chinese restaurants, and Lima has a thriving "Chinatown."

Because of excessive mining and the development of synthetic fertilizers, guano mining has all but disappeared. During its heyday, however, the guano industry provided geographers with a fascinating example of environmental interaction, the development of a rather unique economic resource, and surprising cultural consequences of its use.

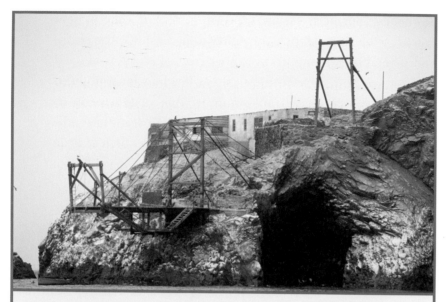

Over the centuries, an abundance of fish attracted millions of birds to the Ballestas Islands, off the coast of Peru. Over time, an accumulation of guano, or bird droppings, built up on these islands. The guano, which served as an excellent fertilizer for agricultural crops, was subsequently mined by Inca Indians and then Chinese laborers. Pictured here is a platform upon which guano was loaded onto ships and sent to other ports.

Secondary industries are those engaged in manufacturing and construction. All large cities will support some manufacturing, but for the most part, such activities are for the production of items for local consumption, rather than export. Most of the countries that are in arid lands (with the exception of the United States, Australia, and Israel) are classified as being less developed countries (LDCs). These countries lack the money to generate much in the way of economic development. Political instability adds to their problems. Few potential investors—whether foreign or domestic—dare risk their money in a place where it might be lost because of conflict. Widespread corruption also scares away investors from doing business in many LDCs. Sadly, most desert countries find themselves high on the list of the world's most corrupt places.

Tertiary industries are those that provide some service. Health care, education, insurance, and sales fall within this category. So, too, do transportation, tourism, and communications. Most desert countries lag far behind the developed world when it comes to tertiary industries. Particularly critical are health care and education. Even in developed countries, the life expectancy of desert-dwelling minority populations falls far below that of the more affluent populations outside of the desert areas. It is difficult to determine literacy figures, but for much of the desert regions, it is alarmingly low. In a number of countries, scarcely half the population can read or write. And in Islamic countries, which in general place little emphasis on educating women, a considerable gap exists between male and female literacy.

A strong tourism industry is often lacking in many desert nations. Many, if not most, desert areas can offer marvelous natural landscapes and scenic wonders, a fascinating local history, and charming people. But tourists are not apt to visit places that lack adequate tourist facilities or are unable to give them some degree of assurance that they will be safe. To add to this, some arid lands have a history of hostile acts against visitors. Sadly, such conditions deprive these countries of what may be their greatest opportunity for economic gain.

Desert Regions

The world's desert lands and peoples are remarkably diverse. Each of the many regions that lie within arid climates has its own distinct features, conditions, and character. In fact, aridity and various types of adaptation to a dry environment are about the only thing they share in common. In this chapter, you will briefly visit the world's major desert regions and learn what makes each of them unique.

NORTH AMERICAN DESERTS

Much of the southwestern United States and northwestern Mexico is occupied by the Colorado-Sonora Desert. In both countries, the desert has experienced remarkable growth in population and economic development during the past 50 years. At first, much of the expansion was based on irrigated farming. Warm winter temperatures made it possible for desert farmers to raise and ship produce to winter markets. And refrigerated rail cars and trucks made it possible to ship perishable produce to distant and hungry urban populations. Another boost came from the twentieth century shift of the "Cotton Belt" from the southeastern United States to the Southwest and adjacent Mexico.

It was really refrigerated air-conditioning that made the population boom possible. People follow jobs and jobs follow labor. With cool, comfortable living (and driving) possible, people began to flock to the North American deserts. Manufacturing and service industries relocated to cities such as Phoenix, Tucson, Albuquerque, and El Paso, fueling explosive population growth. As rapid travel became possible (the jet airplane age began about 50 years ago), millions of people opted for a Las Vegas holiday. Across the border in Mexico, small towns grew to huge cities. Many border cities have grown tremendously during the last 50 years, including Tijuana (near San Diego, California) and Ciudad Juárez (near El Paso, Texas), both of which now have populations that exceed one million. Some people were attracted to the border in the hope of finding work in the United States, legally or illegally. Others were drawn to the border region to work in *maquiladoras*, which are manufacturing plants that make goods for companies in the United States. More than one million Mexicans are employed in the more than 3,000 maquiladoras that dot the U.S.–Mexico border. Several coastal Mexican desert cities have also become popular vacation destinations.

As is true throughout much of the desert world, the only brake that can slow or stop the runaway growth in the North American desert is the water supply. Already, the use of water from the Colorado and Rio Grande has reached the highest point possible.

DESERTS OF SOUTH AMERICA

According to some climate classification systems, South America has one to three desert regions. This provides a fine example with which to illustrate the geographic concept of "region." Regions are nothing more than geographic "convenience packages" that are created to fit particular needs. In the context of this book, it is important to at least mention each desert region as recognized by some authorities.

Lake Maracaibo Basin

A very small portion of northwestern Venezuela, around Lake Maracaibo, is classified as desert by many geographers and climatologists. Here, climate is of little importance. The region's significance lies in the fact that the Maracaibo Basin is one of the Western Hemisphere's leading areas of petroleum production. Venezuela is highly dependent on its petroleum exports to support its economy. Oil accounts for about one-third of the country's gross domestic product, more than half of the government's revenue, and some 80 percent of its income from exports. Venezuela, like many other natural-resource–dependent countries, must add more areas of income to its economy before the oil wells run dry. Otherwise, after the oil reserves run out, Venezuela and other countries with incomes dependent on oil will no longer have any means in place to make money.

Argentina's Desert Lands

From about 20 to 50 degrees south latitude, several areas of desert lie scattered about the western and southern half of Argentina. The largest desert area includes much of Patagonia. This rugged plateau supports a sparse population. A few small oasis settlements struggle to survive along streams that flow from the Andes eastward into the Atlantic. Where they exist, streams have scoured deep valleys into the plateau surface, making north-south transportation difficult. In fact, no railroad and only several gravel roads cross the 1,100-mile (1,770-kilometer) plateau in that direction. Irrigated farming, including Argentina's thriving wine industry, is centered in the northwestern part of the country's desert regions. Sheep grazing is the major economic activity of Patagonia. Argentina's Andean foothills, briefly home to the notorious cowboy outlaws Butch Cassidy and the Sundance Kid about a century ago, have recently been "discovered" by outsiders. Some people from the U.S. entertainment industry are among those who have lately bought large parcels of land, having been attracted to the region by its solitude and natural beauty.

Atacama Desert

Extending from about 5 to 30 degrees south and hugging the Pacific Coast and its cold Peru Current is the world's driest region, the Atacama Desert. Although bone-dry, this desert is cool, cloudy, and shrouded in fog throughout much of the year. In fact, communities that average .01 inch of precipitation a year and may go decades without rain can still average 80 percent relative humidity, a figure comparable to cities along the U.S. Gulf Coast. While in Lima, Peru, in the 1830s, naturalist Charles Darwin had this to say about the cloud cover:

> A dull heavy bank of clouds some 100 feet thick constantly hung over the land. It has become almost a proverb that rain never falls in the lower [coastal] part of Peru. Yet this can hardly be considered correct, for during almost every day of our visit there was a thick drizzling mist which was sufficient to make the streets muddy and one's clothes damp; this the people are pleased to call the "Peruvian dew."

Lima, founded in 1535 by Francisco Pizarro, was the first large city established by the Spaniards on the South American continent. Today, Lima is a booming political, industrial, financial, cultural, and transportation center of about 8 million people. During recent decades, the city's population nearly doubled. Two ultra left-wing groups—the Sendero Luminoso ("Shining Path") and Túpac Amaru (named for the last leader of the Inca)—terrorized much of the country, particularly the Andean highlands. During the 1980s and early 1990s, millions of mountain people migrated to coastal cities, including Lima, seeking safety.

Thousands of years ago, various Indian peoples inhabited the coastal zone. Paired villages were common—one on the coast and a related one some miles up a stream valley. Coastal villages specialized in fishing, and the inland communities were agricultural. Cotton was an important crop. It was used to make nets for the fishermen who, in turn, provided farmers with fish. Today, Peru continues to rely heavily on farming and fishing. Where streams flow across the desert from the Andes, oases flourish. The cold waters of the Peru Current offer a rich harvest of fish—most of the time. Ironically, fishing in Peru is much like a yo-yo, experiencing extreme highs and lows. One year, the country will take the world's largest catch; the next year it may not be listed in the top 20 fish-catching countries. This "feast and famine" is the result of El Niño, the periodic warm current that replaces the nutrient-rich cold water of the Peru Current.

Mining is the primary economic activity in northern Chile's Atacama Desert. Chile is the world's leading producer of copper. The state-owned Chilean National Copper Corporation is the world's largest copper-producing company, and operates the world's largest copper mine. Several years ago, the Chuquicamata mine expanded to devour the community for which it was named. Residents were relocated to Calama, just a few miles distant. During the early twentieth century, a huge portion of the Chilean economy was dependent upon mining sodium nitrate from the northern desert region. This mineral is used as fertilizer and in making explosives. During World War I, however, a process was discovered for making nitrates artificially. Between this development and the war-caused shipping blockade, Chile's economy collapsed. Then, several decades ago, the country's economy was again dependent on a mineral—nearly 90 percent of the economy relied upon copper mining and exports. For some time, many observers feared that the country was setting itself up for another economic disaster. Today, however, about two-thirds of Chilean exports are products other than minerals.

AUSTRALIA'S DESERT "OUTBACK"

Australia holds the distinction of being the world's driest inhabited continent, with roughly half of the country being desert and

The outback region of Australia is roughly half the size of the continental United States, but due to its aridity, it is home to only small pockets of economic activity. One such activity is mining: Australia produces 95 percent of the world's opals and the outback is home to the world's largest opal mine, located near the town of Coober Pedy.

another third being semiarid and subject to repeated droughts. Unlike many desert regions that have river oases, Australia's parched interior does not have exotic streams or other sources of abundant freshwater. Scanning an atlas of economic activity is extremely revealing in regard to just how barren and unproductive the country's desert really is. Only scattered mining centers appear and nearly all of those sites are located at the desert's margins. In an area roughly half the size of the continental United States, there is only one east-west highway spanning the continent and only one railroad that crosses from south to north through the desert. (The railroad, completed in 2006, extends northward from Alice Springs to Darwin.)

This land that once was inhabited solely by various Aboriginal tribes has become one of the world's most productive producers of mineral wealth. Occasionally, mining and native beliefs conflict as proposed developments intrude upon lands held sacred by the Aborigines. Small deposits of petroleum and natural gas lie scattered throughout the region, as do a number of major uranium deposits. The country also has huge deposits of gold and silver, cobalt, iron ore, nickel, and manganese. Lead, zinc, and copper also are mined within the desert region. Export of minerals has helped Australia accumulate the smallest national debt of any developed country.

AFRICA'S DESERT REGIONS

About half of Africa is classified as desert—and much of it is nearly deserted of people and plant life. The two major areas are the Kalahari in the south and the giant Sahara that spans the northern part of the continent from coast to coast. About 95 percent of Africa lies within the dry, seasonally wet-and-dry, or wet tropics. Each of these climates and their resultant ecosystems is an environmental "problem area" that can make development difficult and costly. This has been a major factor in the continent's very slow economic development. In many respects, nature has not treated Africa and its more than 900 million people kindly.

The Kalahari

The Kalahari Desert occupies parts of northern South Africa, much of Botswana, most of Namibia, and reaches northward into southern Angola. Along the coast, the arid landscape is recognized by a local name, the Namib Desert. The Namib's extreme aridity is due to the cold Benguela Current that hugs the continent's southwest coast. This coastal region bears the gruesome name, "Skeleton Coast." Many ships wrecked along this treacherous coastal zone, leaving their stranded sailors to die of thirst.

Traditionally, the Kalahari was inhabited by !Kung (Bushmen) and Hottentot peoples. Eventually, the region was colonized by Portuguese (Angola), Germans (Namibia), British (Botswana, Namibia, and South Africa), and Dutch (South Africa). Desert areas of the respective countries were all but ignored by the Europeans, however, leaving them to native populations until recent times.

The success story of the Kalahari, and indeed of much of Africa, is Botswana. This small landlocked country has a population of about 1.6 million. Race relations in Botswana are among the best on the continent. The country is a model of democracy and political stability. Corruption is low, at least in comparison to other African states. And its economy is the second strongest in the entire continent, trailing only its southern neighbor, South Africa. During recent decades, Botswana has replaced South Africa as the world's leading producer of gem quality diamonds (those diamonds that are used for jewelry). Diamonds are the country's primary source of income. These precious gems account for more than three-fourths of all exports and about one-half of Botswana's gross domestic product. Sadly, Botswana also has one of the world's highest rates of HIV/AIDS. Nearly one out of every four adults has tested positive for this dreaded disease.

The Great Sahara

In terms of human settlement and activity, the Sahara and a donut have something in common: empty centers. With the exception of the Nile River Valley, nearly the entire desert supports a population of less than one person per square mile (0.3 per square kilometer). Some maps show roads crossing the Sahara. But once they reach the desert core, these "roads" turn into little more than "paths" marked only with widely spaced flags to show travelers the route.

Oases associated with the Ahaggar and Tibesti highlands support small populations of subsistence farmers and herders. Among traditional cultures, the Berber (technically, a language,

(continues on page 100)

Tombouctou
"The End of the World"

To Europeans, Tombouctou (spelled in several ways, including "Timbuktu") is synonymous with the "end of the world," a location as remote as any on our planet. Yet this once thriving city lies only a short distance from Europe's Mediterranean shores. How, then, did this West African city earn its reputation? To answer this question, we must turn to a number of geographic concepts and conditions. Physical geography, environmental perception, and cultural adaptation to environmental surroundings provide some of the answers. So, too, do exploration, trade, changing technology, and the clash between folk and popular culture.

For 2,000 years, camel caravans linked the Mediterranean coast with cities on the southern edge of the Sahara, a region called the Sahel. Desert people were not used to the humid conditions of the savanna and rain-forest realms lying south of the Sahara. And the people from the south found the desert to be a totally alien and inhospitable environment. As a result, trade items from the south (such as gold, ivory, slaves, grain, and palm oil) were transported north until the desert was reached. Camel caravans carried trade items (salt and various European manufactured goods) across the Sahara and southward to the desert margin. Between these two extreme environments and on the great bend of the Niger River, Tombouctou was founded, prospered, and grew. The city amassed great wealth and became a leading center of trade and commerce, education, and the religion of Islam. The city's fame spread far and wide, including well into Europe.

Most European explorers followed water routes. But a series of river rapids prevents navigation on the Niger River from the coast to Tombouctou. To the north and west, the desert created a huge barrier to European explorers who were unfamiliar with, what was to them, a harsh and alien environment. Further, Muslims who controlled the Sahara regarded Christians as a threat. And so, although Europeans were aware of this magnificent, booming city, they were unable to reach it. Amazingly, it was not until the 1820s that Europeans first reached Tombouctou. When they arrived, the once proud city had shriveled to a small, poor, dusty city of adobe structures, its past fame having long vanished into the desert sands.

What caused Tombouctou to wither away? Here, too, geography provides an answer. By the mid-1400s, Portuguese sailors reached the coastal region of West Africa near Guinea. Cargo previously carried by foot (from the south) and camel (from the north) could now be carried by ship. Almost overnight, Tombouctou lost its important economic function. It had become a victim of technological change and another step in the transition from folk to popular culture.

During the fourteenth through sixteenth centuries, Tombouctou, or Timbuktu, was a leading center of trade along the trans-Saharan caravan route. The city, which is located in present-day Mali, was designated a UNESCO World Heritage Site in 1988.

(continued from page 97)

but also the term by which these largely nomadic people are recognized) were dominant. Perhaps the best-known Berber group is the Tuareg. For more than 2,000 years, these nomadic peoples traded camels across a trans-Saharan caravan route linking Mediterranean cities with those located south of the Sahara.

Most economic development within the Saharan region takes place in areas adjacent to the desert itself. Exceptions include petroleum and natural gas in Algeria and Libya (the chief source of wealth for both countries), and uranium in Niger. The use of these deposits of natural resources has brought economic, population, and transportation development to areas of production. Libya's monumental Great Man-Made River Project also brought some development to that country's interior.

During the 1970s and 1980s, much of the world learned a new word: *desertification*. The term refers to the creation of desert-like conditions as a result of human activity. It can be caused by such things as over-grazing, firewood cutting, and tilling marginal soils. Steppe (grassland) climates tend to experience drought conditions every three decades. In the Sahel zone that borders the southern Sahara, however, an entire 30-year cycle was missed. This resulted in some 60 years of above-average rainfall. With wetter conditions, settlement began to expand into what formerly (under normal conditions) had been the southern Sahara. Herd sizes grew, new ground was broken for planting, and the human population greatly expanded—resulting, of course, in the need for more cattle, more crops, and more firewood. A human and environmental disaster was in the making.

When the normal drought cycle returned in the early 1970s, environmental conditions and human activity were far out of balance. Astronauts reported seeing "small white circles" in West Africa from their vantage point in distant space. Throughout the Sahel zone, boreholes (wells) had been drilled to provide water for livestock and other uses. Animals, however, could only stray so far from the wells before needing to return in order to replenish their water supply. Over-grazing around the wells is what created the white circles seen from space. What was the response to this growing tragedy? More boreholes were drilled! Very rapidly, much of the Sahel zone became ravaged by over-grazing that resulted in further desertification. As a result, in some places, the Sahara Desert spread southward at a rate of 10 to 12 miles (16 to 19 kilometers) a year. It took many years and billions of dollars to stabilize the region. In the process, pastoral nomadism all but vanished as a way of life in the African Sahel.

EGYPT

Despite its location in the northeastern corner of Africa, Egypt is often included within the Middle East because of its close cultural ties to that region. Here, the country is treated separately. Historically, demographically, culturally, and in many other geographical aspects, Egypt deserves recognition on its own. Few countries have a more fascinating history than does this land that clings to the shores of the Nile and its life-giving oasis. Farming, the very foundation of early civilizations, may have had it start here some 18,000 years ago. Two of the world's Seven Wonders—the pyramids and lighthouse at Alexandria— attest to the country's early cultural development. In fact, to many of us, "Ancient Egypt" and "Early Civilization" are synonymous.

In many respects, modern Egypt began with the opening of the Suez Canal in 1869. This 101-mile-long (163-kilometer) artery that links the Mediterranean and Red seas is one of the world's most important facilities. But it is not Egypt's only engineering claim to fame. The country's Aswan High Dam is one of the largest and most controversial engineering projects of recent times. Initially, Egypt turned to the United States and England to help design, finance, and assist in construction of the dam. When refused by these Western nations, Communist China stepped in, as did the Soviet Union soon thereafter.

These events created an international crisis that took years to resolve. Ultimately, the dam was designed and largely built by the Soviets, giving them a cold war foothold in Egypt (hence, much of the Middle East).

Aswan was finally completed in 1970 and its reservoir, Lake Nasser, filled by 1976. The project brought many benefits to the country, but also some problems. Annual floods on the Nile were finally controlled, but the floodwaters were the source of minerals and other nutrients that replenished soil fertility. Now, for the first time in history, Egyptian farmers had to fertilize their soil, which can be quite costly for poor *falaheen* (peasant farmers). Artificial fertilizers also contribute to increasing chemical pollution in the area. As the waters of Lake Nasser rose, nearly 100,000 people were displaced. Many treasured archaeological sites also were either lost to the rising lake level, or removed to higher ground. When built, the dam supplied nearly half of Egypt's electrical energy needs. Yet with a population that has doubled since its construction, the dam can meet only about 10 percent to 15 percent of the country's electrical needs today.

The dam has contributed to a number of other environmental concerns. Silt that once reached agricultural fields now settles in Lake Nasser, lowering its water storage capacity. In the absence of silt downstream from the dam, erosion has quickened its pace. Fishing in the Mediterranean has declined because important nutrients no longer reach the sea. Valuable agricultural land has been ruined by poor irrigation practices that result in waterlogging and the accumulation of salts in soils. These are just some of the many issues surrounding the controversial Aswan High Dam.

THE MIDDLE EAST AND SOUTHWEST ASIA

One could easily argue that the very complex, troubled, and oil-rich Middle East is the most important region in the world today. There can be little doubt that, with the cold war a thing

The modern city of Dubai, in the United Arab Emirates, stands in sharp contrast to the Middle East's traditional rural villages and age-old regional capitals. Since 2000, Dubai has instituted a large-scale construction campaign driven by its desire to diversify the economy.

of the past, the Middle East is the focal point of global attention and concern. Thousands of years ago, this dynamic part of the world gave root to Western civilization. Events currently happening in the Middle East and Southwest Asia now have a nearly immediate impact on our lives. Newspapers and television tell of the clash between Islam and the West. Words such as *jihad, terrorism,* and *al Qaeda* have entered the common vocabulary or taken on new meaning during recent years. We see the effects of this global struggle everywhere, from the rising costs of gasoline, to the long lines at airport security checkpoints, to stories of the experiences of U.S. soldiers overseas.

The contemporary Middle East is a land of contrasts, many of which lie at the foundation of the region's problems and conflicts. Few places in the world have a greater gap between the wealthy and poor. Western ideas of democracy, social equality, and the economy have not fared well in most Middle Eastern countries. Shining modern cities like Dubai, in the United Arab Emirates, stand in sharp contrast to traditional rural villages and age-old regional capitals. Even within cities such as Cairo, Teheran, Amman, and Damascus, areas of affluence and luxury are surrounded by poverty and squalor. As a region largely dominated by folk culture, many people are reluctant to change. They feel threatened by modernization and globalization and the freedom of options that they bring.

Although news reports often focus on stories about the bitter clash between the Jewish population of Israel and the surrounding Islamic Arab and Palestinian neighbors, it is important to remember that Islam, itself, is a house divided. The ongoing clash between traditional and modern, rich and poor, powerful and powerless, will continue for decades to come. So, too, will conflicts between Sunni and Shia Muslims, Israel and its neighbors, and those lands with or without adequate supplies of water.

All of the foregoing concerns pale, however, in contrast to the importance of oil within the region. More than a half-century ago, anthropologist Leslie A. White spotlighted the importance of energy consumption. He suggested that cultural growth (an increase in the number and complexity of cultural traits) is dependent upon how much energy each person in that culture consumes. Numerous examples suggest that White was correct. Nearly 70 percent of the world's proven energy reserves are in the Middle East, and an estimated 40 percent of the developed world's economy is based on the use of fossil fuels. Stop and think: Where would we be without cars, trucks, ships, planes, and trains—nearly all of which are powered by petroleum? Because of this situation, it is imperative that the Middle East is stabilized. Were the Middle East to fall into total chaos, the oil-dependent industrial West would experience a staggering economic decline. The resulting economic depression would also destroy any hope for economic development and future prosperity within the less-developed world.

As you can see, all of the world's people have much at stake in the Middle East. Middle Easterners, on the other hand, are often resentful over what they perceive to be their role as puppets. Many of them feel powerless in the global struggle for control of their petroleum resources and overwhelmed by the threat of outside cultural domination.

CENTRAL ASIA

The desert areas of Central Asia remain a huge blank spot in the "mental map" possessed by most Northern Americans. Historically, city names such as Tashkent (in Kazakhstan), Samarkand (in Uzbekistan), and Ulan Bator (in Mongolia) may ring a bell of recognition. So, too, might the famous Silk Road (upon which tradesmen traveled between the Middle East and East Asia) and notorious Mongol warriors such as Genghis Khan and Tamerlane. Readers may know something about the distant past of this region. During most of the twentieth century, however, Central Asia was a part of the former Soviet Union and therefore off-limits to Westerners. So, too, were the lands of inner China and Mongolia. Only recently have these remote lands begun to open their doors—and often just by a narrow crack—to foreigners.

The nations in this region face many problems. As landlocked countries, they remain quite isolated from the rest of the world. With few capital resources, there is little wealth to invest in development. Rampant corruption, lack of adequate infrastructure, and inept authoritarian governments discourage foreign investment. Like many other arid lands, this region looks to the future with hope, but great uncertainty.

8

Future Prospects for Desert Lands and Peoples

Water is the key to desert survival. If people are to live in arid lands, they must have an adequate source of water. Oil and other mineral resources are of great importance regionally, but they will soon be gone. For most of the desert realm, oil and water long have been and certainly shall continue to be the most important natural elements and source of human concern. These, and in some cases, other precious resources lie at the very foundation of human settlement, economy, and well-being within the region.

For American deserts, the only limit to growth appears to be an adequate supply of water. The region's economy has become extremely diversified during recent decades. No longer are states such as Arizona and Nevada dependent upon their nonrenewable mineral resources. Currently, enough water exists in the region to support its booming population well into the foreseeable future. But if this is to happen, a very difficult decision must be made. In both the United States and Mexico, leaders must decide which is more

106

Since the early twentieth century, oil has been one of the most important natural elements in the desert region. Because of its importance, it has been a point of contention for generations. Pictured here is a burning oil well on the border of Kuwait and Iraq, which was set ablaze by retreating Iraqi soldiers prior to the second Gulf War in 2003.

important—people and urban growth, or agricultural production. There is not enough water for both to continue growing at their current pace.

In South America, the Atacama Desert region simply needs political stability to thrive. Streams flowing from the Andes provide an adequate and reliable water supply. Because the desert hugs the coast, future development also can draw and desalinize water from the Pacific Ocean. The economy of northern Chile's Atacama region depends largely on copper mining. Although currently thriving, the ore deposits will not last forever. Chile, however, is one of Latin America's most stable democracies. The world's driest desert and its unique conditions and resultant landscapes could be a very strong draw for tourists. All the country needs to do is improve its tourist infrastructure: "Build it and they will come!" The same holds true for Patagonia and its spectacular Andean scenery and rugged plateau landscapes.

The Kalahari Desert region in Africa is also thriving. No one knows, however, how long the diamonds will last. Botswana is politically stable and has a rapidly growing economy. A well-managed national park system with abundant wildlife, the unique Okavango Delta and Swamp, and fascinating Bushman culture can all attract tourists into the region. Peace finally appears to have come to long-troubled Namibia and Angola. Here, too, tourism may provide the capital resources to support the beginnings of development of other economic potentials.

More than a dozen countries lie fully or partially within the Sahara Desert. They all have their own problems and prospects. Generally speaking, they are poor, poorly governed, and dominated by Arabic- or Berber-speaking Muslims. A number of the countries have suffered civil conflict during recent decades. Other than Algeria and Libya, most nations lack valuable natural resources. A rich history, scenic Mediterranean beaches, the high Atlas Mountains, and traditional cultures could serve as the basis of a tourist industry. Again, however, a tourist infrastructure—hotels, restaurants, shops, car rental agencies, and so forth—must be in place before tourists will come. Of greatest importance, of course, is ensuring that visitors will be safe, something that much of the region cannot yet guarantee.

Egypt has most of the "pieces" in place that are essential to success. Today, as throughout history, the Nile River provides an adequate, reliable, and now controlled source of water. During recent years, the country's political situation appears to have stabilized somewhat. It has a thriving tourist industry, some manufacturing, and a growing service sector of the economy.

Egypt's greatest problem is the country's explosive population growth. Its 75 million people constitute one of the world's most crowded populations, and the number continues to grow at a rate of 2 percent per year, nearly twice the world average. It is difficult for the country's economy and services (schools, health care, and so forth) to keep pace with the rapidly growing population. If the government continues to be responsive to the needs of its people, social conditions remain stabilized, and population growth declines, Egypt's future should be bright.

This brings us to the turbulent Middle East. For decades to come, the politics of oil will continue to influence both local and global decisions and actions. Who will be the power brokers and ultimate winners and losers in this struggle? Few Middle Eastern countries have a tradition of political stability or democracy. The petroleum resources that provide many countries with nearly all of their wealth will not last forever. What will happen to these lands and peoples when the wells finally run dry? What future turns might the region's political fortunes take? Will the current push by the United States and its allies for democracy in Afghanistan and Iraq be successful? If it is, will a tide of democracy sweep across the Middle East and into other Muslim-dominated lands? What of Islam itself? Will Shia and Sunni factions put aside their heated differences? Will Islamic terrorists continue to use their faith as justification for their actions? Perhaps Islamic leaders and Muslims in general will finally rise up and say, "Enough!" to the use of their faith as a justification for terrorism.

These are just some of the many questions and issues that arise during discussions of current events in the Middle East. We can be all but certain that, during the foreseeable future, the Middle East will be the world's most critical economic, political, social, and military hot spot. A headline that appeared in the *Arizona Republic* more than two decades ago read: "Water becoming world issue; problems 'boggle the mind.'" (October 27, 1983). Although the article focused on the U.S. water supply, its theme certainly holds true for the world's desert regions. Yet when discussing the problems of arid lands, it is very easy to focus solely on water issues. We must remember that with contemporary technology, fresh-water can be diverted from sources hundreds of miles away, as is already being done in California, Arizona, and Libya. It also can be drawn from seawater through various desalination processes that are becoming economically viable. Agricultural lands can be taken out of production, releasing water supplies for growing urban populations.

Ultimately, the future of the world's desert lands—as is true of all environments—rests more with the people them-selves than any other factor. Among the various problems within the region are inept and self-serving governments, rampant corruption, civil strife, and booming populations that exceed economic growth. Acts of terrorism and other criminal activity (such as the drug trade) are commonplace throughout portions of the arid realm. It is difficult to imagine major changes coming soon to much of the region. Sources of conflict are simply too deeply rooted. And yet, recent decades have witnessed many changes for the better: East Germany, Yugoslavia, and other former Communist countries broke apart, and much of Latin America is becoming more politically stable. Throughout the desert realm, the future is in the hands of the people themselves. For much the world's desert lands and peoples, there may be reason for optimism.

Historical Geography
at a Glance

YBP*	
1,000,000	Early humans inhabit desert regions.
18,000	Evidence of early agriculture in Nile Valley.
12,000	Sheep and goats join the dog as domesticated animals.
8,000	Cattle domesticated.
3500 B.C.	Emergence of early cities in Middle East.
2800 B.C.	Early form of abstract writing developed.
2680 B.C.	Building of pyramids begun in Egypt.
814 B.C.	City of Carthage established.
330s–320s B.C.	Alexander the Great of Macedonia conquers lands eastward to create a vast empire.
A.D. 622	Prophet Muhammad moves from Mecca to Medina in present-day Saudi Arabia.
711	Muslims, having spread across North Africa, invade the Iberian Peninsula.
1095	First of many Christian Crusades that will last for three centuries, attempting to convert the Holy Land and take it away from Muslim control.
1869	Opening of the Suez Canal.
1870s	First oil wells in the Caspian Basin.
1880s	Beginning of Zionist movement; Jews migrate back to Palestine (Israel).
1908	Oil discovered and wells drilled in Iran.

1918 End of World War I and the partitioning of much of North Africa and the Middle East into countries, most of which had been European colonies.

1922 Temperature reaches 136°F (58°C) at Al Aziziyah, Libya.

1948 Creation of Jewish state of Israel.

1990 Iraq invades Kuwait, and the United States and its allies intervene in what comes to be known as the Persian Gulf War.

1991 Collapse of Soviet Union changes global geo-political strategies and allows the former Soviet states to become independent countries.

2001 Following September 11 attacks on the United States, U.S. forces enter Afghanistan marking the beginning of the "War on Terrorism."

2003 United States and its allies invade Iraq hoping to create stability within the Middle East.

* years before present

Bibliography

Bagnold, R.A. *The Physics of Blown Sand and Desert Dunes.*
London: Methuen and Company, 1941.

Beaumont, Peter, et al. *The Middle East: A Geographical Study.* New
York: Halsted Press, 1988.

Briggs, Lloyd Cabot. *Tribes of the Sahara.* Cambridge, Mass.:
Harvard University Press, 1960.

Cloudsley-Thompson, J.L., ed. *Sahara Desert.* Oxford: Pergamon
Press, 1984.

Cressey, George B. *Crossroads: Land and Life in Southwest Asia.*
Chicago: J.B. Lippincott Company, 1960.

Gautier, E.F. *Sahara, the Great Desert.* New York: Columbia
University Press, 1935.

Held, Colbert C. *Middle East Patterns: Places, Peoples, and Politics.*
Boulder, Colo.: Westview Press, 1989.

Hills, E.S., ed. *Arid Lands: A Geographical Appraisal.* London:
Methuen & Co. Ltd., 1966.

Lewis, Bernard. *The Arabs in History.* New York: Harper & Row,
Publishers, 1960.

Longrigg, Stephen H. *The Middle East: A Social Geography.*
Chicago: Aldine Publishing Company, 1963.

Walton, K. *The Arid Zones.* London: Hutchinson University Library,
1969.

Further Reading

Aramco World. Published bimonthly by the Saudi Aramco Oil Company. Excellent source of articles on the Muslim-Arab world.

Bourne, Joel K., Jr. "Eccentric Salton Sea." *National Geographic,* February 2005, 88–107.

Cockburn, Andrew. "Lines in the Sand: Deadly Times in the West Bank and Gaza." *National Geographic,* October 2002, 102–111.

De Blij, H.J., and Peter O. Muller. *Geography: Realms, Regions, and Concepts.* 12th ed. Hoboken, N.J.: John Wiley & Sons, Inc., 2006.

Gore, Rick. "Men of the Sea: Who Were the Phoenicians?" *National Geographic,* October 2004, 26–49.

Leone, Bruno. *The Middle East: Opposing Viewpoints.* St. Paul, Minn.: Greenhaven Press, 1982.

Morell, Virginia. "Africa's Danakil Desert: Cruelest Place on Earth." *National Geographic,* October 2005, 32–53

Spencer, William. *The Middle East.* Global Studies Series. Dubuque, Iowa: McGraw-Hill/Dushkin Company, annual editions, 2004.

Vesilind, Priit J. "The Driest Place on Earth." *National Geographic,* August 2003, 46–71.

Warne, Kennedy. "Okavango: Africa's Miracle Delta," *National Geographic,* December 2004, 42–67

Webster, Donovan. "Journey to the Heart of the Sahara." *National Geographic,* March 1999, 2–33.

———. "The Empty Quarter: Exploring Arabia's Legendary Sea of Sand." *National Geographic,* February 2005, 2–31.

White, Leslie A. "Energy and the Evolution of Culture." Chap. 13 in *The Science of Culture*. New York: Farrar, Straus and Giroux, 1949.

Yellen, John. "Bushmen." *Science,* May 1985, 41–48.

CHELSEA HOUSE BOOKS OF INTEREST

Allen, Calvin H. *Oman*. Philadelphia: Chelsea House, 2002.

Christensen, Wendy. *Empire of Ancient Egypt*. Philadelphia: Facts on File, 2004.

Cottrell, Robert C. *The Green Line: The Division of Palestine*. Philadelphia: Chelsea House, 2004.

Doak, Robin. *Empire of the Islamic World*. Philadelphia: Facts on File, 2004.

Gritzner, Charles F., and Yvonne L. *Peru*. Philadelphia: Chelsea House, 2004.

Gritzner, Janet H. *Senegal*. Philadelphia: Chelsea House, 2004.

Gritzner, Jeffrey A. *Afghanistan*, Second Edition. Philadelphia: Chelsea House, 2006.

———, and Charles F. *North Africa and the Middle East*. New York: Chelsea House, 2006.

Hall, John G. *North Africa*. Philadelphia: Chelsea House, 2002.

———. *Palestinian Authority*. Philadelphia: Chelsea House, 2002.

Harper, Robert A. *Saudi Arabia*. Philadelphia: Chelsea House, 2002.

Hobbs, Joseph. *Egypt*. Philadelphia: Chelsea House, 2003.

Isiorho, Solomon A. *Kuwait*. Philadelphia: Chelsea House, 2002.

Jordan-Bychkov, Terry G. *Australia*. Philadelphia: Chelsea House, 2003.

Kheirabadi, Masoud. *Iran*. Philadelphia: Chelsea House, 2003.

———. *Islam*. Philadelphia: Chelsea House, 2004.

Korman, Susan. *Kuwait*. Philadelphia: Chelsea House, 2002.

Lightfoot, Dale. *Iran*, Second Edition. New York: Chelsea House, 2006.

Marcovitz, Hal. *Jordan*. Philadelphia: Chelsea House, 2002.

Morrison, John. *Syria*. Philadelphia: Chelsea House, 2002.

Ries, Julien. *The World of Islam*. Philadelphia: Chelsea House, 2002.

Skelton, Debra, and Pamela Dell. *Empire of Alexander the Great*. Philadelphia: Chelsea House, 2005.

Slavicek, Louise Chipley. *Israel*. Philadelphia: Chelsea House, 2002.

Wagner, Heather L. *Saudi Arabia*. Philadelphia: Chelsea House, 2003.

———. *The Division of the Middle East: The Treaty of Sevres*. Philadelphia: Chelsea House, 2004.

Weber, Sandra. *Yemen*. Philadelphia: Chelsea House, 2002.

Zeigler, Donald J. *Israel*, Second Edition. Philadelphia: Chelsea House, 2006.

Picture Credits

Index

About the Author

Charles F. Gritzner is distinguished professor of geography at South Dakota State University in Brookings. He is now in his fifth decade of teaching at the college level, conducting scholarly research, and writing. In addition to teaching, he enjoys traveling, writing, working with teachers, and sharing his love of geography with classroom students and readers alike. As series editor and frequent author for Chelsea House's MODERN WORLD NATIONS and MODERN WORLD CULTURES series, and now author of the three-volume set GEOGRAPHY OF EXTREME ENVIRONMENTS, he has a wonderful opportunity to combine each of these "hobbies."

Professionally, Gritzner has served as both president and executive director of the National Council for Geographic Education. He has received numerous awards in recognition of his academic and teaching achievements, including the NCGE's George J. Miller Award for Distinguished Service to geography and geographic education, the Association of American Geographers' Excellence in Teaching Award, and the Gilbert Grosvenor Honors in Geographic Education.

ZERO

TO

IPO

OVER $1 TRILLION OF ACTIONABLE ADVICE FROM

THE WORLD'S MOST SUCCESSFUL ENTREPRENEURS

FREDERIC KERREST

NEW YORK   CHICAGO   SAN FRANCISCO   ATHENS   LONDON

MADRID   MEXICO CITY   MILAN   NEW DELHI

SINGAPORE   SYDNEY   TORONTO

1 2 3 4 5 6 7 8 9   LCR   27 26 25 24 23 22

ISBN: 978-1-264-27766-7
MHID: 1-264-27766-0

e-ISBN: 978-1-264-27767-4
e-MHID: 1-264-27767-9

This publication is designed to provide accurate and authoritative information in regard to the subject matter covered. It is sold with the understanding that neither the author nor the publisher is engaged in rendering legal, accounting, securities trading, or other professional services. If legal advice or other expert assistance is required, the services of a competent professional person should be sought.
—*From a Declaration of Principles Jointly Adopted by a Committee of the American Bar Association and a Committee of Publishers and Associations*

Library of Congress Cataloging-in-Publication Data

Names: Kerrest, Frederic, author.
Title: Zero to IPO : over $1 trillion of actionable advice from the world's most successful entrepreneurs / Frederic Kerrest.
Description: New York : McGraw Hill, [2022] | Includes bibliographical references and index.
Identifiers: LCCN 2021050578 (print) | LCCN 2021050579 (ebook) | ISBN 9781264277667 (hardback) | ISBN 9781264277674 (ebook)
Subjects: LCSH: Business planning. | Entrepreneurship. | New business enterprises. | Success in business.
Classification: LCC HD30.28 .K467 2022 (print) | LCC HD30.28 (ebook) | DDC 658.4/012—dc23/eng/20211015
LC record available at https://lccn.loc.gov/2021050578
LC ebook record available at https://lccn.loc.gov/2021050579

To every entrepreneur battling the odds,
trying to turn their vision into reality.
The world needs you.

———————

One hundred percent of any financial profits I receive from this book will go to **BUILD.org**, an organization that uses entrepreneurship to ignite the potential of youth from under-resourced communities, and to **The Hidden Genius Project**, which trains and mentors Black male youth in technology creation, entrepreneurship, and leadership skills to transform their lives and their communities.

CONTENTS

INTRODUCTION

It was July 2011 when I realized I had failed.

I was driving my ailing, 17-year-old Honda Accord down Harrison Street in San Francisco, and the heavy, gray blanket of summer fog seemed to press down on the city, and on me particularly. I considered just heading back to my apartment and not showing up for the meeting. After all, what was there to say? Our business was doomed.

I had started Okta with my friend Todd McKinnon in 2009. It was a pretty simple idea. We both believed business software was going to move online. The days of getting CD-ROM install discs would end soon. Eventually, somebody had to make sure that we could all sign in to software as it moved online. That had to be useful, right?

Todd and I walked into the small conference room at our cramped office where our board of directors was waiting. They had no idea that the news we were going to share would mean they were about to lose all the money they had bet on us. I tried to remember the moment, to lodge those smiles in my mind. Nobody was going to be smiling when we were done.

"OK, well, I'll dive into the quarterly report," I said.

I had stayed up all night pointlessly adding slides to the presentation, hoping to soften up the directors with minutiae before coming to the bad news. As I clicked through the data, I could see their attention wandering. There was a slide about hiring. Another about client prospects. Finally, we got to the slide I'd been dreading: sales and revenue.

"Yeah, and so, next, I'm gonna highlight that we hit a speed bump with sales," I said. "We missed our projections by 70 percent."

Everybody looked up. That got their attention. They seemed to be wondering if they had misheard me. Perhaps I'd said 17 percent?

I clicked forward, and it was there for all to see. A 70 percent sales miss. Our revenues weren't going up and to the right like all of our planned projections. They had flatlined like someone whose heart had stopped. Nobody was buying what we were selling.

"You show us a bunch of random sh*t before you show us this?" one board member asked, astounded.

"Let me tell you one thing," another board member snapped. "This is the kind of presentation that should only be a single slide long."

Then they told me to get out of the room. They were going to talk to us individually, so they could figure out what was going on. Since Todd was the CEO, they'd speak to him first.

I stepped outside and looked around the office. I was the president and COO. I'd spent two years pouring everything into this company. Now, it was worthless. To make things worse, my wife had just finished her medical residency, and we'd taken on a lot of debt. My stress levels were at an all-time high. I needed some air.

An hour later, I was back in my car, driving aimlessly around the city, when I got a call from Ben Horowitz, one of our board members. Ben and his partner Marc Andreessen had given us half of the $1 million seed money we'd used to start the company. Less than 12 months later, they'd put in another $8.85 million.

"You know that forecasting doesn't translate into sales, right?" he said.

I mumbled something lame, and he cut me off. I figured he was going to fire me and shut the company down.

Instead, he gave me two pieces of advice. I'll get into the specifics of what he said in the following chapters, but here's the upshot: He didn't tell me to work harder or berate me for being an idiot (though that's what I felt like). He drew on his own experience as a founder who'd faced near-bankruptcy himself and gave me specific, tactical suggestions for how we could pull ourselves out of our death spiral. It was wisdom he'd learned the hard way.

Too often in business, this kind of knowledge is only shared among a select few. It's the kind of thing that gets passed person-to-person. And yet, for a founder, it often makes the difference between success and failure. In my case, the advice turned everything around. We immediately implemented Ben's ideas, and things started to look up. Sales increased, and the business began to grow rapidly. Six years after that fateful board meeting, Okta went public. Today, in the fall of 2021, as this book is preparing to go to press, the company is worth over $40 billion dollars.*

If it weren't for that advice, at that moment, I don't think Okta would have survived. It changed the course of the company—and the course of my life.

Too often in business, this kind of knowledge is only shared among a select few. . . . And yet, for a founder, it often makes the difference between success and failure.

* The valuations of public companies fluctuate with the stock market. All valuations in this book are pegged to each company's market capitalization on Nov 15, 2021, which was shortly before this book went to press. The valuations of private companies were taken from funding and acquisition announcements.

We tend
to think of
successful
startups as
businesses that
were bound
to succeed
while failed
companies
were doomed
from the start.
That's not how
it works.

Several times a week, I get calls or emails from aspiring entrepreneurs looking for exactly the kind of advice that Ben gave me on that gloomy day. They're looking for real-world, actionable insights, and they're not getting them from the "Big Idea" business books out there. I read those books—and appreciate them—but when you're in the trenches, you don't want generalities. You need to know what to do *right now*.

That's what this book provides. Over the past 20 years, I've taken notes on the advice I've been given. I've been lucky enough to meet hundreds of business leaders and investors across the country, and I always pepper them with questions. The nitty-gritty tips in this book represent the distilled wisdom of two decades in the business trenches. It comes from people who have built over a *trillion* dollars' worth of wealth for themselves and their investors.

I've battle-tested these ideas myself, so I know their power. And I'm convinced it's long past time to share this wisdom. Entrepreneurs, CEOs, and corporate board members are overwhelmingly people of privilege—mostly men, largely white, frequently graduates of a few select universities, and usually members of difficult-to-penetrate networks. That has to change. Most economic growth—in the United States and abroad—comes from entrepreneurs and the new companies they create. To help more people earn a larger slice of the pie, we need to demystify the world of startups and disseminate the hard-won, closely held secrets of how to grow a business. These lessons should be available to everyone. That's why I created the *Zero to IPO* podcast that preceded this book and why I decided to capture all those insights in a single place, here.

Many people go to business school thinking that an MBA will teach them to navigate the world of finance and management. That may be true if you want to work for an established company. But if you want to start your own—if you have a fresh idea for how to solve a problem—then business school doesn't usually provide a roadmap. I was fortunate to attend MIT's Sloan School of Management, where I received an MBA in entrepreneurship and innovation. I made many lifelong friendships with classmates and faculty. I took amazing classes, including several on entrepreneurship and tech startups. I also ran MIT's celebrated $100K Entrepreneurship Competition. But even with all those experiences, I still emerged from business school with a weak grip on what was involved in building a company from scratch. I had to learn *that* from talking to entrepreneurs who had struggled before me—people I met through social circles in the Bay Area as well as other founders I met through Okta's investors. In this book, I will present their wisdom and advice.

The chapters ahead will guide you through the key steps in launching and growing a company. While I and many of the people featured in these pages have built public companies, a lot of the advice in here applies to founders who intend to get acquired or just stay private. Only a small subset of companies make it to the stock market, after all. Many founders build businesses that eventually get snapped up by larger corporations. And many more remain private (known as "cash-flow businesses"), throwing off enough money for you and your colleagues to do the work you want and live well. You'll see that some of the information in here—like how to raise money from venture capitalists—does only apply to the world of high-growth startups. But most of the advice, from how to choose an idea to how to set your company's culture, is applicable to entrepreneurs starting any kind of business.

This book is organized by topics in roughly the order you'll run into them as you build your business. In the beginning, I'll talk about who should become an entrepreneur and how to tell if you've got a good idea. From there, I'll focus on putting teams together and raising money. After that, I'll discuss sales and building a company culture, and then how to grow your company and how to lead it. I'll talk about what happens when everything goes south and how to take care of your mental and emotional health along the way. Lastly, I'll talk about working with boards of directors and going public.

The material is divided into individual sections, each with its own set of takeaways. Some of the stories in here are my own. Most, however, come from the many founders, investors, and executives I've met throughout my career in Silicon Valley. Some of them told their stories on my podcast. Others shared their experiences specifically for this book. Unless otherwise noted, all the stories and quotes in the book, including those from various experts, come from these interviews.

If you're an entrepreneur who doesn't happen to live in Silicon Valley, New York, London, Tel Aviv, Tokyo, or any of the other major startup hubs around the world, I want you to know that you too can do this. This book will help you, but I need to level with you: Regardless of where you live, your life will be painful and hard if you follow this path. We tend to think of successful startups as businesses that were bound to succeed while failed companies were doomed from the start. That's not how it works. In this book, you are going to hear what *really* makes the difference. This may dissuade some of you from pursuing your idea. Better now than later.

But if you are not dissuaded—if you're ready to withstand years of doubt, instability, and stress—then welcome to the real world of entrepreneurship.

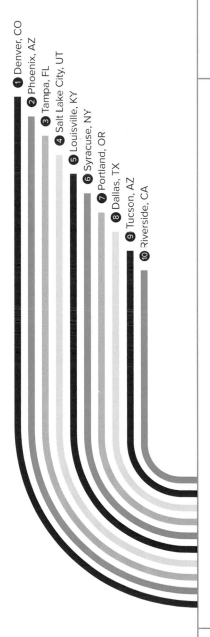

10 US Cities with the Lowest Startup Costs

1. Denver, CO
2. Phoenix, AZ
3. Tampa, FL
4. Salt Lake City, UT
5. Louisville, KY
6. Syracuse, NY
7. Portland, OR
8. Dallas, TX
9. Tucson, AZ
10. Riverside, CA

Source: "10 Best U.S. Cities for Startup Costs," Embroker, October 2021.

Three Rules to Live By

This book is full of great tactical advice, but if you stop reading here, there are three principles I'd want you to leave with, even if you learned nothing else.

TIME IS YOUR MOST VALUABLE ASSET

1 **Time is your most valuable asset.**
If you take money from investors (particularly venture capital firms), that money has a fuse on it. The VCs themselves need to produce returns for the institutions that gave *them* the money to invest in *you* (pension funds and university endowments, for example). So as soon as you take a VC check, there's pressure on you to become wildly successful within a relatively short period of time. How long? It depends, but for the purpose of making this point, think at least five to seven years. That means you're going to have to look at everything you do—from the smallest tactical choice to the biggest strategic decision—through the lens of whether it's helping you move quickly or whether it's slowing you down.

2 Keep the main thing the main thing.

Bill Aulet, a professor at the MIT Sloan School of Management, used to remind me of this when I was in business school. It's so important that I printed it up poster-size and hung it on my office wall. What it means is: prioritize, prioritize, prioritize. Don't get wrapped up in details that don't matter. Always stay clear on what the most important thing is—for the next hour, the next month, or the next year. I take this precept so seriously that, more than a decade into Okta, people around the office still hear me asking myself several times a day (out loud), "OK, what's the main thing I should be working on?" It's my way of helping myself stay laser-focused.

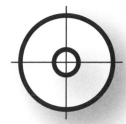

KEEP THE MAIN THING THE MAIN THING

NOTHING HAPPENS UNTIL SOMEONE SELLS SOMETHING

3 Nothing happens until someone sells something.

This is the second poster on my wall. It paraphrases a remark originally attributed to one of IBM's first CEOs, Thomas Watson Sr. Sure, rag on motivational posters all you want, but Old Man Watson had it right. When you first start out, you're going to find yourself dithering over everything from organizational charts to early hiring decisions. But none of that ultimately matters if you never make a sale. The point of your business is to sell your product to customers. Everything else is secondary.

one

SHOULD YOU BE AN ENTREPRENEUR?

My black dress shoes were soaked through. I couldn't feel my toes. But I needed to keep moving. The few vehicles on this stretch of Oklahoma highway blasted through the rapidly accumulating snow. They were trying to outrun the blizzard, but there was no escaping it for me. I was on foot. As the cars passed, they splattered ugly gray-black sludge across my suit and tie.

"I'm going to die," I muttered through a shiver. "What the hell am I doing?"

The answer was simple: I was desperately trying to make a sale.

It was February 2011, a few months before the terrible board meeting I recounted in the Introduction, and we weren't getting a lot of takers for our product. A guy at an oil and gas company in Tulsa had agreed to meet, so I flew out to pitch him.

Unfortunately, the blizzard hit that morning, and when I called a taxi from the hotel, the operator laughed.

"No one's going out in this weather," he said and hung up.

I'd flown halfway across the country. I looked at my watch. It was 9 a.m. I had one hour to get there. I hurried to the front desk and showed the receptionist the address. She said it was maybe a mile or two down the highway, but it was impossible to drive there. Anybody out in this weather was taking their life into their hands.

"Do you think I could walk?"

She laughed but then stopped. "Wait, are you serious?"

"Just point me in the right direction."

Forty-five minutes later, I started to realize a few things. The first was how much wind a semitruck creates as it blasts past you. The second was that this is what being an entrepreneur really looks like. Shivering cold, covered in grime, hoping for nothing more than the chance to convince a stranger to buy your product.

When I miraculously stumbled into our prospect's lobby, the security guard stood up with concern.

"Are you OK?"

I looked at my watch. It was a minute past ten.

"I'm fine," I said, smiling through a chattering jaw.

If you follow the media coverage of startups, you could be forgiven for thinking they're a quick way to riches. When a company goes public or is acquired, there's an explosion of triumphant articles that rarely reveal the journey it took to get there. The truth is that starting a company is a lot more like hiking through an Oklahoma blizzard. You're constantly blasted with bits of gravel, dirt, and garbage, and that's before you even pitch your product.

The data is clear: The vast majority of new companies fail. Others do well and get acquired by larger companies, landing tidy sums for their founders but not the gargantuan paydays of top IPOs. The number of startups that make it to a public stock exchange—and turn their founders into instant millionaires—is microscopically small.

Obviously, luck plays a role, but the personal makeup of the founders is also critical—so much so that it's one of the top factors investors look at when assessing a company. You can have an amazing idea, but if a venture capitalist can't picture *you* having the skills—or the psychology—to carry it out, he or she will pass.

In this chapter, I'll review what it takes to be an entrepreneur: the skills, the mindsets, and the dispositions. Hopefully you'll read this and think, "This is me!" But if it doesn't feel like you or if you start to feel queasy, listen to that inner voice. Odysseus's journey had nothing on the entrepreneur's path, so be certain this is the right fit for you.

"I'm going to die," I muttered through a shiver. "What the hell am I doing?"

Do You Have What It Takes?

A checklist of qualities that founders need to have.

Founders are all unique. Steve Jobs was different from Mark Zuckerberg. Katrina Lake is different from Elon Musk. Bill Gates is different from Arianna Huffington. Despite these differences, though, they all share certain qualities. Does this look like you?

☐ **The ability to thrive in ambiguity.** Running a startup means never having near as much information as you'd like when it comes to making important decisions. Forget about taking 30 data points and running a regression analysis. You'll be lucky to have three. You'll effectively be guessing most of the time. Are you comfortable with never knowing anything for certain?

☐ **A knack for salesmanship.** You're going to be selling every moment of every day. Not just to customers. Also to investors: Why should they back you? To talent: Why should they abandon their secure jobs to come work for you? To vendors: Why should they give you favorable terms? And don't forget your spouse or partner (if you have one): Why should they agree to let you imperil your family's future with this crazy dream of yours?

☐ **Equal parts EQ and IQ.** Most great founders aren't the stereotypical socially awkward geeks. They're actually great with people. They know how to inspire and motivate. They can put their egos aside and listen to their teams, advisors, and investors. So be sure your EQ (emotional intelligence) rivals your IQ.

☐ **Organization and discipline.** When you're the boss, no one is going to get on your case if you're disorganized or slack off. You have to be your own backstop. Do you naturally create plans and knock things out on your own? Can you keep track of the big picture while also figuring out what needs to move forward in any given week or month?

☐ **Energy and drive.** You've probably heard the expression, "It's not a sprint; it's a marathon." That's true, except that founding a company is a marathon made up of seven-minute miles.* You need to keep moving, at all times.

☐ **Inspirational leadership.** Can you set a vision—and a mission—and get people excited to follow you? This doesn't necessarily mean pulling off a Henry V on St. Crispin's Day† (though kudos if you can). Inspiring people come in all kinds of packages. It's not about *how* you do it. It's just *that* you do it.

☐ **Self-confidence.** When I started Okta, I always said I was "betting on myself"— that I had what it would take to grow Okta into a successful company. Sure, that confidence wobbled in our darkest times. But I always believed that if I just kept chipping away at our problems, I would find a way.

☐ **Resilience.** Napster founder and early Facebook president Sean Parker famously said running a startup is like chewing broken glass—to succeed, you need to fall in love with the taste of your own blood. And it's true. You're going to get punched in the mouth every day. Are you the kind of person who'll just keep getting up? Or will it eventually flatten you?

* **How fast is that?** The average marathoner runs a 10-minute mile.

† **This is Shakespeare's famous "band of brothers" speech from the play *Henry V*. Look it up.**

More Skills You Need to Master

A lot of people think being an entrepreneur is just about coming up with a great idea. (In the tech industry, they often think it's about having a great idea *and* being a great programmer.) But taking your idea from zero to IPO involves so many more tasks than simply building out the concept you've thought up. Take a look at this checklist, and ask yourself: Can I do that? Am I going to *enjoy* doing that? Because these things are what your job is *actually* going to consist of, especially the bigger you get.

☐ Can you **recruit** a team, especially people willing to leave safe jobs at established companies, when you can't pay them as much and you can't guarantee they'll have a job a year from now?

☐ Can you **attract investment capital**, or at least convince a bank to give you a loan?

☐ If you'll be selling to corporations, can you figure out the right executives to **approach** *and* **convince** them to give you time to pitch them?

☐ Once you have a prototype, can you **persuade customers** to test-drive it? Or better, to *pay* you to participate in a pilot program?

☐ Can you **build** a financial model, **learn** to forecast, and **manage** a budget, cash flow statement, balance sheet, and income statement?

☐ Are you comfortable with conflict? Can you **resolve conflicts** between people, such as differences of opinion among senior leaders in your organization who have competing goals?

☐ Can you **tell a compelling story** about your company, so that the media will want to cover you?

What do you think? If you were set loose today, could you do all these things? More importantly, would you *enjoy* doing all these things?

What Makes an Entrepreneur Tick?

Wisdom straight from the founders' mouths.

JULIA HARTZ, EVENTBRITE

Serial entrepreneurs are missing a chip in their brain that says, "This might not work out." That chip is just not there. They don't tend to see the ways in which something might fail. They only see possibility. It creates a sort of infectious optimism.

THERESE TUCKER, BLACKLINE

I like to make decisions. I like to be in control of my own time and life. I don't answer well to others. I'm confident. I feel like I have the best idea, and everybody should buy into it. It's completely unfounded, of course, but it carries you through when nothing else does.

SEBASTIAN THRUN, UDACITY AND KITTYHAWK

I live to empower people. When you come across something as powerful as hundreds of thousands of people all around the world all of sudden being able to participate in the gift of great education, there is no way you can't do it.

JOSH JAMES,
OMNITURE AND DOMO

I remember being in my freshman year in college, and we'd go sit up on top of the mountain and look down over the valley and be like, "Someone's got to be on top. Why not me?"

MELANIE PERKINS,
CANVA

I really like thinking about the future. I love spending a lot of time imagining what the world would look like.

FRED LUDDY, SERVICENOW

An entrepreneur is somebody who so passionately cares about solving a problem that they will disregard a large percentage of what otherwise might be their life. I've had my electricity shut off, I've been evicted, I've had my car repossessed—not because I didn't have money but because I didn't take the time to pay my bills. The bills would come in, and if the envelope wasn't pink, I didn't even think to write the check.

Why a Founder Is Like a Navy SEAL

It's all about "focus over time."

In 2005, Keith McFarland, author of *The Breakthrough Company: How Everyday Companies Become Extraordinary Performers*, gave 250 leaders of Inc. 500 companies the Test of Attentional and Interpersonal Style (TAIS). This personality assessment is frequently administered to professional athletes, elite military units, and corporate executives to evaluate their ability to stay focused, make good decisions, and communicate in high-stress situations.

TAIS measures 20 different personality factors. McFarland looked at three in particular that represent key attributes of successful entrepreneurs. The first is what he calls "focus over time," which is an individual's ability to go all in on a goal, including making extreme sacrifices to achieve it. McFarland used Inc. 500 leaders (the heads of privately held companies who are frequently also those companies' founders) as proxies for entrepreneurs in general. He found that they scored higher than traditional CEOs in "focus over time." As he wrote on Inc.com at the time, that meant they "have more in common with military commandos and athletes than with other business executives."

Next, McFarland looked at the Inc. 500 leaders' tolerance for risk. Entrepreneurs are often seen as having a greater tolerance for risk than the average person, but McFarland made a surprising finding: They weren't all natural-born bungee jumpers. McFarland—whose firm, the RED Strategy Group, works with entrepreneurs—has a hypothesis about this: while founders aren't more likely to be risk junkies, they are better than others at *calculating* risk. "They see connections in the world that other people don't," he says. "That gives them a better grasp of probabilities that they can't always articulate—or might not even know they have."

Finally, he looked at how entrepreneurs respond to stress. One of the personality factors that TAIS measures is "performance under pressure." The Inc. 500 leaders scored in the eighty-third percentile—45 percent higher than the average corporate CEO. Founders actually seem to enjoy facing adversity, McFarland says. "These are the clutch players. When the chips are down and the stakes are high, they actually really want to have the ball and take a shot."

Visionaries Versus Operators
Both can be founders.

The media celebrates the visionaries: Steve Jobs, Mark Zuckerberg, Sara Blakely, Marc Benioff. But not all founders are brilliant conjurers of futuristic dreams. Take me. I'm not particularly visionary. Todd, my cofounder (and Okta's CEO), is. He has a great sense of where our industry is going and what a winning company will look like in this space. I don't have that knack. But what I do have—and what is equally critical to our success—is the ability to get things done. In fact, our partnership is what you'll often find in successful startups: a founding team in which one person dreams up great ideas and at least one other person brings it to life (the latter is often called "an operator"). So don't write yourself off if you're an operator. Just make it your mission to team up with a visionary.

Got Anything Planned for the Next 5 to 10 Years?

Clear your calendar.

The minute you take venture capital money, a clock starts ticking. That's because VCs have to return money to *their* investors within a specific amount of time. This creates pressure on founders to have an exit strategy (usually getting sold to another company or going public) fairly quickly. VCs usually want this to happen within seven years, although the actual time horizon varies based on several factors, including what industry you're in and where they are in a fund's life cycle.

And the pressure isn't to grow just a little bit, but to grow enormously. You might have heard the term "10×"—which means VCs are hoping the startups they invest in will grow to be 10 times larger than they were when the VCs put their money in. If your company is valued at $40 million when the VC cuts their check, they'll want you to be worth $400 million in just seven years. To do that, you'll have to grow your customer base, expand your product offerings, and fine-tune your internal operations to handle that enormous growth. It's an extraordinary undertaking.

To achieve this, you have to be willing to work on nothing but your startup for the next 5 to 10 years. No hobbies (other than those that help keep you sane). No side hustles. You can have a family, of course—my physician wife and I got married in Okta's Year 1 and had children in Years 4, 6, and 9, all while we both kept working. It was demanding, but we made it work.

You need to ask yourself: Do you love the idea of being an entrepreneur so much that you're willing to do this and only this for the next decade? If the answer is no, or even maybe, you might want to reconsider this path.

Note: Even if you're not considering a venture-backed startup, these points still apply. While you won't have VC investors, starting a company of any size usually takes all your time and attention in the first 5 to 10 years. Don't believe me? Walk into any restaurant or small business and ask how long it took the owner or owners from the time they started until they felt they could stop and take a breath.

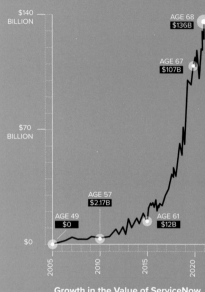

Growth in the Value of ServiceNow
(since Fred Luddy founded it at age 49)

When 50 Is the New 37

Fred Luddy started ServiceNow just shy of his fiftieth birthday. The company is now worth $136 billion. Fred told me it never occurred to him not to start a company in middle age, despite the mythology about young founders: "At age 50, I felt like I had a shot." (He'd had a long career in tech before that, including holding some very senior positions.) "I told myself: I'm going to do this," he says. "I've learned a lot. I've observed a lot. I think I know enough."

Busting the Myth of the Boy-Genius Founder

Most great founders aren't 20-year-old college dropouts.

The Age of Startup Founders

The average age of people who founded the highest-growth startups is 45.

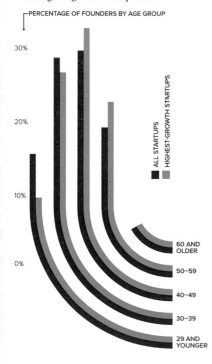

PERCENTAGE OF FOUNDERS BY AGE GROUP

30%

20%

10%

0%

ALL STARTUPS

HIGHEST-GROWTH STARTUPS

60 AND OLDER

50–59

40–49

30–39

29 AND YOUNGER

"The cliché of a founder is a kid with a crazy idea," says Marc Andreessen, legendary cofounder of Netscape and Ben Horowitz's partner at Andreessen Horowitz. But that's not the reality. "Usually, it's someone who's thought about their idea for 5, 10, or 15 years. By the time they start their company, they have a level of competence that even we investors can't imagine."

MIT professor Pierre Azoulay found that the average age of a founder at the start of a company that later becomes a successful high-growth startup isn't 25 or even 35—it's 45. In a 2018 *Harvard Business Review* article, Azoulay and his coauthors observed that the stereotype of the brilliant young founder is belied by the data. "If you were faced with two entrepreneurs and knew nothing about them besides their age, you would do better, on average, betting on the older one," the piece argued.*

Paul Arnold, a friend of mine who runs Switch Ventures, arrived at the same conclusion when he developed a model to predict which founders to bet on: higher levels of education, especially at elite institutions, and more years of work experience at high-performing organizations—especially experience in a senior position—are correlated with startup success.

"Somebody who worked for Google, Facebook, or McKinsey & Company is much more likely to build a big company," Paul says. The reason is pretty basic: they know how a high-functioning, highly effective organization works. "If you're just walking out of college, you might stumble onto success like Mark Zuckerberg did," he adds. "But generally, you have no idea what a successful organization should look like. People who worked for a Google do."

Source: Pierre Azoulay et al., "Age and High-Growth Entrepreneurship," NBER, nber.org, April 2018.

* Pierre Azoulay et al., "Research: The Average Age of a Successful Startup Founder Is 45," *Harvard Business Review*, July 11, 2018, https://hbr.org/2018/07/research-the-average-age-of-a-successful-startup-founder-is-45.

two

IDEAS

"Anyone who's taken a shower has had an idea."
—Fred Luddy

In the fall of 2008, I was starting my second (and final) year of business school. My colleagues at Salesforce thought I was just taking time off to get an MBA and then would return to the company. I, however, was pretty sure that after graduation, I was going to start my own thing. And I had a good idea of what that would be: a financial services product for kids and their parents. PayPal meets Mint.com, but for 5- to 13-year-olds. It'd be a way for adults to teach their children how to save and invest money.

The reason I was drawn to this idea was personal: my upbringing had been filled with finance education, but I later learned my family was unusual. My father was an immigrant who'd arrived in the United States with just $500 in his pocket. While he ended up doing extremely well as the CFO of six publicly traded companies, he always made sure my siblings and I understood the value of a hard-earned dollar, and he taught us how to manage our personal budgets and cash flows.

Online financial services were still fairly new back then. PayPal had been around for a while, but Mint.com, a website for tracking your finances, was only a few years old. Before that, people had only used desktop software or, more commonly, paper spreadsheets. The idea of doing this stuff on the web was still pretty radical. I knew my idea was going to be a home run.

I surveyed friends with kids. I worked on figuring out how big the market could be. I researched what application programming interfaces (APIs, or digital gateways) were available for transferring information to and from banks and other financial institutions. I even hammered out an initial business plan. But then I talked to some experts: Jeff Jordan, former president of PayPal, and Kevin Hartz, cofounder of Xoom (a way to send money overseas). They both told me the same thing: "Online payments are really hard." They warned me that my idea was horrible (yes, *horrible*) and strongly advised me not to do it.

I was crushed. I had just spent six months researching this idea. I had visions of this amazing company I was about to build. And yes, I'd even pictured myself standing in the New York Stock Exchange, ringing that famous bell when my obviously groundbreaking company would inevitably go public. But I trusted Jeff and Kevin. They knew the space much better than I did. So I had to face the hard truth that no matter how much I wanted it, it wasn't going to work. (And sure enough, more than a decade later, while various apps have emerged to help children manage money, not a single one has grown to the size and impact I'd imagined.)

That winter, I was back in San Francisco, having lunch with a Salesforce executive who was trying to convince me to come work for him after business school. "No way," I told him. "I'm going to start my own company." Which one? he asked. I had, in fact, a second idea in mind, one that fell not far from the Salesforce tree. "Enterprise infrastructure software," I answered. I hadn't thought about it as deeply as the financial services idea, but I had enough experience watching Salesforce's early customers struggle with all kinds of software integration issues. I was pretty sure it would be something worth pursuing. As it turns out, my lunch date knew that Todd, who was still at Salesforce, was similarly jonesing to do his own thing. Soon after, Todd and I met up, and the rest is history.

Ideas are, as they say, a dime a dozen. As Fred Luddy, founder of ServiceNow, once told me, "Anyone who's taken a shower has had an idea."

The key question is: How good is your idea really? Is it actually doable? And if it's doable, can it be profitable? And if it can be profitable, how big is the total addressable market (TAM)*? The TAM of a consumer item with only 10,000 possible buyers is too small. But if potentially 100 million people might possibly want or need the item, that's a much more attractive TAM.

Next question: Even if the TAM is big enough, will there be enough demand for your product? Just because 100 million people could possibly use it doesn't mean they're actually going to buy it. If there's enough demand, will you be able to build an operation capable of producing tens of thousands (or hundreds of thousands, or millions) of the item, with a meaningful profit margin, so that your company will eventually be worth many times what your investors put into it?

Silicon Valley mythology would have you believe that great ideas magically occur to founders—particularly young college-age founders—who whip up pitch decks and then are suddenly off to the races. In reality, however, founders usually come up with ideas because they are intimately familiar with a certain industry or space. Sometimes they are able to see a gap in the market that no one else has yet identified or that the industry thinks is simply not fillable.

Sometimes (as happened with Todd and me), founders perceive a shift in the current paradigm or ecosystem that's about to clear the way for new opportunities. Think about Apple and its first computer back in 1976. Both Steve Jobs and Steve Wozniak were computer geeks who had spent enough time tinkering around to realize that it was financially and technologically possible to build a personal computer for the masses. Or, more recently,

> Just because we'd landed on a great idea, it didn't mean it was the right business for *us*.

* "Total addressable market" refers to the total possible demand for your product. The TAM for leather jackets for Shih Tzus is very small. The TAM for dog food for all dogs is huge.

think about Melanie Perkins, who started working on Canva in the early 2010s. While studying at university, she taught people how to use graphic-design software programs. She could see how difficult these programs were for the average person. After building a yearbook-publishing company with its own proprietary design software, she realized she could build a version of that software that everyone could use.

Sometimes, the founder starts down one path, but in working through an idea, he or she realizes there's an even bigger—or much more feasible—opportunity in another approach. Max Levchin and Peter Thiel joined forces in the late 1990s to produce encryption software for handheld devices, only to discover there wasn't much interest. The following year, they regrouped and launched a new product that people could use to send money wirelessly, an insight that led to PayPal.

Although Okta became a multibillion-dollar business, Todd and I didn't actually start out with a great idea. We initially thought companies would want cloud-based versions of the system management tools that they used to manage their on-premise ("on-prem") software—software that ran on in-house servers that were owned and operated by companies themselves. But after we ran our idea by 75 different IT executives, we learned that wasn't what they really needed. "It's interesting," they'd say, "but it's Problem #4."

What they most needed was a way to manage employee access to the software they were using in the cloud. We grasped the problem immediately. Together, Todd and I had more than 20 years' experience in online enterprise software. We knew these customers. We understood their world. It was also immediately clear how big this business could become. Every company, university, and government department would eventually be using online software. All of them would have this same need.

But there's one more thing we had to consider—and that you will too. Just because we'd landed on a great idea, it didn't mean it was the right business for *us*. We needed to do some soul-searching. Building a startup is crushing work. At best, it's years of exhaustion. At worst, it will burn through your resilience, optimism, determination, and personal savings—and leave you with nothing.

So any idea you embrace has to be something you care about so much that when every door in front of you is slamming shut, you won't stop. When you've just lost your top engineer, or the funding you were counting on falls through, or a giant customer abandons you, you'll still keep going because you believe so deeply in what you're doing.

Once you identify a great idea, you're still going to have to refine it into something you can build a business around. We're not going to talk about that here. There are many great books written on this topic: Steve Blank, a professor at Stanford University and one of the fathers of the lean startup movement, wrote a good one called *The Four Steps to the Epiphany*, which we used at Okta for early customer discovery.

What we are going to explore in this chapter is the more fundamental question: How can you tell if an idea is worth pursuing at all? Let's dive in.

Any idea you embrace has to be something you care about so much that when every door in front of you is slamming shut, you won't stop.

Yes, It's Too Soon to Ask for an NDA

At a conference in Perth, Australia, future Canva founder Melanie Perkins met Silicon Valley investor Bill Tai. She made enough of an impression that he told her to look him up if she ever made it to California. But then she made a rookie mistake: Melanie sent Tai a nondisclosure agreement. "I was like, 'I've got the secret to the future of publishing.' Once you sign the NDA, I can tell you about it,'" she says. How did that work out? "I sent it to him twice, and he didn't respond."

Melanie decided to hop on a plane to the United States anyway, and when she asked Tai for a meeting—no mention of an NDA this time—he agreed. They met in person in Palo Alto, and that meeting led to other introductions, which helped get Canva off the ground.

Melanie's thinking about NDAs at the idea stage has changed dramatically. "I sent out those first documents, so that he wouldn't steal my idea," she says. Now, several years into building her company, she knows how unlikely that would have been. "I didn't realize how hard it would be to actually build the future of publishing."

As I explain in the next section, if your idea is really good, no one's going to steal it. They'll be happy for *you* to give up the next 10 years of your life trying to bring it about. They might even give you some money. But no one's going to ditch what they're doing to go launch a startup, much less one they don't have nearly as good a grasp on as you.

Treat Your Idea Like a Houseplant

Give it plenty of sunlight.

I can't tell you how often would-be founders tell me they don't want to say too much about their idea because they're afraid I'm going to steal it. Holding your cards close to your chest, however, only hurts you. Your idea won't get better unless you run it by a ton of people. Outside perspectives can help you learn the history of similar products, so you can avoid their mistakes. They can help you understand how production, manufacturing, and distribution work in your sector. They can flag any regulatory issues you should plan for. And they can introduce you to other people working in your space who might be able to help or who might make great hires.

Sure, there are the rare exceptions where theft has taken place. But founders should usually err on the side of being open rather than close-mouthed because in the vast majority of cases, other people won't want—or won't be able—to steal your idea, for these reasons:

- **They don't have the time.** Any startup worth its salt will take 10 or more backbreaking years to build. Am I going to quit Okta to start another company from the ground up? Absolutely not.

- **They don't know nearly as much about your idea as you do, and they will never catch up.** Most founders have spent *years* thinking about their idea. They know their industry and their customers inside and out. No one they talk to is going to have their depth of expertise. So even if someone did try to run with your idea, that person is *years* behind you.

- **They aren't going to be as passionate about it as you.** Building a startup is going to knock you down and kick you about—repeatedly. You can't do it unless you genuinely *care* about the idea you're working on. Someone else might recognize that you've got a great idea, but if they aren't consumed by it the way you are, they won't get very far.

- **They actually won't think your idea is any good.** Most people can't actually recognize a really good idea. It's more likely that the majority of people you talk to will spend all their time telling you why your idea will never work.

A Shining Vision of the Future Does Not a Business Make

There's such a thing as looking *too* far into the future.

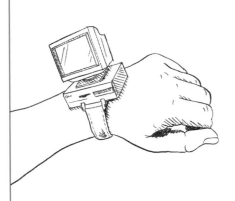

Alex Asseily was a senior in college in 1997 when he came up with an idea for his senior thesis. "It was an Apple Watch–style interface that connected to a headset that you could use to control your digital life," he says.

The technology that would have made this possible didn't exist at the time. But Alex was enthralled by the mobile revolution that was just beginning to take shape. "The idea of wearable technology was exciting to me," he says. When he presented his idea to his senior thesis judges, he was met with deafening silence. One of the judges finally took pity on him. "Is there any part of this you think is actually possible in the next 10 to 15 years?" she asked. Alex paused before answering, naively, "I haven't really thought about that."

Still, Alex was convinced he had a brilliant idea. And technically, he wasn't wrong. (See: the now-ubiquitous Apple Watch.) In 1999, he co-founded AliphCom to create a communicator watch controlled by speech recognition. He set up meetings with angel investors who responded excitedly to the picture he painted. But no one wrote him a check.

"We began to realize that their loving the vision didn't mean they wanted to invest," Alex says. By his own admission, he wasn't presenting a business. It was just "a potential product idea." A great idea, maybe, but one with no way of becoming a reality in a reasonable amount of time, given where technology stood then.

Eventually, AliphCom went in a different direction. After being inspired by a cutting-edge voice sensor technology under development at Lawrence Livermore National Laboratory—technology that actually worked and which AliphCom decided to license—Alex and his team began working on a breakthrough noise-suppression technology for the Pentagon's famed Defense Advanced Research Projects Agency (DARPA). The work was underwritten by a series of Defense Department contracts—and eventually by some prescient angel investors as well. The company was renamed Jawbone as it shifted to producing what was arguably the first-ever high-quality Bluetooth headset for consumers. In the process, it created an entirely new category of products. It just wasn't what Alex originally had envisioned.

"One of the biggest lessons I've learned in the 20 years I've been working in and investing in startups," Alex says, "is how to help people think realistically about what they're working on."

When Good Ideas Look Like Bad Ideas (to Others)

And how to know the difference.

The thing about good startup ideas is that, if they're really good—meaning they're a 100 percent leap over what already exists—most people won't recognize them. As Marc Andreessen says, "If your idea is any good, you're going to have to beat people into accepting it." Why? Because great ideas come from people who see something that others don't. To quote the hockey great Wayne Gretzky: "I skate to where the puck is going to be, not where it has been." Founders with really valuable ideas can see where an industry is headed, and they don't let naysayers throw them off. Instead, they consider the other person's objections and figure out if the feedback is based on a useful analysis or on just "not getting it." Here are some common reasons your idea might be dismissed:

- The person is an expert in your industry, and they think they understand how your idea works. Unlike you, however, they haven't noticed how the technology or economic conditions are shifting and how those changes are creating new opportunities for ideas like yours. **Your Next Step:** Probe their assumptions about how the industry works and then compare them to yours. The farther apart those assumptions are, the less useful their response is for you.

- They're aware of regulatory hurdles you haven't considered. If you haven't factored existing regulations into your calculations, it could be a deal-breaker. **Your Next Step:** Go back to the drawing board and assess the impact of regulation on your timeline and cost structure.

- They might have seen something like your idea fail before. Tech experts wrote off Google when it first launched because previous search engines had struggled to find viable business models. Google, however, figured out a revolutionary revenue opportunity that others hadn't considered. **Your Next Step:** Compare the objector's assumptions with yours. The closer they are, the more likely the objector is right. The farther apart they are, the less relevant their objections might be.

- They flat-out don't understand your idea. Instagram's product seemed silly and inconsequential to many. Few grasped how important visual communication would become for smartphone users, and how brands could use these tools for marketing. **Your Next Step:** If you've created something that is seemingly trivial, focus on sussing out demand. If you can generate demand, you might be onto something, and the naysayers might be wrong.

Architecture Is the Mother of Invention

And of a bazillion new companies.

Marc Andreessen is convinced there aren't any truly new ideas. If you think you've magically unearthed one, Marc will tell you you're probably wrong. More likely, you haven't done your homework and researched your idea's lineage. But if that's the case, you might ask: How come no one else has successfully translated this genius idea into a business? According to Marc, it's because three things must come together before an idea's time has come:

TECHNOLOGY: Is the tech available to make this idea happen?

ECONOMICS: Can it be produced and distributed at a price that customers will pay?

PSYCHOLOGY: Are people ready for it?

Without all three syncing up, your idea has little chance of success.

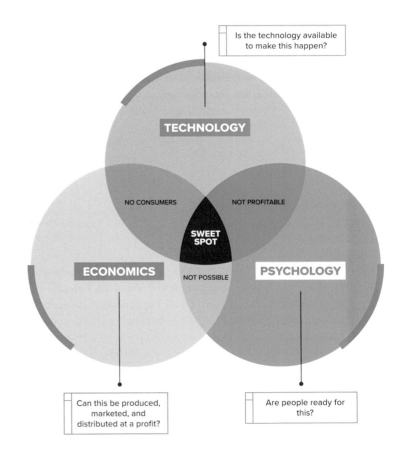

Is the technology available to make this happen?

TECHNOLOGY

NO CONSUMERS

NOT PROFITABLE

SWEET SPOT

ECONOMICS

NOT POSSIBLE

PSYCHOLOGY

Can this be produced, marketed, and distributed at a profit?

Are people ready for this?

Fundamental architecture shifts create giant opportunities. Corporate computing once required large mainframe computers so big they had to be housed in their own rooms. As chips got smaller, so did computers. Desktop computing created a new market for business software. And as consumers started buying them for use at home, another new segment emerged: personal software. With even smaller chips came smartphones, and with them, the explosion of the app industry.

Startups have an advantage in these shifts. Existing companies might have more money, but they can't rapidly retool themselves to tackle new opportunities, a concept Clayton Christensen famously introduced in his book *The Innovator's Dilemma* (read it!). The shift from on-prem business software to cloud-based tools is what created a giant opportunity for Okta—as well as countless other startups, including Fred Luddy's Service-Now and Workday, founded by Aneel Bhusri, one of Okta's early board members. It's a great example of how architectural shifts open up a flood of new opportunities for entrepreneurs.

THE WAY IT WAS

For decades, businesses had to run business software on their own servers. The cloud didn't exist. The internet was new. Businesses had to buy and install software on their own servers, the way consumers used to buy software on CD-ROMs and install it on their own computers. **This is the Technology part of Marc's triad. Cloud-based business software wasn't possible until the internet and connectivity speeds grew large enough to support it.**

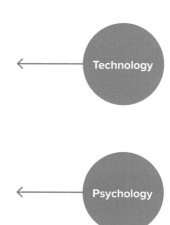

Even as the internet developed in the 1990s and 2000s, the technology wasn't powerful enough for people to use it for anything other than email and chat rooms. But then, even when speeds increased, users didn't *trust* web-based tools. (There was a time when people were even skeptical about *buying* things online.) **This is the Psychology part of Marc's triad. Even after the Technology had arrived, humans weren't ready for it.** It's crazy to think about this now, but back in 2009, when Todd and I were pitching our idea for Okta, a lot of people we talked to simply didn't believe businesses would migrate their operations to web-based tools.

The idea of creating the kind of business software that exists today seemed ludicrous. People thought it would be harder to use than the tools they were used to, and they were afraid of transferring their business data to a website's databases.

THE WAY IT BECAME

Still, visionaries like Fred, Aneel, and my old boss, Marc Benioff, who co-founded Salesforce in 1999, looked into the future and could see that business software would, in fact, eventually move online. The naysayers were focused on things they thought would be problems. But Fred, Aneel, and Marc could see all the advantages online software would bring.

For example, it was really hard to update on-prem software. Whether you wanted to fix bugs or add new features, you had to get copies of the software from the vendor and then install it, manually, on your own devices. It was a nightmare for everyone. Once everything was online, Fred, Aneel, and Marc knew, all changes would be made behind the scenes by the vendors—the way services like Gmail, Dropbox, and Airtable do today. The customers wouldn't have to do *anything*. Life would be so much easier!

Benioff was one of the first to dive into this new world, and we and others followed in the 2000s. The tipping point didn't really come until the early to mid-2010s, however. Before then, executives weren't psychologically ready to make the leap. No CIO was going to get fired for sticking with on-prem tools, but they definitely would lose their jobs if they jumped to the cloud, and something went terribly wrong.

WHAT IT IS NOW

Today, cloud computing is ubiquitous. The companies where you've worked or the universities where you've studied probably all use cloud-based tools such as Microsoft Office 365, Salesforce, Amazon Web Services, Google Workspace (formerly called G Suite), Slack, Zoom, Box, and even Okta.

There's been a resulting explosion in business software. Previously, the expense involved in building on-prem tools limited the number of companies able to get into the game. Cloud-based tools, on the other hand, are so much easier and cheaper to build. Before the cloud, you couldn't whip something up on your couch—or in your parents' attic, as Aaron Levie and one of his Box cofounders did—and toss it on the internet. In the on-prem world, you needed at least $10 million to pay for all the equipment and people you would need—just to get started. Today, you can start working on a cloud-based idea with $100,000 from angel investors (and sometimes even less). **This is the Economics part of Marc's triad. It had to become cheaper to build and to buy cloud-based tools for this industry to take off.**

There's been a commensurate rise in demand. On-prem software was hugely expensive. Companies couldn't buy a lot. Now that many cloud tools are so cheap, companies can use a lot more of them.

The founders who recognized that these shifts were taking place—and who had the courage to dive in—have done amazingly well. Sure, there were some very lean, nail-biting years early on. But companies like Salesforce, Workday, ServiceNow, and Okta have become hugely valuable. Getting in early solidified our lead, and now many of those companies are the leaders in what they do.

Economics

Go Big or Stay Home
Ten percent better is not good enough.

Ask yourself this question: How different is your idea from what already exists? If it's only a 10 percent improvement over the incumbent, it's not a good idea. If your idea is only incrementally better, one of two things will happen:

 1

 2

Your potential customers aren't going to care enough about that extra 10 percent that they'll ditch whatever they already use to buy your product. This is particularly true when you're talking about business systems, but it often applies to consumer goods as well.

Even if customers *do* seem willing to ditch their old thing for a modestly better new thing, a larger competitor with more resources and bandwidth will likely get it to market faster and sell it more cheaply than you can. Anything that's a 10 percent improvement is something that's obvious. And if it's obvious, then big established players are probably already working on it.

Instead, your idea needs to be 100 percent better than what already exists. This usually requires some kind of a leap. Airbnb was a leap in the hospitality industry. They didn't simply build a hotel that was 10 percent cooler than any other hotel out there. They completely reimagined what hospitality could be and who could provide it.

Where Great Ideas Are Born

Some come from a classroom. Others from prison.

MELANIE PERKINS, CANVA

I taught people how to use design software like InDesign and Photoshop when I was in college, and I saw how much students struggled to learn even the basics. At first, I came up with an online tool to design college yearbooks. But by the time I came to Silicon Valley in 2010 to meet investors, I'd already realized we could take the ideas behind the yearbook tool and use them to reinvent all kinds of design.

FREDERICK HUTSON, PIGEONLY

I served almost five years in prison for dealing marijuana. I personally experienced how difficult and expensive it was to stay in touch with my loved ones. I also noticed that the people who had the financial means to make phone calls (which were very expensive) were the people who, once their sentence was up, never came back. But the people who couldn't afford to make those calls, I would see them end up back in prison. I later discovered that there is a lot of research on this—that people who are in touch with their families, who have a lot of support, tend not to fall back into crime once they leave prison.

AARON LEVIE, BOX

In 2004, I was in college at the University of Southern California, and one of my best friends from high school, Dylan Smith,* was at Duke University. File sharing was weirdly hard at the time. You had to either email files to yourself or use a thumb drive or an FTP site. We basically said, "There has to be a better way to do this." We were sure it could become a $50 million business. [It's now worth $4 billion.] We were wrong about the projections, but we were right about the underlying idea, which was that all data should be stored online in a secure way.

* Dylan would go on to cofound Box with Levie and two others.

FRED LUDDY, SERVICENOW

The way my company started was that the company I was working for went bankrupt. The equity I had had in the company had been worth $35 million, and then it went to zero. I found myself unemployed at 49 years old, so I said to myself, "I've worked for enough people. Let's see if I can make a go of it on my own." I had enough money to last about 36 months. I didn't have a business problem in mind, but I'd been a programmer since I was 16, and every day I'd wake up hoping to get time to code. So I started exploring all the new languages and technologies that had emerged while I'd been working at that other company. And then I started thinking about what problem they could solve.

JASMINE CROWE, GOODR

In 2013, I drove by a parking lot and saw hundreds of people who were homeless. It pulled at my heartstrings. I started feeding people out of my apartment. I would make spaghetti dinners and set up a table on the street handing out to-go boxes. Then I started renting tables and chairs so people could have more of a restaurant experience. In the meantime, I was fascinated with the emergence of food delivery apps. I realized there needed to be something similar for restaurants, to get their excess food to people in need. There could be an app where restaurants could say, "I have extra XYZ," and someone could pick it up and deliver it to nonprofits.

SEBASTIAN THRUN, UDACITY AND KITTYHAWK

I didn't really choose to create a startup. It chose me. I was in the midst of running Google X,* while also still teaching occasionally at Stanford University. I decided to put my class on artificial intelligence online and offer it free of charge. I wrote a single email to some friends, telling them their students could take this class online, and they would get the same instruction that students at Stanford were getting. The email went viral. By Friday afternoon, 5,000 people had signed up. By Sunday morning, it was 10,000. The enrollment swelled to 160,000 students from around the world. I remember going to a Lady Gaga concert around that time and looking at the 45,000 people in the arena and thinking that was nothing compared to the number of people in my online class.

* Now simply called X (or X Development LLC), this is the "moonshot" arm of Google's parent company, Alphabet, which does R&D on radically new technologies.

three

TEAMS

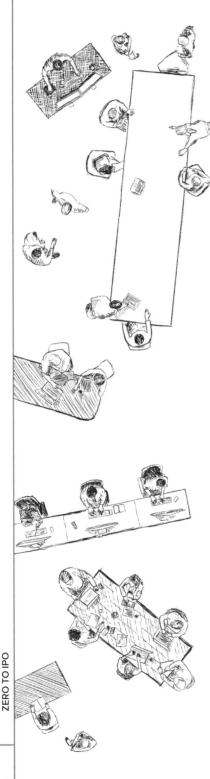

In the Introduction, I told you about how our investor and board member Ben Horowitz called me as I was driving aimlessly around San Francisco and how he gave me two critical pieces of advice about how to pull ourselves out of our death spiral. I'll share the first piece of advice now.

When Ben called, I assumed he was going to fire me. After all, Todd and I had just told the board that we'd drastically missed our sales targets—and I was the person responsible for sales.

But instead of showing me the door, Ben asked me to describe my job. I explained what he already knew. I was the Chief Operating Officer.

"What else are you doing?" he asked.

Our company was still pretty small. We only had about 30 employees. Todd and I were taking on a lot of extra roles. I headed up sales, and Todd was both the CEO and the head of engineering. We were effectively working two, maybe three jobs apiece.

"So here's your problem," Ben said. "You can't do multiple key jobs at the same time and do them well. Very few people can. Which means that you have to hire experts—and fast." He suggested that I shouldn't be the head of sales, especially since I'd never run a sales organization. "That's why your pipeline management, sales process, and forecasting are terrible," he said. Ben went on to say the same about Todd: he couldn't be both the CEO and the head of engineering. "You guys need to build out your executive team," he advised. "Otherwise, you're toast."

Todd and I took his advice to heart. We immediately started a search for two new vice presidents and filled both positions within six months. The impact was dramatic. Okta's sales started to pick up, and the product improved rapidly.

Many entrepreneurs try to do everything themselves for as long as possible. Partly out of necessity: you don't have the money to hire people. But often, it's because you think you can do it better than anyone else. So I'm telling you this from personal experience: You can't. Doing everything on your own doesn't work. As you grow, you need to start assembling a team of people who are better at other pieces of the puzzle than you. This is one of the most profound lessons I've learned. A company isn't about one person. It's about a team of highly talented people.

Who you hire matters a *lot*. Mature companies can afford to hire people who are merely "just fine." You can't. You've got too much to do in too short a time. The right people help you move fast. The wrong people—no matter how nice or talented—drag you down like a lead balloon. If you've never hired people before, it's easy to make mistakes. Even if you have experience, it's not always clear what to look for. In this chapter, I'll share what characteristics to look for in people and how to vet them. I'll also talk about letting people go because you will invariably end up making some bad hires.

First, though, I'll talk about cofounders. You might be dreaming of going it alone, maybe even becoming the next Elon Musk. But research shows that teams of two to four usually do better than single leaders, so I'll talk about why that is and how to find the right partners.

"You can't do multiple key jobs at the same time and do them well. Very few people can. Which means that you have to hire experts—and fast."

One Is the Loneliest Number

Thinking of going it alone? Think again.

The media likes to celebrate individual heroes, but in most cases, starting a company alone isn't advisable. Ed Roberts, the David Sarnoff Professor of Management of Technology at MIT and a longtime mentor of mine, researched the optimal size of founding teams in high tech. "Two cofounders do better than solo founders," he says. "Three cofounders do better than two, and four cofounders seem to do better than three." Beyond that, however, "it's a crowd," he says. The chaos introduced by larger teams begins to outweigh their added benefits. "More cofounders become troublesome and harder to manage."

It makes sense: if you're going to try to grow a company to 10× its original size in a ridiculously short period of time, you need at least one other person to share the burden. And maybe another one or two others on top of that. It's not just about dividing up labor, though that's important. You're going to be buried under a tsunami of tough decisions, most of them things you've never faced before. Having another person to bounce ideas off means you're more likely to land on the right answer. Two brains (or three or four) are likely to come up with a wider set of solutions than a single person brainstorming solo.

This jives with Ed's research into high-tech teams. Typically, the more diverse the skills and expertise of a founding team, the better it performed. And the team performed especially well when it included someone with technical expertise and someone with a sales and/or marketing background. This latter part is important: The important business expertise wasn't general management. It was someone who had sales or marketing experience. Those are customer-facing roles. Someone on your team needs to know how to find and talk to customers. I performed that role at Okta in the early days, when we were still talking to smaller companies. Once we started targeting enterprise-sized customers, however, we had to bring in someone with that expertise.

Cofounders are also necessary for moral support. There are going to be many times when you feel hopeless or overwhelmed. Usually only one cofounder feels this at a time. The one who's not spiraling down can pick the other up and help keep them going. "You need a partner, so you'll have a shoulder to cry on," Ed says. At a minimum, your partner will be able to keep the ship moving forward until you de-panic and calm down.

It's easy to overlook the fact that most successful startups have multiple founders. The media likes to focus on a single heroic leader. It makes for a better story. Facebook is synonymous with Mark Zuckerberg, but he actually had four cofounders (Eduardo Saverin, Chris Hughes, Dustin Moskovitz, and Andrew McCollum). Google had "Larry and Sergey" (Page and Brin). Intel had Gordon Moore and Robert Noyce. Everyone thinks of Larry Ellison when they think of Oracle, but Ed Oates and Bob Miner also launched it. Think Microsoft and you think Bill Gates, but Paul Allen was right there next to him.

Of course, successful companies have also been built by single founders. Jeff Bezos of Amazon is probably one of the most famous. Sara Blakely started Spanx with $5,000 and a prototype consisting of nothing more than a pair of hose with the feet cut off. In 2021, she sold a majority stake in her company for $1.2 billion. David Karp founded Tumblr and later sold it to Yahoo for $1.1 billion. And Aaron Patzer founded Mint.com, which he later sold to Intuit for $170 million.

So yes, a single founder can make a go of it. But doing it with others is advisable—provided, of course, that the cofounders are a fit.

If you're going to try to grow a company to 10x its original size in a ridiculously short period of time, you need at least one other person to share the burden.

We Don't Need No Stinkin' MBAs (Yet)

If you're a technical founder, like an engineer, you don't necessarily need to find someone with an MBA to join your team, at least not immediately. For the first 12 to 18 months, your primary focus is going to be on refining the product idea—working with prospective customers and users to get it right. There won't be a lot of work for people with MBAs.

That said, someone on the team needs to have some degree of business acumen. Someone needs to be able to calculate projections—what your costs are, what revenue (if any) you're going to generate, how much money you need, and when it's going to run out. Someone, in other words, needs to be able to sketch out a business plan.

The Cofounder Next Door

How 10 sets of founders met their matches.

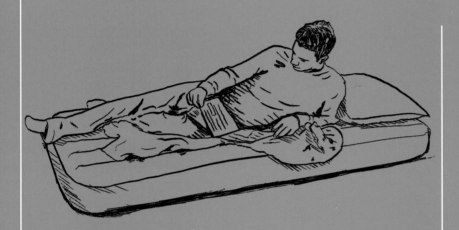

MEDALLIA

CEO Amy Pressman started the company with her husband, Borge Hald.

NETFLIX

Reed Hastings and Marc Randolph came up with the idea for Netflix while carpooling to work at another company.

AIRBNB

Nathan Blecharczyk and Joe Gebbia became roommates via Craigslist. When Blecharczyk moved out, Brian Chesky moved in. They started Airbnb, after Gebbia and Chesky let a conference-goer sleep on an air mattress in their living room because all the city's hotels were sold out.

SALESFORCE

Parker Harris, Dave Moellenhoff, and Frank Dominguez had a consulting company that built software for other companies. One of their clients introduced them to Marc Benioff, who was then an executive at Oracle.

APPLE

Steve Jobs was in high school and Steve Wozniak was a freshman in college when a friend, who knew they both liked playing around with electronics, introduced them.

RENT THE RUNWAY

Jennifer Hyman and Jennifer Fleiss were classmates at Harvard Business School in the mid-2000s. Once a week, they met to brainstorm business ideas and had their eureka moment after Hyman's sister splurged $2,000 on a dress for a wedding.

FACEBOOK

Mark Zuckerberg, Eduardo Saverin, Chris Hughes, Dustin Moskovitz, and Andrew McCollum were all friends at Harvard University.

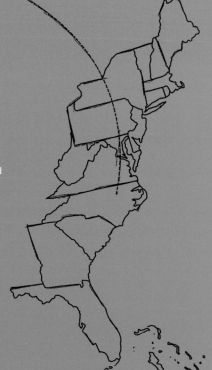

BOX

CEO Aaron Levie and his three cofounders, Dylan Smith, Jeff Queisser, and Sam Ghods, knew each other growing up in Seattle. When Aaron and Dylan were in college on separate coasts and had a hard time sharing files, they came up with Box.

GOOGLE

Larry Page and Sergey Brin met as graduate students at Stanford University in the mid-1990's.

WORKDAY

Aneel Bhusri and Dave Duffield worked together at PeopleSoft, which Dave had cofounded. By 2004 when PeopleSoft faced a hostile takeover, both men had already left the company, but they came back to fight the takeover.

Choosing a Mate
How to know if you've met the right cofounder.

Companies with multiple founders work great when the founders work great together. But poor collaboration among cofounders is a top reason for startup failures. So how do you know if you've found "the one"?

I didn't know Todd well before we started meeting for coffee in early 2009. Our paths had crossed at Salesforce, but we didn't work closely. We were put in touch by a mutual colleague who knew we were both thinking about branching out on our own. The fact that we were both interested in doing something in enterprise software was mere table stakes. We had also both helped build Salesforce from the ground up, and that meant we had a common understanding of how a startup should work. Since we had colleagues in common, we were able to vet each other and find out if there were any red flags. The last thing we did was go out to dinner with our wives and have our better halves interview the other person. Who better to assess whether the other would be a good fit for their spouses?

As you look for a cofounder, keep the following questions in mind. If you have doubts about any of these, think hard before joining forces:

☐ **Can you *trust* this person?**
If you had to take off for two months and leave the company in their hands, would they make the best possible decisions for the company, and look out for you as well?

☐ **When you disagree, are you able to come to a resolution in a mature way that enables you to keep moving forward?**
You can't get stuck in disagreement—or in resentments about the decisions that do get made. Find someone you're able to negotiate with and who can move on quickly from differences of opinion.

☐ **Do you *like* this person?**
Is being around them a net positive? If you don't like them now, you're not going to like them any better when things get tough.

☐ **Does this person know how to be supportive?**
Each of you will hit periodic troughs of despair. Is this someone who'll take on some of your load while you sort yourself out? Or better yet, know how to cajole you out from under a dark cloud?

☐ **Does the person care as deeply about the business as you do?**
Are they as excited about the actual thing you will be building as you are? Do they think about it all the time the way you do? A cofounder who doesn't care that much will almost certainly leave the company within a couple of years (or worse, start undermining you or advocating to take it in a different direction).

☐ **Do you have any reason to second-guess this person as a cofounder?**
Do a gut check. Is your Spidey-sense telling you this isn't a good fit? Are you trying to talk yourself into this partnership? Heed those signals. If you feel like something's not right, it probably isn't. Face up to it now, not two years down the road.

Why You Should Be a Snoop

While you're doing your own gut check on these questions, do due diligence on your potential cofounder. Find at least three people (preferably six) to ask what your prospective partner is really like. Don't get those names from your would-be cofounder. Talk to people who haven't been teed up for you. (And don't worry about coming across as sneaky. If your potential partner is good, he or she is doing this too.)

Find a Fairy Godmother

If you don't know how to evaluate certain candidates, find someone who does.

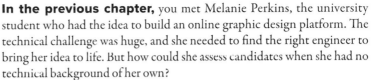

In the previous chapter, you met Melanie Perkins, the university student who had the idea to build an online graphic design platform. The technical challenge was huge, and she needed to find the right engineer to bring her idea to life. But how could she assess candidates when she had no technical background of her own?

There were so many dimensions to consider: Would they know the correct coding languages, or be able to learn new ones that might be needed? Were they more than just programmers—were they architects who could design complex systems? Did they have the skills to manage a growing team? Melanie didn't have enough tech experience to figure out who should be the right partner—and this was going to be a make-or-break decision.

Fortunately, Melanie was resourceful. After meeting Bill Tai, the Silicon Valley VC at a conference in Perth, she boldly hopped on a plane to California. Tai introduced her to Lars Rasmussen, a storied engineer from Denmark who had cofounded a mapping tool startup in 2003. That company was later bought by Google and became Google Maps. By the time Melanie met him, Rasmussen was a lead engineer at Facebook.

Rasmussen agreed to help Melanie vet potential technical talent. (He later became an investor.) "It ended up being a full year of him just rejecting every single candidate that I brought him," Melanie says. "I'd send him people I found on LinkedIn, résumés people had sent to me. I even walked people straight into his office." But no one was good enough. "I just wanted to get started, but he kept saying that the people I brought him weren't up to the challenge of the huge technical project we were about to undertake."

Eventually, Rasmussen introduced Melanie to someone he'd worked with at Google, Cameron Adams, a world-class designer who'd shaped Google Wave and was currently leading his own startup. After months of back-and-forth, Melanie eventually convinced Adams to join forces, and he came on as a cofounder and chief product officer.

Without Rasmussen acting as her consigliere, she may never have found Adams. And without Adams, she may never have built Canva into the $40 billion business it is today.

Share and Share(s) Alike

Why cofounders should receive equal shares.

You're probably going to read a ton on the internet and elsewhere about how to divide your company's equity (or shares of stock) among founders. People will suggest all sorts of complicated permutations and convoluted strategies to come up with something "fair."

I'll save you the time—except in a few rare edge cases, give everyone equal amounts of equity.

Startups fail when founders don't get along. By giving different people different ownership stakes, you're immediately setting up a power dynamic that says one person is more important than the other(s). Why would you do that? You did your due diligence, right? The people you chose as your cofounders are all rock stars. They're all going to be working just as hard as you to ensure the company's success. If so, then no one is more important than another.

If one founder insists on taking more equity, you're simply planting a seed that will someday grow into a thicket of resentment. Strife slows you down. Why would you willingly introduce that? You won't get nearly as far as you will if you and your partner(s) are in harmony. As the saying goes: a smaller portion of a giant pie is a heck of a lot bigger than a larger portion of a much smaller pie.

If, despite all your due diligence, a cofounder ultimately doesn't work out and ends up leaving early, they won't leave with all that stock—only the amount that's vested. For example, if a cofounder leaves after a single year, they only vest 25 percent of their founder's stock (the typical vesting period is four years), and their remaining ownership stake (75 percent in this example) goes back to the company.

If you're going
to move
fast, each
cofounder
needs his
or her own
sphere of
responsibility.
You can't be
tripping over
each other
in the same
areas.

There's Plenty of Room
in the Sandbox
The case for dividing responsibilities.

If you're going to move fast, each cofounder needs his or her own sphere of responsibility. You can't be tripping over each other in the same areas. It will slow you down. The division of labor between Todd and me worked well. He was responsible for the company vision, the product, and engineering. I took on sales and company operations—finance, HR, legal, and so on. He was the visionary and had tons of experience building products. I had experience on sales and business-development teams. As for the rest, I knew I could just figure it out—I'm a get-stuff-done guy, so I wasn't worried about managing those areas.

Of course, there are times when founders have to make decisions about the company in general that transcend their functional areas. Most of the time, Todd and I were in sync. There were a handful of situations where my opinion diverged from Todd's. I made my case—perhaps even "energetically"—but at the end of the day, Todd went in the direction he believed in.

Was it humbling? Sure. But the CEO is the CEO. As in any company, that's where the buck stops. That's who has to make the calls. The investors had invested in us based on that lineup. As legendary Intel CEO Andy Grove famously advocated, teams need to be able to "disagree and commit." Not everyone might agree with a decision, but once the decision is made, everyone must get behind it.

Build Inclusive Hiring Strategies from Jump

Your first 10 hires set the tone for your later ones.

Silicon Valley has historically been overwhelmingly male and overwhelmingly white. Maybe your industry is the same. For a long time, the powers that be in Silicon Valley didn't think much about it, but in recent years, our industry has been paying more attention to the ways in which its companies' cultures have not always been welcoming places for people who didn't look like the founders.

These days, no matter your industry, you must start thinking about these issues from the moment you start hiring. Not from a defensive stance, as in "we need to make sure we don't get sued." But because you won't be able to hire the smartest and most talented people if those people don't want to work for you.

Researchers at North Carolina State University studied the output of 3,000 publicly traded companies from 2001 to 2014. Their findings? Companies with explicit commitments to building diverse workforces—as defined by indicators like: women and people of color get promoted to business leadership positions, policies support LGBTQ+ employees (like domestic partner benefits), and people with disabilities are actively recruited—were more innovative and launched more products.

Your first 10 hires will be your most critical. If your first 10 are all men, a later fantastic female candidate might question whether she'll be truly welcomed. If your first 10 are all white, a person of color might wonder whether your company will allow them to thrive. Plus, you're going to be drawing on the networks of those first 10 people to find your next 100 hires. If they all come from similar backgrounds, that will limit your ability to cast a wide net.

Follow these tips to ensure you end up with a diverse "first 10":

1 Don't start interviewing candidates until you have a truly diverse applicant pool.

2 Reach out to a wide variety of networking groups (such as groups for women, people of color, LGBTQ+, and people with disabilities) to let them know when you have open positions.

3 Use one of the many web tools available to ensure your job descriptions don't use language that is inadvertently exclusive.

4 Set up a system where an intermediary strips out demographic information from the résumés you receive, so you only respond to what candidates bring to the table, rather than who they are.

The I'm-Too-Slammed-to-Hire-Anyone Fallacy

In the early days, you're moving so fast, it's hard to focus on hiring. Especially since it falls entirely on your shoulders. (You likely won't have an HR lead for a while.) So here's a quick tip on how to recognize when it's time to hire your next person: when you're too slammed to even write the job description. Once so much of your time is consumed with doing rote work that could easily be delegated to someone else, that's when to bring on a new team member. Yes, you may fall behind while you do the search. But think of it as a brief pause that will let you invest in your future success.

Rethink Your Job Descriptions

Tien Tzuo and I worked together at Salesforce. More recently, he founded Zuora, a $3 billion enterprise software company that helps businesses manage subscription services. Most companies list generic responsibilities in their job descriptions, but Zuora highlights the *outcomes* they want their candidates to produce, including the specific projects or results the person will be expected to drive in the coming year.

Tien says it's more effective. Knowing that someone has held a job with the same title elsewhere doesn't tell you much about whether they'll be successful (or even motivated) at your company. Similarly, the absence of certain experiences doesn't always mean a candidate can't do something new at your organization. Plus, how a candidate responds to outcome statements is highly telling. "The right candidate usually responds really positively," Tien says. "They'll say something like, 'That's a challenge I can see myself doing for the next few years.'"

Look for "Great Athletes"
Surround yourself with people who have mastered hard things.

Maggie Wilderotter, the former CEO of Frontier Communications, says she always sought to hire "great athletes." Not necessarily in the sports sense—you didn't need to have played college ball to get hired by her (though some people did). Maggie meant that you had to be a person who naturally sought to continuously learn, practice, and get better at whatever they set their mind to. She called such people "students of the game." "They're always expanding their minds and their horizons," she says. They're often also very competitive, or at least hugely ambitious. "You have to have that fire in your belly."

In job interviews, Maggie would probe to see if a candidate had ever pushed to do something that required enormous persistence. "Did they have a craft or a hobby or a sport or an instrument that they were committed to? Was there something that took hours and hours of practice for them to get good at?"

She would ask them to tell her a story about one of the toughest things they'd ever had to deal with at work and to walk her through how they'd handled it. "Being in a growing company is a little bit like being in the military," she explains. "We're going to get into firefights. I want to know who's in the foxhole with me. I need to make sure they've got my back, as I will theirs."

Many candidates won't fit this mold. Not everybody can handle the confusion, chaos, uncertainty, and rigor of an early-stage company. It's not useful—either for the candidate or for your company—to bring in people who can't handle the unique demands of a startup. "Great athletes" can go the distance.

Hire for Core Competencies
Then outsource the rest.

A common mistake new founders make is thinking they need to hire an employee for every task on the company's plate. Sure, you need all your core competencies in-house. But many positions can be outsourced.

Jobs to Outsource	Here's Why
Chief Financial Officer	A whole industry has emerged in which external finance professionals provide the CFO function—financial strategy and planning—to small companies like startups.
Accounting	These vendors manage tasks such as bookkeeping and accounting for small companies.
Human Resources	Many third-party companies manage core HR functions, such as payroll and benefits, for companies that are too small to staff these functions in-house.
Legal Counsel	If you need to file patents, but only a few times a year, just hire an outside lawyer who specializes in intellectual property. And if you're in the United States, consider looking for someone in the Midwest rather than in the Bay Area or New York. They'll be significantly less expensive.
Branding	We used a company called A Hundred Monkeys to come up with our name.* We're glad we hired them. They're pros at this work, and the name they came up with was much better than anything we thought up ourselves.
Marketing	You'll periodically want to revise your brand messaging—the words and images you use to express your company's vision and how people feel when they're interacting with your products and services. While the vision should obviously come from the founders, until you're really big, you should use outside pros to help refine it.

* Okta is a meteorological term used to express the amount of sky covered in cloud (1 okta = one-eighth of the sky). Our company was designed to provide "cover" for our customers in the cloud, so we became Okta.

Off with the "Heads"

When a company hires an executive, they sometimes give the person a title that begins with "head of"—Head of Marketing, Head of Sales, Head of People—instead of a more conventional "manager," "senior manager," "director," or "vice president" title. Often, this happens because when you're first starting out, you're not bringing on very senior people (you don't need a vice president of sales with 10 years' experience before you have anything to sell). Yet once that more junior person is on board, they'll be running their department. Because of that leadership role, many candidates ask for more senior titles. Their experience might only merit a "senior manager" title, but since they're going to be driving the group, they want "director." Giving them a "head of" title can seem like a reasonable compromise.

But there's a problem. Eventually, as you get bigger and the challenges the company faces become more complex, you'll need to bring in someone more senior. Unfortunately, your "head of" person often won't see it that way. They'll have assumed that they would continue to run the show. Few people appreciate having someone brought in above them.

So don't kick the can down the road by avoiding the tough conversations up front. Insist on titles that are commensurate with people's experience. Make sure your hires are on the correct track from the beginning.

Go Behind Your Candidates' Backs

Talk to at least three people *not* on their list of references.

When you hire employees, you do reference checks. This you know. People give you a list of references who will inevitably say nice things about your candidate. Most recruiters stop there. They check that box and move on with the hiring process.

But when it comes to hires for key executive posts, you can't afford to do that. Unlike at a large, well-established company, every single person in a startup has an outsized impact on its success. A middling manager can coast in a large, slow-paced organization that doesn't have to move as fast as you do and that isn't figuring out everything on the fly.

In a startup, your early hires—particularly your early executives—need to be rock stars with the chops to handle the work. They need to be responsible and reliable. They need to be able to roll with the inevitable failures of early-stage life. Ideally, they have worked on the most important, core initiatives at their previous companies, not on sideshows that didn't matter. Typically, you'll want people who got promoted and took on bigger roles and responsibilities as they grew.

How do you figure out if your candidate is that person? You can't just ask them, of course. Anyone can come across well in a job interview. And you can't just ask the references they provide. Those people are teed up to sing their praises.

Instead, just as you did with your cofounder(s), go behind your candidates' backs. This is sometimes called "backdoor reference checking." Find at least three people who have worked with the candidate recently and can talk about what they're really like, how they work with others, how they handle setbacks, and, ultimately, whether they'd be a good fit for your world.

Sometimes, your network and the candidate's will overlap sufficiently that you'll actually know people who know them. If so, reach out to those people. But even if you don't know anyone within a degree of separation, use tools like LinkedIn to find colleagues who can give you candid assessments. Don't extend an offer to a candidate until you've spent at least 30 minutes really digging deep with each of those backdoor references.

Startup Hiring Basics

Advice on how (and who) to recruit.

FRED LUDDY, SERVICENOW

In the beginning, you don't need the absolute top tier of engineering talent. You need people who are extremely dedicated and who are going to just love, love, love the problem that they're solving and want to pursue it to its end.

AMY PRESSMAN, MEDALLIA

I look at people's résumés and ask why they decided to leave one job and go to the next. One of my pet peeves is when they say, "A recruiter called me." People with the founder mentality we're looking for in our early employees don't sit around waiting for a recruiter to call. They decide it's time to do something new, and then they go figure out what that is.

PATTY MCCORD, NETFLIX

In the beginning, you're hiring people to solve problems of difficulty. They're people who can take your crazy idea and hone it into something that could actually get customers and make money. Later, when you start growing, you need people who can solve problems of scale or complexity. At that point, you need to hire people who have seen those problems before.

MARIAM NAFICY, MINTED

Do reference-checking early, before you fall in love with a candidate. If you wait until you've convinced yourself to hire someone, you'll be less able to hear honest feedback. Also, listen really carefully to what their references say. Nobody wants to give a bad reference, and that includes backdoor references—people the candidate didn't supply, but who you'll call anyway. If someone wants to signal that they can't give a 100 percent positive reference, they might provide feedback that is vague or indirect. If you hear anything that is not a total endorsement, dial up the volume on that. Every single time someone has hinted gently at something negative, but I went ahead with the hire anyway, it has turned out badly.

Firing Best Practices
There are good ways to do it—and bad ones.

It once took me 12 months to let go of an executive who simply was no longer the right fit for the position or our company. I'm embarrassed it took me so long. Being decisive is one of my biggest strengths. But this decision? I just kept putting it off. Partly because firing someone is really hard to do. We're human. Who wants to tell an employee that you're about to take away their livelihood—and potentially their pride and sense of self?

It's so easy to come up with rationalizations as to why now is not the right time to let someone go: There's a product launch or rebrand coming up that you need the person for. Or the end of the quarter is around the corner, and it would be disruptive to the team. Or the holidays are coming up, and it's just wrong to fire someone then. In my case, I was also afraid of having that critical position empty while we looked for a replacement.

In the end, though, it set us further back to keep the wrong person in that job than if it had sat vacant briefly while we recruited the right person. I hope you will be braver than I was. It's the right thing to do, both for you and the employee you have to let go. Sometimes you'll even discover that the employee already knows it's not the right place for them, and they might actually be relieved that you're doing something about it. While letting someone go is never easy, there are ways to do it that are better for everyone—and ways that are worse.

- First, consider whether the person is simply in the wrong role. If they're a good fit for your company but not for the position they have, is there a job that will be a better fit?

- If you do decide to let an employee go, it shouldn't be a surprise to them. You should have been having regular conversations with them about where their performance was lacking, so that they had a chance to improve.

- Once you've made the decision, don't belabor your feedback. You are no longer in performance-review mode. Going over what didn't work is just going to make them feel worse.

- Bite the bullet and get it done quickly. Letting these decisions linger is damaging to the company.

- Always fire on a Monday and never on a Friday. You want them to have the whole week to start moving forward. If you let them go at the end of the week, they'll stew on it the entire weekend.

- Give them a proper severance and, if they have equity, vest the appropriate amount of their shares.

How to Have "The Conversation"

Shashank Saxena's VNDLY is a cloud-based system that allows companies to manage contingent workforces. (Okta is an investor.) When Shashank first started the company in Cincinnati, Ohio, a fair amount of his early hires didn't last more than a few months.

"People read TechCrunch, and they think startups are glamorous and guaranteed overnight success. And then they get here and realize how hard it is," he says. If it quickly becomes clear that a person isn't suited to the startup pace, Shashank or another manager will pull the person aside and have a candid conversation.

"First, we'll say, 'This is what we expect of you. This is where you are today. This is the gap you have to make up. Are you willing to step up to that?'" If the answer is no, Shashank will let the person know there's an option B: a healthy severance and positive references for their next jobs. "We hired them because they were skilled," Shashank says, so there's no problem singing their praises to another company. "If you didn't realize what you were getting into, and you can't step it up, that's fine. We're going to wish you all the best."

four

FUNDRAISING

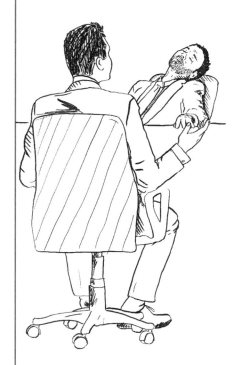

I thought I knew what I was doing. I had read the business books. I knew the "12 Essential Slides" you needed in any fundraising pitch. I could talk at length about the problem we saw, the solution we offered, the market opportunity, and the competition. But here I was at a famous Sand Hill Road* venture capital firm pitching my heart out, and the guy across the desk was asleep.

Not metaphorically asleep. He'd literally fallen asleep in the middle of my presentation. Needless to say, he did not invest.

It was the summer of 2009. Todd and I were trying to raise seed funding for Okta, and it wasn't going well. We had pitched dozens of VC firms, but nobody was interested. I want to repeat that to make sure you understand the pain: we'd pitched more than 25 firms, and not a single one followed up.

Sure, we were in the middle of the recession brought on by the financial crisis, but that wasn't the problem. Investors actually often look for opportunities during downturns. The problem was us. We'd walk in, shake hands, and fire up the presentation. Todd and I would go back and forth, reading from the slides. We followed the format the books laid out. But none of it worked.

The business we pitched then is now worth over $40 billion. It did so well that each of the lead investors in our first four financing rounds made back their *entire* fund by just investing in our company.† I'm not trying to puff myself up. I just want to drive home the point that the blank stares didn't mean we had a bad idea. Or that the investors were idiots—far from it. Rather, it was our approach that was failing.

As the summer rolled on, we were running out of options. Then we heard about a new firm that had just opened. We asked for a meeting, and they agreed to see us. It felt like it might be our last chance. On the way to the meeting (and I still remember exactly where we were on Highway 101), Todd told me he was worried we might never raise any money. "What will we do then?" he wondered.

"We're going to be OK," I said optimistically. Then I had an idea: "Let's just ditch the presentation and wing it."

He glanced at me and nodded. "We have to try something else for sure."

We parked at the office complex that housed the new firm. A piece of paper was taped to their door. Someone had handwritten the name of the company on it. It felt like we had reached the end of the line of VC firms. But it was all we had.

We walked into their conference room. There was a plastic folding table from Costco and a handful of folding chairs. No flat-screen monitor on the wall. No projector to plug our laptops into. We shook hands as usual, but instead of staying standing up, we just sat down. Todd and I looked at each other. We felt unsteady without our deck. Then Todd took a deep breath and started speaking.

"I guess we'll just tell you about our company," he said.

And we started talking. We explained why we felt so strongly about our idea. We had a firm grasp of the details (hashing out the 12-slide deck had served its purpose). But what had been missing in our previous meetings was our passion. We'd never told the story of the company. We hadn't made it exciting. In fact, we'd done the opposite: we'd put people to sleep.

This time it was different. In part, because we felt like this might be our last chance. It also helped that we weren't talking like robots. We let our enthusiasm shine through, and it made a difference.

At the end of the meeting, those venture capitalists—Ben Horowitz and Marc Andreessen—handed us a $500,000 check. It was our first round of real fundraising.

Our story isn't unusual. It's rare to land an investment on your first pitch. But each meeting is an opportunity to make your pitch better. It took me too long to learn that lesson, so I hope you'll benefit from the pain I went through. And it's not just my pain. This chapter is filled with plenty of other agonizingly earned lessons from successful entrepreneurs.

Money is the gas for your startup engine. Without it, the car doesn't go. For your first 10 years or so, thinking about how to raise money will consume every waking hour. (Okta, for example, didn't even become cash-flow positive until *after* we went public.) You'll get a brief respite the first few weeks after you raise a new round, but then the clock starts ticking again. Rounds are usually designed to last 18 months or so, two years tops. This chapter highlights some of the key things to think about as you go trawling for money.

Note: Everything here is geared toward high-growth startups that raise venture capital. This information won't necessarily apply if you have a cash-flow business or are self-funding a company that you're grooming for acquisition.

* Sand Hill Road is a thoroughfare in Silicon Valley where many of the tech industry's top-tier venture firms are located.

† Venture capitalists raise funds, or pots of money, from large institutions like university endowments and pension funds. Then they invest that money in startups. They hope that the companies they invest in will, collectively, do so well that the value of the fund grows many times over. So when I say that Okta made back "the entire fund," what I mean is that, for example, if a fund had $300 million in it, and the firm invested $30 million of that in us, our company did so well that that $30 million was worth $300 million by the time the fund liquidated.

Ready to Raise?

Before entering the venture capital hunting grounds, study this checklist.

You should start thinking about raising venture capital when you've reached a point where you think you'll be able to grow your company—and its value—to 10 times (10×) its current worth within 10 years or less. That is an extraordinary goal to achieve. So why do you have to aim so high?

Because the money VCs invest actually belongs to other organizations, such as pension funds, university endowments, and foundations. Those entities know that investing in startups is risky. They typically allocate about 10 percent of their assets to what are known as "alternative assets," which includes private equity, of which venture capital is a subset. Even though they know startups are risky (and that most will fail), they expect that a VC fund's failed investments will be more than offset by "outsized" returns from the few companies that do well. That's why VCs aren't interested in companies that only have the potential to grow two or three times their current size. They need ambitious companies with the potential for giant success—the Facebooks, the Teslas—to compensate for the Juicero-like outcomes in their portfolios. (Google it.)

Here's a checklist to help you decide if you're ready to start raising money:

☐ Do you have an idea that is so promising, and whose total addressable market (TAM) is so big (meaning it starts with a $B) that your company could in fact grow 10× quickly, and then, hopefully, 10× again?

☐ Do you have your entire founding team in place? Will a firm look at your team and say, "Yes, these are exactly the people we believe can make this happen"?

☐ Do you have material evidence that your idea is a good one? In some cases, if you're already selling, you'd want to see sales traction. In other cases, it could be a mountain of enthusiastic feedback from your prospective customers.

☐ Have you crafted a story around what your company is about and why it will succeed? Can you tell it persuasively at the drop of a hat?

☐ Do you have a realistic business model?

☐ Are you prepared to do nothing but this for the next 10 years? No vacations. No weekends. Missed birthdays. Sleepless nights?

IF YOU ANSWERED YES TO EVERYTHING, CONGRATULATIONS. YOU'RE READY TO START RAISING.

* Term sheets are a type of "letter of intent" that a VC firm gives you when they want to invest. They spell out how much of your company they want to buy and under what terms. When you accept a term sheet, it means you are agreeing to their terms. The next step is for the lawyers, yours and theirs, to hammer out an actual contract for the sale.

Roadmap to Raise

How to stack your pitches.

I recommend a pretty straightforward strategy for running a fundraising process: identify your 15 favorite VC partners (the people, not the organizations), and then approach them in groups of 5, starting with the ones lowest down on your list and working your way up to your top choices.

For example:

WEEK 1 Reach out and set up meetings with firms 11–15.

WEEK 3 Refine and repeat with firms 6–10.

WEEK 5 Refine some more and repeat with firms 1–5.

Here's why: Crass as it might sound, you're using firms 11–15 and 6–10 to fine-tune your show. Your meetings with numbers 11–15 will help you figure out what's working in your pitch and what's not, as well as give you practice answering tough questions. Use those experiences to refine your narrative (and revise your slides). Your meetings with numbers 6–10 will enable you to see if you've worked out all the kinks. Spend this time honing your 60-minute meeting. By the time you've completed these 10 dry runs, your pitch should be a work of art. (I hope I don't have to say this, but *don't tell* the first set of firms that you're using them for practice. The VC industry is a tiny world. People talk. Plus, you might need one of those teams to become your lead investor, if firms 1–5 give your idea a pass.)

Finally, schedule your meetings with firms 1–5. Try to get them scheduled as close together as possible. Your goal is to move through their process—from introductory meeting to second pitch to due diligence—at a fast pace. The final step in this process is the "partner meeting." It usually takes place on Mondays, and it's where you pitch your startup to the entire partnership. After you leave, the partners will discuss among themselves whether to invest in you.

In your ideal world, the meetings at firms 1–5 will take place within a few days of each other. That way, you'll get any term sheets* at around the same time. At a minimum, you want them to come in within the same week. Within a day or two of each other is better, so you can negotiate for the best possible terms. (Term sheets usually expire in 48–72 hours, or, at the latest, "at the end of the week.") The more of them you receive at the same time, the greater your chances of getting your favorite firm to accept terms that are more favorable to you. What you can't do is ask a firm to wait another week (much less two), so that you can "see if anyone else is interested." As much as venture capital is about making money, ego also plays a big role. No one wants to be someone's second choice.

TKAD: "Time Kills All Deals"

There's a saying in the sales world: "Time Kills All Deals" (TKAD). It means that you're more likely to close a deal if you do so quickly, when the customer is at the height of their interest, than to let discussions drag on, allowing cold feet to set in.

The same applies to raising money, which is its own kind of sales process. As such, you need to maintain momentum. As you begin talking to investors, you'll hopefully notice rising interest in your company. As you move from pitching one firm to another, you'll sense if they've already received a heads-up about you from other investors and whether the interest level is rising. If you're lucky, that energy will continue to grow during the length of your fundraise. That growing enthusiasm will let you keep moving up the investor food chain and, hopefully, snag one of your preferred VC shops.

On the other hand, if you begin to sense that your momentum is slowing, strongly consider compromising and accepting a term sheet from one of the firms in the 6–15 slots. There's something ephemeral about momentum: once it starts to dissipate, it can evaporate quickly. And once momentum's gone, it doesn't come back. Your number-one job as a founder is to make sure your company always has enough money on hand. Beggars can't be choosers. A check from any VC is better than a check from no VC. Don't be left without a chair when the music stops.

How to Vet an Investor

Because it's not *just* about the money.

If you should be so lucky as to receive term sheets from multiple VC firms, you should go with the investor at the most prestigious firm or the one offering the biggest check or highest valuation, right? Not necessarily.

Remember, your investors will be part of your life for a long time. The money they bring your startup is only a fraction of the value you'll get from them. They will (most likely) join your board and become some of your closest advisors. As they say in Silicon Valley, you can divorce your spouse, but you can't divorce your investor. Plus, your company is your baby. If it goes well, you'll probably never have another startup. (VCs, on the other hand, get to participate in dozens—or even hundreds—of startups.) So choose wisely.

Here are some things you should suss out in conversations with investors:

- Does the investor have experience in your industry? Those who do can hit the ground running. They'll have invaluable insights into how the industry works, where the opportunities are, and what risks to consider. They'll have wide networks they can use on your behalf, whether it's in making customer introductions or giving you leads on great hires. The absence of such experience isn't a deal-killer, but it's not ideal.

- Have they invested in companies that have a similar business model to yours? If so, they'll be able to help you fine-tune yours and identify any pitfalls you'd otherwise have to discover the hard way.

- Do their strengths balance out your weaknesses? If you are great at product development, you might want to look for investors with sales backgrounds. If you're great at marketing, you might want someone with depth in engineering. It's like putting a sports team together. You want a wide variety of skills. You won't get very far if everyone plays the same position.

Next, you'll want to do some sleuthing to learn things investors won't tell you (at least not directly). Reach out to a few other founders in the investor's portfolio, preferably those whose businesses have struggled—or even failed altogether. You want to find out how the investor handled the challenging times:

- Were they supportive? Or did they ghost the founder when the going got tough?

- Did they find ways to help? Or did they struggle for answers themselves?

- When they had tough conversations with the founder, did they do so respectfully and clearly? Or did they yell and berate? Was it difficult to even understand what they were trying to communicate?

- Did they respect the fact that their role always needed to be that of an advisor? Or did they try to take control and start steering the company themselves?

With all this information in hand, then and only then should you choose which term sheet(s) to accept.

With VC Funds, Size Matters. So Does Vintage.

As I mentioned earlier, the money VCs invest in you comes from their individual funds. The firm's limited partners ("LPs" in VC talk) put money into a particular fund, and then the fund invests that money in startups. One fund at a firm might do great while another only so-so, depending on which companies each fund bets on.

As a rule of thumb, funds last about 10 years. VCs will spend the first three years of a fund investing half the fund's money in new startups. (That collection of startups is called the fund's "portfolio.") Then they'll spend the next three or four years using the remaining money to double down on the best-performing startups in the portfolio. The hope is that, during the last three years of the fund, at least one of those companies will have a huge exit event, which is where most of the fund's returns are made.

So here are two more factors to keep in mind as you're researching potential VCs:

1 **The vintage of the fund.** The fund's "vintage" means the year in which the fund was started. Your goal is to get backed by a fund with a recent vintage—one that was formed in the last year or so—so that the VC firm can reward your early performance with more money during those middle three to four years. If you get in at the *end* of that first period, you might not have enough time to demonstrate how well you're doing, and you could lose out on any follow-up funding (the "doubling down" money) from the VC.

2 **The size of the fund.** Avoid funds that are too large for the amount of money you're raising. For example, if a fund has $500 million and you only need $3 million, you likely won't receive their maximum attention—advice and help that could be critical to your success. You're just not big enough to justify their investing time in you when they have much bigger companies that also need their help. On the other hand, if you get $10 million from a $250 million fund, you can bet you'll be important to them, and you'll be more likely to get ongoing support.

Don't Change Horses Midstream

Know *which* partner in a firm
you want to work with.

A common mistake founders make is to think of VC firms as regular companies where executives are interchangeable. They think they can approach one partner—maybe because they've had a warm introduction to that person—and start selling him or her on their startup. But then, after they've made that connection, they ask to be passed to a different partner in the firm, the one they really want to work with. Don't do this.

Venture firms aren't companies. They're collections of individual partners who each build their own portfolios.* These partners also usually have very healthy egos. It doesn't go over well to establish a relationship with one, only to ask to be handed off to another. If you have a warm connection to one partner but are interested in another partner, go ahead and ask them to introduce you to the second person right at the beginning, before they've spent any time on you, especially if you offer a reasonable explanation about why that second person would be the right fit.

Codicil: It's often useful to get the most senior partner possible in a firm to be your investor. They have more juice to get you both your initial funding and any potential follow-on dollars. In most firms, decisions about who to back aren't made by some central group. Rather, the partners negotiate among themselves about where their (finite) investment dollars will go. As you can imagine, the further up the pecking order a partner is, the more likely they are to get their way.

True story: I once saw a promising startup lose out on a Series B simply because a more senior partner at their VC firm was having a bad day. The partner who represented the startup (and who was the primary investor on their board) was more junior at the firm. The decision about whether to put money into their Series B came up at a Monday partner meeting. Unfortunately, the more senior partner had totaled his high-end sports car the previous weekend. He arrived at the meeting ornery. The partners were supposed to make investment decisions on two companies, one in the senior partner's portfolio and the other in the junior partner's. Three minutes into the meeting, out of nowhere, the senior partner announced that the firm would fund his company but not the junior partner's. And that was it. End of discussion.

It's scary to think that the fate of your company could rest on something as capricious as the mood of a VC partner, but it does. In this case, it had serious ramifications for the startup. They struggled to raise any money at all on their Series B, because when a Series A lead investor declines to participate in a follow-on round, other investors suspect there must be a fly in the ointment. The company ended up having to agree to a much smaller round, with bad terms, from a fringe fund. Shortly after, they were gobbled up by a larger company in a fire sale, effectively ending their startup journey.

* The term "portfolio" can get confusing because it refers to three different things in the VC world: the companies that a specific partner has backed, the companies that the entire firm has backed, and the companies that a specific fund (within a firm) has invested in.

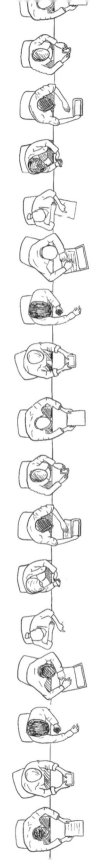

Keep Your Cool

Get comfortable being uncomfortable.

One day, when Todd and I were trying to raise our Series C (our third major round of financing), we showed up for an appointment at one of Silicon Valley's top VC firms. We were shown to a giant conference room with one of the longest tables I've ever seen. At the far end sat 20 people from the firm, some of whom I had only seen in business magazines. On our side was . . . Todd and me. Talk about intimidation.

Then the firm's most senior partner walked in. This guy was a tech legend. He'd made some of the Valley's most historic investments. But instead of heading down to his team, he came over to us and pulled up a chair right next to Todd and me. The man was friendly and relaxed—he even made a few jokes. The entire mood in the room shifted. Out went the inquisition, and in came something much more collegial.

Pitch meetings will always be scary. Why wouldn't they? You show up, hat in hand, often to a very impressive office, with glass walls and wood paneling, and very expensive cars parked out front, begging for money from people with hundreds of millions (sometimes even billions) at their disposal. They can change your life in an instant. Thorough preparation will help calm your nerves, of course. Revise your pitch deck until it's bulletproof, and practice answering any and all possible questions until you can deliver answers in your sleep. Research the firm—its partners and staffers, current portfolio, and investment interests—so you can speak directly to the points that will resonate with them.

But no matter how well you prepare, there will always be curveballs. In another pitch meeting, Todd and I arrived to discover that the senior partner—the person we had to woo—was going to dial in by phone. Our anxiety went through the roof. How would this guy be able to absorb everything we needed to communicate? But the meeting went fine. The partner masterfully directed the meeting from afar, and we hit all the important points. Later, the partner even decided to back us.

So be ready for the unpredictable. And when it happens, don't lose your nerve. Just roll with it. It may turn out better than you think.

Keys to the VC Castle

**The four pieces of collateral you need
before approaching investors.**

THE ELEVATOR PITCH

Imagine you're in an elevator with your dream investor, and you only have the length of the ride—about 30 seconds—to convince them to meet with you for a pitch. What would you say?

You're not going to give them a giant spiel. Instead, in 100 words or less, you're going to tell them something so compelling about your startup that they're going to be dying to know more. Maybe something about the market and the idea. Maybe something about your performance so far. Be specific. Avoid jargon. Say it so an eighth grader could understand.

Write down your elevator pitch and memorize it. You never know when you're going to run into a potential investor.

THE EXECUTIVE SUMMARY

This is a document (a one- or two-page PDF that you can attach to an email or hand out as a hard copy) or a short video (three minutes max) that summarizes all the key information about your company. It should include your big-picture vision; the problem you're solving; the product or service you're creating; the names and short bios of your founding team and any key hires; the total addressable market; your business model; your competition; any notable angel investors; and the amount of money you're looking to raise.

The summary's job is to whet your readers' appetite and make them want to schedule a meeting with you. Make sure it's attractively designed. Like a travel brochure, you want to entice your reader into learning more.

Never send a pitch deck by email. If an investor asks for one, send the summary. If they press you on the deck, they're clearly interested. Insist on scheduling a meeting if they want to see the whole thing.

THE BUSINESS MODEL

Your in-house business model is a spreadsheet with the detailed financials of your business for the next 24 months: your expenses, headcount, projected sales, and how long you expect the money you are raising will last. The one you give to investors, however, is a simplified version. Just detail how much cash you have left, your monthly (or quarterly) burn rate, your current headcount, and the projected number of customers (or subscriptions, sales, or whatever your key metric is) by quarter for the next eight quarters.

Feel free to add some broad-stroke Year 3–5 ranges for headcount, revenue, and free cash flow to give investors an idea of what your business might look like and how big it could get. You don't need to have this hammered out in detail. Investors know that a lot of this is technically unknowable. But do make sure you can explain how you arrived at the numbers.

THE PITCH DECK

Most pitch decks follow a standard format. They include slides on: Vision, Problem, Market Size and Opportunity, Product or Service, Business Model, Traction (or other proofs of validation), Team, Competition, Financials, and Amount You're Raising. Keep it succinct, however. Twelve slides max. No one will sit through a 30-slide deck.

More importantly—and I cannot stress this enough—learn to tell your story without your deck (as Todd and I did when we pitched Ben and Marc). When you're standing in front of a group of investors, you need to be a storyteller. You need to enthrall them with your vision of where your company is headed in order to persuade them that this is an amazing opportunity and to help them see why you and your team are the only people to tackle this. Once you master this, the slides in your deck simply become the background to your talk.

Lastly, bring hard copies of your pitch deck to leave behind so they can remember your amazing story.

Okta's Original Elevator Pitch

Business software is moving to the cloud, and businesses are going to need a way to manage their employees' logins to all those systems. It's already a big problem, and it's going to get a lot bigger as companies start running their businesses with online tools. Okta has built the first-ever centralized online "identity management" system. Todd and I helped build Salesforce from the ground up and through its IPO. We know how to build online infrastructure like this, and we've already raised $1 million in angel money to start the company. We have 12 employees, 10 customers, and $100,000 in annual revenue, with a clear path to get to $1 million.

Master Your Story

"If you can't tell something, you can't sell something."

"Story is everything," says Beth Comstock, the former vice chair of General Electric who once ran GE Business Innovations. "If you can't tell something, you can't sell something."

Beth is a master marketer. She began her career as a storyteller, first on public radio and then in television. After joining GE, she quickly rose to become its chief marketing officer. At GE Business Innovations, Beth saw founders make a common mistake when they spoke about the companies and programs they wanted to launch: "I often saw founders and leaders get stuck talking about the 'gee whiz' of their technology," she says. "They lost sight of the fact that they needed to convince their listeners to care."

Mastering your story is crucial in fundraising, but it will be important in other areas too. You'll need to tell it to the first employees you try to hire. To customers, especially early ones who take a risk in handing over money to an unproven entity. To the media. At conferences. To potential partners. Even to your own family.

Here's one winning startup story, as told by Jasmine Crowe, the founder of Goodr, an Atlanta-based B Corporation focused on reducing food waste and solving hunger. I asked Beth to listen to Jasmine's story and then weigh in on what makes it so effective.

JASMINE'S STORY

In 2013, I started feeding people who were experiencing hunger and homelessness out of my apartment. I didn't have a ton of money, but I knew I could cook. I posted on Facebook, "Next Sunday, I'm going to go downtown, and I'm going to feed on the streets, if you want to join me." I had about 20 volunteers. I made a spaghetti dinner, and I brought out my little Beats Pill speaker. We played The Jackson 5, Aretha Franklin, James Brown, like it was an old-school Sunday dinner. I started renting tables and chairs and linens to give it a restaurant experience. **1**

Meanwhile, I started researching food waste and got really upset. I couldn't believe how much food goes to waste, when here I am, putting together $5 donations and my own money, trying to feed 500 people. At the same time, food delivery apps were starting to emerge. I was getting those referral codes for DoorDash, Uber Eats, and Postmates. I started thinking, "There needs to be something like this for restaurants to get their excess food to people in need."

Then I found out that one of my friends from college, who was well educated and worked in the film industry, was between jobs and struggling with hunger. That was the pivotal moment where I decided I had to go build this app. **2**

I entered into a hackathon that Google for Startups held at Georgia Tech. I began drawing out the little screens of what this app would look like, and I started working with engineers to build it.

The Atlanta airport launched an innovation program where they were trying to become a zero-waste facility. They put out a call for new contracts that could help them get there. I pitched them, saying: "This is the world's busiest airport. You've got over 115 restaurants. At the end of every day, they're wasting food that could be going to people in the community." The airport sits in College Park, Georgia, where about 65 percent of children live in poverty. I said, "There's no reason for any food from this airport to go to waste when there are all these children and families right around your airport who are going hungry." **3**

The restaurants that worked with us didn't just get the tax write-off for the donations. We also gave them data about how much food they were letting go. So now they could start to make reductions in their food production, which helps them save money on food costs. We started with one concessionaire who had about 25 restaurants. At the next concessions meeting, they told the others, "We've gotten all this insight, and we've saved $80,000 in three months." That encouraged the other concessionaires to sign up too. **4**

Beth's Feedback ↓

1 **The founder is part of the story.** The fact that Jasmine started this on Sundays, played The Jackson 5, and had spaghetti dinners—I'm never going to forget that about Jasmine and her passion. Already, it's telling me about her.

2 **The story has to have personal authenticity.** Jasmine's story makes you believe she's going to get to where she says she's going.

3 **The story should be aspirational.** It doesn't have to be true yet. Founders sometimes get nervous about this. Because while you're building a vision, you're also saying, "Help me." Being open and saying where you're going, but that you're not there yet—that truthfulness is persuasive.

4 **She's putting out a vision.** Part of what you do with your story is you say, "Here's where we're going." Jasmine's not just looking to feed people. She's a productivity solution for businesses. You're starting to believe, "Wow, Jasmine can make the future."

Collusion Actually Happens, But It's Hard to Prove

Never tell a VC who else you're talking to.

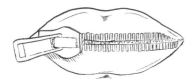

In the United States, price fixing is illegal. Companies are prohibited from joining forces and deciding collectively what they will charge for a specific product or service. This applies to venture capitalists as well. They're not allowed to decide among themselves how much your company is worth and how much they're going to pay for a piece of it.

But do they? You didn't hear it from me, but let's just say it's been rumored to happen.

Your goal, as a founder, is to avoid having VCs do this to you for the obvious reason that it works to your detriment. So how do you prevent it? By not telling investors who else you're talking to. That's the only way they'd know who to confab with.

Inevitably, of course, an investor, or two or three, will ask who else you're talking to. They'll make it sound like a casual question, and you'll feel awkward about dodging it. So let me give you the magic words to say in that moment: "As you might imagine, other fine firms." That'll do more than simply get you out of an awkward pickle. It will also signal to your questioner that you're aware of the game being played. They'll back off.

Don't worry that it will hurt your chances with them. They'll actually respect you for being clued in. And if they're genuinely excited about your company, they'll write a check either way.

It's Raising Season!

There are two preferred "seasons" to raise venture capital:

Martin Luther King Jr. Day	Memorial Day	Labor Day	Thanksgiving

Try to kick off your search for funds either in late January (around Martin Luther King Jr. Day) or in early September (after Labor Day). People go on vacation in the summer, so it's hard to get enough partners around the table to sign off on a new deal. As for the end of the year, everyone loses momentum around the holidays. These recommendations aren't set in stone, of course. You're welcome to start anytime. But if you have the flexibility, use these dates as guides.

1 **Research y**
ground. Ma
as an investo
town. You might h
for clues.) All of th
tity" and toward sc

2 **Highligh**
clearly re
degrees, t
held, any awards yo
sports. And finally,
to your audience an

3 **Turn to th**
raised mo
will know
sented founders and
into those networks

4 **Anticipate**
Research h
founders al
women tend to get q
ference in framing al
wants to park their n
is a way around this, l
their answers to discu
money.

5 **Become a**
but great ex
least a few d
aggressive and to attac
to not let this rattle y
and unbeatable energ
language, facial expres
of doing so. Whiffs of
handle the rigors of sta
without batting an eye

* **Some investors justi**
that, since founders w
jerks in the course of t
see how the founder w
of them are just jerks t

A Million Ways to Say No

Venture capitalists who decide not to fund you are like the date who won't tell you they're not into you. Few investors will ever turn you down outright. They might reply to a pitch by saying, "We're in between funds." (Even though they did listen to your pitch and might even have started to do due diligence, which usually only happens when there's money on the table.) They might tell you, "We need more time." They might say they need to talk to more people or that they're focusing on a few other deals right now. They might say, "It's Tuesday and it's raining." Whatever they say, it all adds up to the same answer: No.

In their defense, VCs don't intend to string you along. It's human nature to avoid rejecting people directly. More than that, though, VCs are terrified of burning bridges. They live in FOMO. If you suddenly become a hot commodity, they want to keep the door open so they can get in on this round or your next one.

So keep this in mind: Time, as I've said before, is your most precious asset. Don't waste time wondering if a firm is really into you. As with dating, you'll know if they are. They'll invite you for a meeting and then another, and eventually you'll pitch to the partners.

But if you're getting evasive answers and happy talk but no action, put them on the back burner and move on.

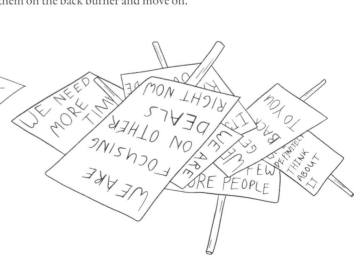

Don't Forget Your Angel Investors

Bring them along as you grow.

When you first launch your company, you will probably need to turn to angel investors, those high-net-worth individuals who help startups get off the ground.*

You pitch these informal networks the way you'd pitch a VC, so they can learn about your company and decide if it's a good bet. But, unlike at a VC firm, angel-investment decisions are made on an individual basis. You don't have to convince everyone in the network. Just enough people to make your nut.

As startups get bigger, some founders begin to overlook their angels. If you're lucky enough to make it to a Series A and then a Series B, you're going to be dealing with VCs who don't want to share the wealth; they want to keep the entire round for themselves. It's understandable. Their decision to back you might be based on an internal goal to own a certain percentage of your company (often 10–25 percent, depending on the round and the firm). They don't want to parcel out any of that equity to other players.

And yet, it's in these later rounds where the real money is made. Your angels might have invested early on with a convertible note—a form of debt that converts into equity at a later date—but the value of that early equity is diluted with each additional financing round. As your company shows increasing promise, some angels might want to put additional money into subsequent rounds as a way of maintaining their ownership stake in the company (called "pro-rata"), which means they'll get higher returns if the company has a successful exit.

A Million Ways to Say No

Venture capitalists who decide not to fund you are like the date who won't tell you they're not into you. Few investors will ever turn you down outright. They might reply to a pitch by saying, "We're in between funds." (Even though they did listen to your pitch and might even have started to do due diligence, which usually only happens when there's money on the table.) They might tell you, "We need more time." They might say they need to talk to more people or that they're focusing on a few other deals right now. They might say, "It's Tuesday and it's raining." Whatever they say, it all adds up to the same answer: No.

In their defense, VCs don't intend to string you along. It's human nature to avoid rejecting people directly. More than that, though, VCs are terrified of burning bridges. They live in FOMO. If you suddenly become a hot commodity, they want to keep the door open so they can get in on this round or your next one.

So keep this in mind: Time, as I've said before, is your most precious asset. Don't waste time wondering if a firm is really into you. As with dating, you'll know if they are. They'll invite you for a meeting and then another, and eventually you'll pitch to the partners.

But if you're getting evasive answers and happy talk but no action, put them on the back burner and move on.

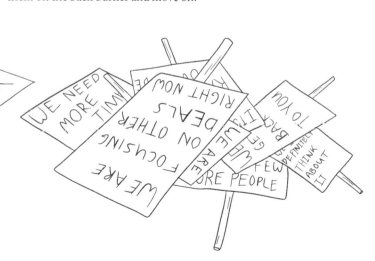

How Underrepresented Founders Can Unstack the Deck

Five ways to fight implicit bias.

Fundraising is never easy, but research has shown it's generally harder for women and people of color. I'm fully aware of that. While Todd and I struggled to raise money, the fact that we're both white men who attended schools like Stanford, MIT, and CalTech undoubtedly eased our path in innumerable ways, such as helping us get in the door to make a pitch in the first place.

Much has been written about cognitive biases in the venture community and how they may influence who gets funded. Many venture capitalists rely on two factors to reduce their sense of risk, even if they're not always conscious of it: warm introductions and pattern recognition. These appeal to a person's primal, risk-averse lizard brain. Someone who is introduced to you by someone you know has "social validation." Someone who has no connection to you is an unknown quantity. That's why warm introductions help a great deal, even though they're vastly unfair to those who aren't already plugged into the right networks.

"Pattern recognition" just means you use your knowledge of the past to predict the future. Consider driving, for example. When you first get out on the road, you pay attention to everything. After a while, pattern recognition helps your brain learn what it can safely process in the background (regular flows of traffic) and what it needs to bring to the forefront, so you can act on it (a child running into the road). When founders walk through the door who seem similar to other founders who've been successful, VCs might be more open to their pitch. When founders seem very different, VCs sometimes have more questions.

Much of venture investing depends on gut instincts. While investors crunch a lot of numbers, in the end, as with the stock market, they're really just making educated guesses about who's likely to succeed. To overcome this built-in fortress of unconscious bias, consider these tips:

1 **Research your audience.** Look for ways to create common ground. Maybe you attended the same university or graduate school as an investor you're pitching. Maybe you're from the same hometown. You might have common interests or hobbies. (Troll social media for clues.) All of this helps move you away from being an "unknown quantity" and toward something more familiar.

2 **Highlight attributes that give you credibility.** Foreground clearly recognizable signs of authority: your educational degrees, the companies you've worked for, the positions you've held, any awards you've received—whether at work, in school, or even in sports. And finally, highlight the people in your network who are credible to your audience and who can vouch for you.

3 **Turn to the whisper network.** Women founders who have raised money before you, Black founders, Latinx founders—they will know which firms have better track records with underrepresented founders and which ones might not even be worth contacting. Plug into those networks. They will save you time.

4 **Anticipate their questions and master your responses.** Research has shown that investors are more likely to ask male founders about the *opportunity for gain* in their business, while women tend to get questions about how they'll *protect against loss*. The difference in framing almost dooms women from the start. What investor wants to park their money with someone they're afraid will lose it? There is a way around this, however. Research has shown that when women pivot their answers to discuss the opportunity for gain, they end up raising more money.

5 **Become a master of body language.** I hope you have nothing but great experiences with investors, but odds are there will be at least a few downers. Some investors think it's their job to be aggressive and to attack pitches or even the founders themselves.* Learn to not let this rattle you. Instead, always project confidence, enthusiasm, and unbeatable energy. Investors notice nonverbal cues, such as body language, facial expressions, and vocal affect, even if they're not conscious of doing so. Whiffs of dejection can make them question your ability to handle the rigors of startup life, while watching someone take a blow without batting an eye often impresses them.

* Some investors justify this behavior by saying that, since founders will inevitably cross paths with jerks in the course of their jobs, they are testing to see how the founder will handle it. Of course, some of them are just jerks themselves.

Don't Raise Money for the Heck of It

Or to save your butt.

Venture capital is strategic money. You raise it to help you achieve a specific goal that isn't attainable with the money you have in the bank, combined with your future expected revenues. For example, you might want to enter a new market. Or you might realize it's time to begin working on a new product that doesn't currently have demand, but will in a few years. Those are legitimate reasons to seek investment because those projects will help strengthen and solidify your company.

Here are a few reasons *not* to try to raise venture capital: because you're flailing, because you haven't figured out your business model, because you're burning through your existing cash without showing any results.

If you aren't running your company well, venture capital won't help. It will just prolong the problem. It's like giving money to someone who hasn't demonstrated the ability to make sound financial decisions: The money just allows them to continue making bad choices. Similarly, money can't fix what's wrong with your company. It only amplifies what's already there.

If things are going well, if you're firing on all cylinders, if you have a well-run operation, an infusion of outside funds accelerates your growth. If things are going poorly, if your organization is dysfunctional, if there are fundamental issues you've avoided addressing, new money just allows you to continue avoiding your issues. It doesn't solve your problems. It only exacerbates them. So do a gut check when you start thinking about more money. If there are internal problems that you haven't dealt with, fix them first.

In Defense of Bootstrapping
Because venture money isn't always the solution.

Amy Pressman and her husband and cofounder, Borge Hald, didn't plan on bootstrapping Medallia, the startup they founded in 2001. Like most new companies in the heady days of the late dot-com boom, they envisioned fueling their business with venture capital.

But then 9/11 hit. Medallia had been created to give brands real-time insight into their customers' experience, and hospitality was one of their first target industries. The terror attacks all but shut down that sector, while also obliterating the venture markets. "9/11 took all the air out of the internet bubble," Amy says.

They were forced to get very lean very fast. "We'd sold our house, and we were living off our savings," Amy adds. Everything had to be scaled back: the size of the product, their staff, their operating costs.

The enforced scrappiness ended up having a silver lining: Medallia built enough traction with customers to survive on its own for *10* years. Along the way, Amy discovered something that's not always widely understood in the startup world—selling to customers took the same amount of time as pitching investors. And after a sale, they still owned as much of the company as when they'd started, which would not have been the case if they'd been getting their money from VCs.

Medallia only turned to the capital markets in 2011, when the emergence of social media meant they had to rapidly expand their product in new directions. By then, the company was doing so well, they ended up getting term sheets from five of the six firms they pitched, giving them a lot more leverage to gain favorable terms. In 2021, the company was sold for $6.4 billion.

* For finding talent in unusual places, Amy Pressman recommends *The Rare Find: How Great Talent Stands Out* by George Anders.

Here are Amy's five key tips for bootstrapping:

1 Find prospective customers who are really into what you're doing. "If you can't do that, then you probably need to find a new business."

2 Stay close to your customers to learn not just what they need but what they're willing to pay. "You don't want to spend a ton of time on products that people don't really want to pay for."

3 Know that overseas developers can lower your costs, but it helps if you have local knowledge. Medallia worked with teams in Norway (where Borge is from) and Argentina (where their head of engineering was from).

4 Expect to still face competition when hiring overseas, especially from big companies like Google and Facebook. You won't be able to compete with them on salary, but you can compete on the quality of work you offer. At the big companies, overseas developers rarely get the juicy projects. But at your company, they will be integral to the main efforts.

5 Get creative when hiring locally. Medallia found great hires among women returning to work after having children, veterans getting out of the military, and spouses of international graduate students, who often have work permits.*

Don't Forget Your Angel Investors

Bring them along as you grow.

When you first launch your company, you will probably need to turn to angel investors, those high-net-worth individuals who help startups get off the ground.*

You pitch these informal networks the way you'd pitch a VC, so they can learn about your company and decide if it's a good bet. But, unlike at a VC firm, angel-investment decisions are made on an individual basis. You don't have to convince everyone in the network. Just enough people to make your nut.

As startups get bigger, some founders begin to overlook their angels. If you're lucky enough to make it to a Series A and then a Series B, you're going to be dealing with VCs who don't want to share the wealth; they want to keep the entire round for themselves. It's understandable. Their decision to back you might be based on an internal goal to own a certain percentage of your company (often 10–25 percent, depending on the round and the firm). They don't want to parcel out any of that equity to other players.

And yet, it's in these later rounds where the real money is made. Your angels might have invested early on with a convertible note—a form of debt that converts into equity at a later date—but the value of that early equity is diluted with each additional financing round. As your company shows increasing promise, some angels might want to put additional money into subsequent rounds as a way of maintaining their ownership stake in the company (called "pro-rata"), which means they'll get higher returns if the company has a successful exit.

This is the point where some founders make a shortsighted mistake—and leave their angels behind. They might be too intimidated to stand up to their new VCs and advocate for their angels. Or they might suffer from Shiny Penny Syndrome and be more excited about the new VC than the dentists and real estate developers who wrote the "friends and family" checks when no one else would. The angel investors served their purpose, and now their services aren't needed. Many an angel has called up a founder at this point, looking to get into the new round, only to be turned down.

But here's what that founder is missing: angels didn't simply write checks that enabled you to get off the ground. They recommended you to other investors. They answered your calls when you needed advice. They introduced you to potential customers or gave you leads on great hires. And now you're going to cut them out once there's real money to be made?

While I often remind entrepreneurs and colleagues that "it's not called show *friends*; it's called show *business*," it's still important to remember that angels are the people who made your company possible. These are the people who bet on you. They're the ones who believed in you. In Silicon Valley, they say, "Life is long, and the Valley is small." In such an insular sandbox, you want a reputation as a person who treats other people well. So make it a practice to reach out to your angels when a new round is on the horizon, and then advocate for any angel who wants to join in. Their checks will barely be a rounding error to your VC. You might get pushback, but the best VCs will understand, and most will accommodate you.

In Silicon Valley, they say, "Life is long, and the Valley is small." In such an insular sandbox, you want a reputation as a person who treats other people well.

* Google the name of your city and the words "angel network" to find one near you.

You're Flush, Now What?

Save your nest egg—except for these five things.

You closed your round. The money's in your bank account. Congratulations! You're on your way. Time to put all that green to good use, right? Sign the office lease with the skyline views! Invest in some high-end furniture! Call the catering companies! Bring on a yoga instructor and give them stock options! Right???

Wrong!

It's easy to get dazzled by that giant bank balance—and other startups' spendthrift ways. But don't be fooled. That money is going to have to do a ton of work in the next 24 months, before you have to go out and start looking for more. Stay lean and thrifty. Go crazy only on these five things:

1

A really good, full-time, in-house recruiter. Your company is only as good as the people you have in it. A top in-house recruiter (with stock options to motivate them) will repay their cost many times over.

2

A stupidly expensive espresso machine—seriously. No more productivity lost on staff trips to the local coffee shop. Plus, break areas often spark conversations, which lead to closer relationships and breakthrough ideas.

3

Really nice Aeron chairs. (And footrests for those who want them.) When people are comfortable, they're more focused. (And they avoid getting carpal tunnel syndrome.)

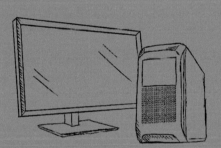

4

Developer-grade computers and monitors. When your employees have the right equipment, they're more effective *and* happier, which drives better performance.

5

Great equipment for people who work from home. Spring for great chairs and monitors, as well as desks, lamps, and chair mats if an employee doesn't already have them. The more comfortable (and happy) your team is while they're working, the more energy and ingenuity they'll bring to their work.

five

SALES

By 2012, things were looking up at Okta. We'd pulled out of our death spiral and had started to win a bunch of contracts. We were finally offering a product that fit the market. I began to feel good: we might actually survive.

So I was floored when things went south again.

I had flown to Louisiana to make a final pitch to a company there, and it had gone great. The deal was going to propel us forward, and I knew we were well positioned. I asked who we were competing against, and when they told me, I smiled smugly.

"That's great," I said. "We love competing against them because we beat them every time." Two weeks later, the prospect called and said they'd given the contract to our competitor.

"You sure you dialed the right number?" I said, flummoxed. "You should be telling that to the other guy."

"No, I dialed the right number," the executive said sharply. I felt a knot in my stomach and got off the phone. I couldn't believe we'd lost.

The next day, I called the prospect back. I wasn't trying to change his mind. (Who am I kidding, of course I was!) But I also wanted to know why he'd gone with the competition. "You were too arrogant," he said bluntly. "This is a new technology, and we're going to have to work closely with the winning company to implement it." He said he didn't like our attitude. "We thought you'd be a bad partner."

It hurt, but I needed to hear it, as did my whole team. Being aggressive is fine. But, unfortunately, we'd also signaled we weren't listening. The loss led me to change the mentality of our sales group. We needed to focus on partnership, not bombastic pitches. It took a while, but once we reoriented, our sales started to accelerate.

Sales is a complicated topic, and there are entire books that cover it. In this chapter I will focus on enterprise sales, which means selling to companies and government agencies, often very large organizations. It's very different from consumer sales, but it's what I know best.

I'm going to talk about some of the most important things I've learned about selling to other organizations, like how it's a people-to-people business and how you must focus on building relationships above all else. I will explain why you, the founder, need to stay extremely close to your sales team. I will share some tricks about how to close deals and about how you must go above and beyond to make your first customers extraordinarily successful.

For some of you, sales will be a new experience. Some will find it awkward. Others might even find it distasteful. But for a founder, it must become a way of life. I hope you get to the end of this chapter and feel more empowered. If your stomach starts churning, however, pay attention. Sales is the foundation of your business. As I said in the Introduction, "nothing happens until someone sells something." Unless someone buys what you produce, there is no business. You don't get to work on your idea. You don't get to grow. And you definitely don't get to IPO.

Being aggressive is fine. But, unfortunately, we'd also signaled we weren't listening. The loss led me to change the mentality of our sales group.

People Buy from People

Exhibit A in why relationships matter.

About that blown deal I mentioned earlier: it has an epilogue. Another company came along soon after and did end up becoming our customer. It was a business in Boston. The deal was worth a lot less than the Louisiana one, only about $30,000. Though it wasn't a huge amount of money, I still ended up flying across the country to walk them through the product. They agreed to do a paid test run, which worked out great, and I flew back to Boston to check in on how things were going. A little while later, they called and told us we had a deal.

Much later, one of the company's executives explained to me that we had been competing for the deal with another company, also based in San Francisco. "Your product worked fine," the customer told me, "and the other guy's product worked fine." So why did they go with Okta? "Because you came in person to see us—twice."

Sales really are all about relationships. People buy from people. When you buy commodities—be it pencils or duct tape—that's just transactional. It's impersonal. You, the customer, know what you want. You find someone who's selling it. You place an order. You get your purchase. There's no interaction with another person.

But enterprise sales are different. They're time-intensive. You have to invest hours, days, and months persuading your prospects that your product is something they want and can trust. With some companies, you only have to work with a single person. With the largest organizations, however, like those in the Fortune 500, you could have 2, 3, or even 10 different people to convince. Some will be fans who will help you move through the organization. Others might resist. Some do so simply because your product threatens some part of their fiefdom. You have to spend time trying to downshift their objections enough to get the sale, even if you never turn them into actual supporters. By definition, you need to build relationships with those people the same way you do with the fans, and it's how you nurture and handle those relationships that often makes the difference in whether you get a deal or not, as well as how big it is and how fast it grows. The team at that Boston company decided to buy from me because they had met me and they had confidence in me.

The last reason for building relationships is that the individual executives who buy from you today will move to other companies. If you do a good job of creating a relationship with them now—and of proving, over and over, that you're awesome at listening and serving their evolving needs—they will continue buying from you at the next two, three, four companies where they work.

The Two Books You Must Read

No matter what kind of selling you do, mark these words.

How to Win Friends and Influence People by Dale Carnegie

Sure, it was written nearly a century ago, but it's as useful today as it was back in the 1930s. Nobody explains better than Carnegie what succeeding at sales is fundamentally about. It's not about what you want to sell. It's about what other people want to buy.

Little Red Book of Selling by Jeffrey Gitomer

It covers the most high-level principles about sales that you should know, especially in the early years of your company. Okta does more than $1 billion in annual revenue these days, and we have hundreds of sales reps around the world. But even with that big a team, I'm still constantly on the phone or in meetings with CEOs and CIOs who are considering using our products. You really never stop selling.

Scare 'Em with Scarcity

Another litmus test for customer seriousness.

Your first big deals are going to feel like they're make-or-break. And they kind of are. You're going to feel like you'd do anything to make them work: come down on price, give your prospect extra product, show up at their homes and shine their shoes for a month. But don't give in to that impulse. In fact, do the exact opposite. First, do your homework. Make sure your prospect is a serious potential customer. Then, after you've gone to see them, demonstrated the product, discussed how they might use it, and sketched out the beginnings of an implementation plan, introduce the Scarcity Argument.

Here's how Carl Eschenbach, who led VMware from 200 to 20,000 employees and grew sales 100× from $40 million to $4 billion, puts it: "You tell the customer with conviction and confidence that, 'Listen, I don't have a lot of resources to do implementations right now. We have a massive amount of customers interested in this, and I can only focus on the biggest ones. If you're not serious about this, it's OK. We'll come back at a later time.'"

It's not that different from nailing down a contractor to remodel your home. If you want a good one, you have to work according to their schedule. In this case, it's reverse psychology. You tell them you can take them on now, but given how many people are closing deals, you might not be available in a month. Take Carl's word for it. He's now a successful venture capitalist with Sequoia Capital and sits on the boards of Zoom, Workday, Palo Alto Networks, and Snowflake, among others. "I have seen this work so many times," he says.

Get Ready to Sell

A few basic principles for identifying and wooing your target customers.

1 Don't "Spray and Pray"

While enterprise products are usually intended to be used by large companies across many industries, smart startups begin by targeting just one or two sectors. The specific needs and use cases vary too widely across industries. It's hard to master them all immediately. Plus, your product will be a more obvious fit for certain industries than others. Start by choosing the industry that seems to be the best fit or has the most potential. Go after prospects in that field, focusing (if you can) on the top three or five companies. These are called "lighthouse accounts." If you can win them, you can often own the whole vertical. Smaller companies in any industry often follow the top dogs, including buying the products they buy. Once you have a foothold in that vertical—and plenty of proof of how great your system works—start thinking about expanding into a new industry.

2 Find a Champion

Large companies are complicated organisms. You won't be able to close a deal without an ally on the inside pushing for you. This person is your internal advocate, making your case to other stakeholders who need to sign off on the deal. They know how to navigate fiefdoms and politics. They likely have a sense of major initiatives within the company that could benefit from what you're selling. And they have a level of credibility that you, as an outsider, do not.

Aneel Bhusri, cofounder of Workday, talks about how he was able to connect with the CIO at Chiquita Brands. Like Okta, Workday was an early mover in the enterprise cloud.* When Aneel started the company, many businesses were still unconvinced by the cloud and stuck to their on-prem tools instead. The CIO at Chiquita, however, understood where things were headed. Over a steak dinner in the Bay Area, he told Aneel and his team, "I know this is the right direction, and I'm willing to bet on you." It was Workday's first big deal—but not their last—with that CIO. He later moved to two other companies, including a multibillion-dollar consumer products firm, and he's brought Workday with him to each one.

One caveat is to make sure your champion is a real champion, and not simply a "coach." A coach is someone who'll give you advice about how to navigate his or her company. A champion is someone who has the power—and the interest—to make the case for you when you're not there. I made this mistake with the Louisiana deal. Part of why I thought the deal was in the bag was because I thought our contact was a champion. In reality, he turned out to be more of a coach. He was happy to help us, but he wasn't in a position to go to the mat for us. When a more senior colleague in another group decided that we wouldn't be a good partner, our coach didn't have the juice to get us the win.

> * These companies are sometimes referred to as "SaaS" companies, short for "Software as a Service," because they run on subscription business models.

3 Don't Promise Your Product Can Do Things It Can't

It's tempting to nod your head when a customer asks if your system has certain features, and then rush home and try to figure out how to make them happen. But it's not a good idea. First, unless it's a very simple feature, Murphy's Law will probably bite you in the rear. Second, a prospect will call your reference customers and can easily discover if you're lying. Lastly, and most importantly, you actually gain more credibility with customers when you're candid about what you can and can't do.

Fred Luddy of ServiceNow tells a story about trying to make a deal with a very large international bank that asked if his software had certain capabilities. "We didn't just tell them we couldn't," Fred says. "We told them we had no idea how to do that." Being candid like that is a risk. You'll definitely lose some deals. But what you'll gain is even more important: trust and credibility. "When that happens," Fred says, "the person says, 'I'm going to remember you because the next time I need something, I know you're going to be honest with me.'"

4 But Do Work with Customers Who Will Help You Grow

Aneel told me about how he locked a deal with his first Fortune 500 company, an international electronics manufacturer. The company had 80 different HR systems in use in 35 different countries. They wanted to consolidate everything down to a single system. The problem was that the company had 200,000 users, and, at the time, the maximum number of users Workday had ever handled was 10,000. Fortunately, the CIO was relatively young and new. He was not wedded to the old, on-prem way of doing things and was willing to take the time to make the shift.

Aneel's team drafted a plan for how long it would take to build out the capabilities required to handle that large a leap. The customer decided to move forward, even though it would clearly be a while until they could actually use the system. Even more, they agreed to help Workday design and develop their product. "The CIO was a great advisor on how we needed to build it for a Fortune 500–type company," Aneel says. In a sense, he became both a coach and a champion for Workday, helping it grow into the juggernaut it is today.

No Free Pilots

Why gratis is never a good look.

A funny thing happens when customers get stuff for free: they tend to dawdle. Your pilots will get sidelined for other, more urgent projects. And that hurts you.

Pilots are a common step in the enterprise sales process. Buying a new product is a complicated endeavor for a large company. They need to be sure it works before they agree to bring it on board, so they have numerous rounds of vetting and approvals. That puts early-stage startups at a disadvantage. Without paying customers, there's no proof your product really works. But a large company can't simply roll the dice on you. If you crashed, it would disrupt their business. So how do you work through this Catch-22? The answer: pilots.

These are short-term assessments of how a piece of enterprise software will work in which a discrete group or department agrees to give it a whirl. The pilot helps the company figure out what's involved in implementing the software and how it can best be used. A successful pilot can bolster the in-house champion's argument.

New startup founders are often so eager to do these pilots that they'll offer them for free. But don't do that. Always insist that the customer pay for the pilot.

Here's why: Unless the customer has skin in the game, the pilot will be a net drain on you. A funny thing happens when customers get stuff for free: they tend to dawdle. Your pilots will get sidelined for other, more urgent projects. And that hurts you. It will stretch out the time to an actual sale, but it hurts you in another way as well. Pilots are also your opportunity to do research: to get your product into the hands of real-world customers and see what really works and what doesn't. If the customer isn't using it, you can't learn.

If a customer pays for a pilot, however, they'll start cranking. The person who signed the purchase order is on the line for the money they're paying you. They need to have something tangible to show to *their* boss. The contract lights a fuse that works to your benefit.

Lastly, insisting the customer pay helps you figure out whether a company is really serious about giving you a shot. Many executives will take your meetings even when they have no intention (or budget) to actually move forward. Talking with you helps them stay current on the changing marketplace. They can afford to spend that time, but you can't. Bringing up money becomes a litmus test. The customers who aren't serious will start backpedaling. "It's not the right time for us," they might say. "I'm not sure it's our highest priority right now." You now know you can put them on the back burner while you pursue more promising leads.

One tip: If a customer tells you they aren't ready to pay for what you're offering, ask them what they *would* pay for. That's how you discover their biggest pain points and highest priorities. It's how Todd and I figured out that our first idea for Okta was a dud. When we asked IT executives about their biggest needs, they told us about identity management. After we heard that from enough people, we changed course and started building the company that is Okta today.

A last thought: In the beginning, it's intimidating to ask people to pay for pilots. You think they're doing you a favor by testing your product. But if you actually believe in what you're building, you have to believe that it's *you* who are doing *them* a favor by solving their problems. Take Brian Halligan at HubSpot. In 2006, Brian and Dharmesh Shah cofounded the company (now worth almost $40 billion) to build online marketing tools. In their early days, Brian would show up at customers' offices with an old-school credit-card imprinter (the kind that made carbon copies of credit cards) to collect payments. His customers would complain about bugs in the system (typical of early versions of new software) as if to suggest he shouldn't charge them. Did Brian back down? Nope. Instead, he gave them the option of simply canceling. Few ever did. Bugs or not, Brian's software was better than their old way of doing things, and most still pulled out their credit cards.

Listen Like a Fox

There's a metaphor I use all the time: as a salesperson, act more like the fennec fox than an alligator. The fennec fox is a mammal native to the Sahara that has these giant ears and a tiny little mouth. An alligator, as you know, has tiny ears and a giant mouth. The best salespeople act like the fennec fox: they listen a ton and talk very little.

If you let your customers talk, you'll learn what they need, and then you can better show why your product will help them achieve their goals. Be like the alligator, however, and you can kiss your company goodbye. Popular culture might portray sales professionals as big talkers, but those kind of people don't actually succeed in the real world.

How to Push Past the No

A little chutzpah goes a long way.

Carl Eschenbach of VMware has one of the most amazing sales stories I've ever heard. As he was building the sales team in the company's early days, they'd gotten some traction with a large pharmaceutical company for their server virtualization technology. The company, which was on the East Coast, had added a couple dozen user licenses, so it was clear they were ramping up usage. Carl decided to propose a new kind of deal, one that would cover all the customer's usage needs for the foreseeable future: VMware would significantly slash the price in return for an upfront commitment. If Carl could close the deal, it would be the biggest VMware had done yet.

Carl and a junior sales rep headed east for a meeting with the key decision makers. "We get in there, and they start beating us up over pricing," Carl says. "They beat us up over the fact that we were a young startup. They asked whether they could really commit to us, whether we had the resources to back up the deal we were proposing."

Carl could tell the customer really wanted to use their product, but they were insisting on a lower price. Carl wouldn't budge. "We could actually show them the value and all the cost savings," Carl says. The customer wasn't impressed. "Finally, they just said, 'I'm sorry, we're not going to do it. The price just isn't right.'"

As the executives filed out of the room, Carl sat in shocked silence. He didn't doubt his strategy, and yet there they were. Then Carl had a stroke of brilliance. He told his rep, "Let's just sit here." Someone would eventually ask them to vacate the conference room, of course. But in the meantime, Carl figured, why not just stay, pretending to finish up their work, and see what happened.

Fifteen minutes later, Carl's main contact showed up. "Are you guys going to leave?" he asked.

Carl asked if they could stay for just a little bit. The guy said OK.

Fifteen minutes later, the contact came back and asked if they were done.

Carl told me what happened next: "Usually, I have this rule in negotiation that the first person to talk loses. But in this case, we were already losing, so I just said to the guy, 'Can we talk this through for a couple of minutes?'" Deal or no deal, he wanted to understand where the sticking point was. The guy explained that it wasn't about the price. Actually, it had nothing to do with the price. It was the size of the discount. The company was simply used to getting much bigger reductions. It made them feel like they'd "won." VMware hadn't played ball, so they were passing.

Carl listened and then explained how he preferred to structure deals: He didn't like to give discounts, he said, but he was happy to throw in more product. The guy listened and then said he'd run it by his team. A while later, he came back and said they had a deal.

I like this story for several reasons:

- **When you get a No, always try to find out the Why.** If you don't understand the customer's reason for turning you down, you can't possibly change their mind. And even if you can't flip them, you'll at least learn something that will help you next time.

- **Pride plays a bigger role than you might think.** For some buyers, it really is about the game. Customers want to feel like they got a good deal. Figure out how you can make your buyers feel like they've "won" while still getting the deal you need and want.

- **There's no substitute for chutzpah.** Not a lot of people would feel comfortable camping out in another company's conference room, especially one that'd just thrown a big deal back in their face. But docility gets you nowhere. Don't be a jackass, of course. But get comfortable being uncomfortable. A good chunk of your deals may depend on it.

- **All good deals die five times.** Most deals will seem dead in the water several times before they finally close. Never take a No as final. It usually just means there's some aspect that doesn't work for the customer. Try to identify the sticking point. It could be a legal clause in the contract. It could be the payment terms. Maybe it's something else. Most of these can be adjusted—or discarded entirely.

After the Yes

Three steps to seal the deal.

Congratulations! A customer has decided to give you a try. You're on your way, but the Yes is just the first step in closing the deal. There's still a lot of work ahead. Here are some key next steps:

1 Make a MAP (Mutual Action Plan)

Actually, make two of them: one for closing the deal and another for getting the customer up and running.

Mutual action plans, or MAPs, are essentially project plans in which you and your customer are joint partners. The goal of the first MAP is to get the deal closed. That doesn't happen when the customer says Yes. It happens when the contract is signed and a purchase order is created. Once you have the Yes, you need to figure out which departments have to sign off and in what order. Who are the signatories? What are the customer's processes for reviewing contracts? What do you need to provide them? If you can, check with colleagues at other companies who've done business with your customer, to find out how the process usually goes and where the hiccups might be.

The second MAP focuses on getting the prospect up and running on the system. You'd think this would be straightforward, but customers are easily distracted. Without a written roadmap and explicit buy-in from both sides, the implementation can drift.

If your customer does start dragging their feet even on the MAPs, you can motivate them by finding something important to tie it to. They might have promised their CEO they were going to launch a new customer-facing app by the holidays, and they need your service for that. Or they're buying a new company that they now need to integrate. Or maybe they simply said on a recent earnings call that they're going to reduce costs by X percent in Y quarters. Whatever it is, link the need to finish drafting the MAP to those larger goals.

2 Schedule "Show Backs"

These presentations show the customer data to prove they are indeed getting the value you promised. Set up systems and processes to track that value, and then schedule these meetings every 6 to 12 months. Carl Eschenbach loved doing these at VMware. "They let you strengthen the trust and the relationship," he says. Plus, "you've positioned yourself for the next sale."

3 Make Early Customers Commit to "Must-Haves"

All contracts with early customers should include at least *one* of the following items, which you'll need for future marketing or fundraising efforts. In order of priority, they are:

- **Participation in a case study or a video testimonial.** The customer will let you write a case study on them or will allow you to produce a video testimonial about how well the system works for them.

- **Three to five customer reference calls.** The customer will take calls from other companies that are considering using your product or service.

- **Three to five press or investor calls.** The customer will take calls from media outlets or from investors who are considering putting money in a future round.

What's in it for you is obvious: You need happy customers to confirm all the great things about your product or service. They help you gain traction with ever-larger customers and will more than repay any discounts you've given them.

Many customers will be used to these requests, since other enterprise companies will have asked for the same. Plus, it's in their interest to help you. If they love what you do, they'll *want* you to stay in business. The more customers you have, the more solvent you'll be. Some might hesitate. What if they end up not liking the product? Assure them you won't hold them to their commitments if they feel they can't endorse it.

Commit to "Unnatural Acts"

How to ensure the success of early customers or die trying.

A best practice that Todd established at Okta that has worked well for us is that we don't consider a new product to be fully launched until it's operating successfully in at least five companies. By definition, with the first few customers, you're going to discover all kinds of problems in the product itself and in the implementation strategy. Hopefully, these are not huge problems. Just small- to medium-sized kinks that are hard to uncover until your product is being used under real-world conditions.

But you want those early customers to be happy despite the hiccups, right? These are your reference customers. So for those first five customers, you need to pull out all the stops and throw maximum manpower, time, and creativity to problem-solve any issue, so the customer experiences as few interruptions as possible. Those efforts are called "unnatural acts," a term-of-art in the business world that refers to above-and-beyond efforts you make on behalf of the first users. ("Natural acts," by contrast, are what you plan for, which don't require extraordinary effort.)

In Okta's early days, if a customer ran into a bug, we would put them on the phone directly with a programmer so it could be fixed as fast as possible. We obviously stopped doing that once our products reached maturity. With 10,000+ customers, it's simply not scalable. (It's also not necessary. A mature product is one where the bugs have already been found and fixed.) Still, we follow that protocol every time we launch a new product. Once five customers are fully up and running, and we've addressed any important issues, only then do we consider the product ready for a broader rollout.

Another example of an "unnatural act" from our early days was when we'd have customer support calls go directly to my personal phone. At first, we didn't have much of a support team. I also wanted to make sure I was staying on top of any issues our customers had. (Sadly, this left me with an understandably disgruntled wife when one of our early customers, who was based in Japan, made frequent calls during their workday, which rang in the middle of our night. Just one more reason your spouse needs to be on board when you decide to launch a startup.)

Unnatural acts will run you ragged and are unsustainable for the long haul. But they're much bigger than simple customer service. They're more like the last stage of your research and design process. You need to plan for these, so you have the people and the bandwidth on hand for when they're needed.

How to Hire
and Manage a Sales Team

Starting with the Rule of Three.

If you've never built out a professional sales team, get help from someone who has, like one of your investors or advisors. They can help review résumés and give you a gut check on candidates. Mistakes in this space can be expensive. Here are some of the most important lessons I've learned about hiring and incentivizing salespeople:

HIRE SALESPEOPLE IN THREES

Salespeople are competitive by nature. Everyone wants to be top dog. From day one, each is gunning to be the best. Therese Tucker, founder of cloud-based accounting and finance company BlackLine (now public and worth over $7 billion), told me a story about the first salesperson she hired. The man talked a great game during the hiring process (not surprising since salespeople are trained to sell), but once on board, he ended up never actually bringing in business. She had to fire him. Then she replaced him with another salesperson who turned around and hired three others. At first, she balked at the size of the team, especially since she was bootstrapping, but she soon saw the positive impact of the intra-team competition.

STUDY EACH SELLER'S PROCESS

In your early days, you're not just trying to sell. You're also developing internal processes that you'll later standardize so they can be used by your dozens and then hundreds of sales reps. Each one of your early sales reps will have their own way of doing things, and by having several people working simultaneously, you'll be able to determine which approaches work well and which are less effective.

BE FLEXIBLE WITH TARGETS

Sales reps operate on quotas, or targets, that are quantifiable, like dollar volume of sales or numbers of demos scheduled. Figuring out reasonable targets is part science but mostly art. Should a sales rep be able to organize 5 or 25 demos within a prescribed period of time? Should they be able to close $500,000 or $1.5 million in revenue per year? Should it take them three months or six to get up to speed in the job? Having more than one salesperson on your team allows you to see what's actually possible and establish appropriate targets.

GIVE SALESPEOPLE QUOTAS FOR ITEMS THAT AREN'T SALES

Early on, you won't be able to give your team sales quotas because you won't be closing actual deals yet. Instead, give them quotas for other items, like getting in the door to give a demo, and then for booking proofs of concept, and then for commitments to paid pilots. Keep the time spans for those quotas short—the next six months, for example, instead of a full year. Your company will be growing quickly, and you'll want to be able to rapidly adjust the targets accordingly.

ASK ABOUT A RECENT LOSS

I like to ask candidates to tell me about a deal they were going after in the last few years that they lost out on and what they learned from that. If they say they can't recall any, they're almost certainly lying. Every salesperson remembers big losses—often in much greater detail than the big wins. And if they say they didn't lose any, they're definitely lying.

BRING ON SALES VETERANS TO TARGET FORTUNE COMPANIES

If you're selling into Fortune 1000 or 2000 companies, it helps to have someone who's sold to these companies before. Salespeople with that kind of experience have networks they can draw on to sync up with the C-level executives you'll need to talk to. They'll also be able to find out details like whether there are any major projects going on at the company that aren't yet public, where your product could be of use. You don't necessarily need to hire this person full time. There are many retired or semiretired executives who will be happy to do your initial legwork in return for a consulting fee or a small chunk of equity.

six

CULTURE

"Todd and I decided to do something we had never done before: be fully transparent."

In July of that terrible year 2011, things went from pretty bad to even worse: one of our most senior developers told us they were leaving. This was a critical employee, a seasoned enterprise software developer who ran our back-end engineering team. Once the developer left, the rumor mill started. Because Todd and I were struggling to figure out how to right the ship, we hadn't shared the company's situation with the team. In the absence of information, they assumed the worst. They weren't far off. The company *was* going to fold if we couldn't find a way out of this mess.

Todd and I decided to do something we had never done before: be fully transparent. We would explain exactly where things stood. Throw numbers up on the board. Spell out the problems. Reveal the magnitude of the hole. There was nothing to lose. Startup employees have an uncanny ability to sense when the ship is sinking. We needed to pull them into the problem—and the problem-solving—before they started fleeing en masse.

At the next all-hands meeting, we presented a slide that showed our glorious sales projections and our catastrophic actual performance. Remember how I told you that we missed Q2 of 2011 by 70 percent? Imagine being one of our employees and seeing that gap for the first time. You could have heard a pin drop. The fear was palpable. Our employees had given up short-term money (the higher salaries they could have gotten elsewhere) in exchange for the potential upside* should our startup succeed. The team now saw that upside cratering.

But here's what happens when you entrust smart, motivated, creative people with a problem: they get to work. Our sales and marketing team identified companies in the sales pipeline that could produce enough revenue to carry us through the near term. In the meantime, our engineering and product team drafted a list of features we'd need to produce to close deals further down the line. Everyone worked together to fix what was broken.

I hadn't thought much about culture when we launched Okta. I just thought we needed to hire smart people, explain their duties, and then sit back and watch them work wonders. I'm not sure why culture wasn't on my radar. I'd played sports all my life. It should have been obvious that how well or poorly a team performs stems largely from the coaches: how they act, the values they insist on, the tone they set. But none of this registered until we were in the hole and had to rely on our team's ability to get us out. Today, I tell new founders that culture is something they need to start thinking about from jump. They should invest time considering what values they want to promote and what practices they want to emphasize.

"Culture" is an amorphous word. Many people struggle to nail down what it really means. Here's one way to think about it: Picture the family you grew up in, and then the families of three of your closest childhood friends. Each family probably operated differently. Some parents were strict. Others were relaxed. Some valued money, others prioritized experiences, some emphasized learning, and others celebrated achievement. Actions that were frowned upon in one household were tolerated or even encouraged in another. The way each family operated influenced how you and your friends behaved, even when you were away from your families. As a result, even among a close group of friends, some were more disciplined about homework, others wanted to socialize, some had after-school jobs, and others played on every school team.

A company is not a family, of course—it's more like a team. But a company's values, like a family's, ultimately dictate which behaviors are celebrated and which are frowned upon, what is expected of each member, and what they will be held accountable for. Your culture becomes how you want employees to behave, especially when the boss isn't around. It's key to hone this early, when the company is small. Later, as your company grows, your culture will propagate itself on its own. It's essential to build your culture in good times, because it could be the key to saving you in bad times.

Successful companies give culture as much thought (and make it as central to performance) as their sales and engineering goals. It's not an afterthought. It's not delegated to HR. It comes from the top—and continues to be cultivated and fostered from the top.

> Your culture becomes how you want employees to behave, especially when the boss isn't around.

* "Upside" is shorthand in Silicon Valley for the amount of gain you'll receive when the value of your stock options increase. The potential for upside is what entices some people to leave a safer job and a higher salary. If you, as an employee, are granted 5,000 stock options at $1 apiece, and the value of the stock increases to $10, your upside (before taxes) is $45,000 ($9 × 5,000 shares = $45,000).

Your Company's Operating System

The dos and don'ts of drafting core values.

Okta's Core Values

——

Love our customers

——

Never stop innovating

——

Act with integrity

——

Be transparent

——

Empower our people

Most companies these days draft core values, usually three to six qualities to which a company aspires. You may choose anything you want for your core values, but they should be principles you think will both drive business results *and* create the environment you want for your company.

Most importantly, however, you and your cofounders must be able to walk the talk. "Don't write down anything that you can't live with," Netflix's former Chief Talent Officer Patty McCord says. Your team will watch what you do, not what you put on paper. "If you say 'Integrity' is one of your core values, and one of your executives is a liar—even about the littlest thing—your employees will pick up on the cynicism," she says. "They can smell it a mile away."

At Papa, an eldercare startup, founder Alfredo Vaamonde created a five-person committee that tracks the company's culture as intentionally as they do sales and operations. Both of the company's cofounders sit on the committee, along with three other regular members. Once a month, they bring two randomly selected employees into the discussion. "We talk about what we want Papa to be in the future, and how we see our culture growing," Alfredo says.

Papa reinforces the culture by celebrating one core value each month. For a month focused on wellness and fitness, for example, they offered a Fitbit to the first employee who ran a total of 50 miles. "Having people talk about a value each month makes it more than just a word or phrase posted on a wall," Alfredo says. "It's something everyone is aware of."

Finally, make sure you create a culture in which everyone feels comfortable speaking up when they see behavior inconsistent with your core values. At VNDLY, a platform for managing contingent workforces, the culture manifesto ("The VNDLY Way") concludes by declaring, "Every VNDLY colleague is empowered to question actions inconsistent with our values." And they do. "I can't tell you the number of times I have been called out at an all-hands meeting or privately," founder Shashank Saxena says. "That's super important."

How Culture Can Save a Company

Eventbrite has a 90 percent rating on the Great Place to Work Survey, which measures how much people enjoy the companies where they work. (The average for a US-based company is more than 30 points

Julia's Five Lessons on How to Build Culture

1 Culture has to be a living thing. "I'm allergic to the idea that you make a handbook and put your values on the wall, and you're done," she says.

2 Don't outsource the creation and maintenance of values to HR. It has to come from the founders.

3 Walk the talk. The most fundamental thing for you, the founder, is to live and model your company's values every day. "Many people get offtrack because they say that they want their employees to do one thing, but they do another," Julia adds.

4 Hire for culture. Once you've vetted a candidate for skills and experience, assess whether the person's values, mindset, and behavior match your company's. "We don't hire a**holes," Julia cautions. "Destructive egos get rooted out very quickly."

5 Give your employees ownership over your culture. They will build on it, as well as identify and tackle issues they see emerging, without you having to get involved.

lower—just 59 percent.) At Eventbrite, more than 9 in 10 employees say they believe their fellow "Britelings" care about each other, and a similar percentage say they believe their executives are honest and ethical. Those are phenomenal numbers, and they're coupled with great business performance. Founded in 2006, Eventbrite went public in 2018 and is worth about $2 billion today.

The company's great culture didn't happen by chance. It was the result of a conscious effort on the part of cofounder Julia Hartz. In 2009, she noticed that some of the other companies founded around the same time as Eventbrite were running into internal problems. "A lot of those companies had raised money and scaled, and then had to go back and correct their cultures," she says. Eventbrite had grown more slowly. It only had about 30 people at the time. There was still time to proactively build the company's culture—but not much. The startup planned to triple in size in the coming year. So Julia set about defining the personal qualities Britelings needed to have if the company was going to be as successful with 100 employees—or 200, or 1,000—as it was when it was still small.

Britelings needed to be innovative, of course, but also dedicated. They had to be authentic and genuine, as well as the kind of people who didn't just excel in their own work but who empowered others. As Eventbrite went on its hiring spree, managers vetted for those qualities as rigorously as they did for functional skills and experience.

Another thing the company did was deprioritize outside trainers. Instead, they created "Brite Camps," which gave employees the freedom to set up and run their own classes about whatever they wanted to pass on to their peers. And when concerns about communication crept in after the company exceeded 100 employees, Julia and her cofounder (and husband), Kevin Hartz, started weekly in-person question-and-answer sessions (aptly named "Hearts to Hartz"). Programs like these created a culture of trust and transparency that helped produce those Great Place to Work scores. In fact, the company was so successful in building a strong culture that the president of the Great Place to Work Institute, which publishes the survey, eventually came to work for them as their Chief People Officer.

The real test of Eventbrite's culture came when the pandemic hit in early 2020. "In two weeks, our company went from a $30 million a month net revenue business to minus $7 million," Julia says. "It was a beyond worstcase scenario." The transparency and trust Eventbrite had built over the previous decade—as well as its "make it happen" culture that resulted from hiring people who were as dedicated as they were ambitious—now paid dividends. Within a week after the lockdown began, a team of 50 Britelings had developed a new strategy. And over the next few weeks, they figured out how to cut $100 million from their operating budget for the year, while also raising a new round of funding to extend their runway by six years.

"When I look back, I'm like, 'How did we do that?'" Julia says. "I know it was all the investment we'd put into our people coming back tenfold."

Don't Be the Cowboy, Be the Stampede

The value of winning—and losing—as one team.

One of my great mentors, Roger Goulart, was Salesforce's first vice president of alliances (sometimes known as "strategic partnerships") during the company's IPO period, when I was a young executive there. (He went on to be a vice president at Okta and two other software companies during their IPO periods as well.) Roger used to hammer away at one concept, which I have carried with me to Okta: "We win as a team, so don't lose alone." Simply put, when you're struggling, ask for help.

The "Looking Out for Number One" culture you often see in the corporate world quashes that tendency. No one wants to show weakness for fear it'll be used against them. But Roger urged us to think differently. "The person who wants to be a cowboy and do everything themselves—they tend not to survive," he says. "If you're trying to be a hero and do everything yourself, you're not leveraging the team."

For a startup to succeed, everyone needs to be pulling in the same direction—together. But there are two sides to that coin: everyone needs to be willing to collaborate at some times, and willing to be helped at others.

At Okta, I cultivate the idea of "One Team," in partial homage to Roger. It's become a call to arms. "One Team!" I'll say at all-hands meetings. "One Team!" I'll say to my colleagues walking down the hall. "One Team!" I'll write in emails about customer wins. I say it not just to remind people to help each other but also to remind them to ask for help when they need it.

Prize Goals Over Promotions

Canva, the cloud-based design software founded by Australian Melanie Perkins, embraces a similar "one team" ethos. They try to keep the focus on wins and milestones, rather than on individual achievements. "I think companies often get it wrong," Melanie says. "They focus on things like titles and promotions. I want to make sure our company is striving toward goals." So Canva has wild celebrations when teams hit major milestones. When Canva launched its first paid product, they released doves. The first Spanish-language release was marked by a mini-version of Spain's La Tomatina Festival (which famously involves massive, joyful tomato fights). When they launched their Android app, Canva set up a drone-racing obstacle course, so employees could test their piloting skills. For another project, they bought a bunch of Greek plates and, as is the custom in Greece, threw them down on the floor, shouting, "Opa!" "We wrote our hopes and ambitions for the project on the plates and then smashed them," Melanie says.

What you celebrate is what people strive toward, she explains. If you trumpet promotions, people only push themselves up the ladder. If you celebrate team accomplishments, people pull together. "Having the goal and the teamwork be the most visible part has had a huge cultural impact," Melanie says. "It inspires people to work together."

Winning the "Ball Bearing Awards"

Celebrate the people who make the work *work*.

One of the ways we promote the "One Team" concept at Okta is to hand out "Ball Bearing Awards" every quarter. Ball bearings are the metal components that reduce friction in a machine and keep it operating smoothly. Every company is made up of tons of these people. They aren't the star salesperson who nabs that million-dollar contract. They're the project manager who organizes the team to support the salesperson. They're not the lead architect who creates brilliant software designs. They're the technical operations engineer who builds and maintains the servers. They're not the CFO who comes up with an ingenious cost-cutting strategy. They're the junior accountant who makes sure employees and vendors get paid on time.

At Okta, we didn't want a culture that focused on the flashiest people or the squeakiest wheels. We wanted to emphasize that our ideal organization is one that actually works well. And it can only work well if everyone is taking care of their part of the machinery. So every quarter, we hand out Ball Bearing Awards across the company to a handful of amazing employees who are nominated—and celebrated—by their own teams.

Integrate Social Impact from the Beginning

It's a good strategy *and* the right thing to do.

When Okta went public, we took the highly unusual step of setting aside 300,000 shares for our philanthropic arm, Okta for Good. To do this, we had to print new shares, which (modestly) diluted the value of the shares everyone was buying in the IPO. Doing it as part of the public offering sent a signal to Wall Street about the kind of company they were buying into—one that was committed to creating social impact as well as shareholder wealth. We wanted to do it with shares rather than cash contributions (as is customary) because equity meant that, as the company grew, so would the value of Okta for Good's shares.

It wasn't our first stab at philanthropy. In 2012, as we were coming out of the terrible year 2011, we told our board we wanted to set aside Okta shares for SF Gives, a tech-community initiative to combat poverty.

Our board scoffed at the idea and told us we should probably concentrate on making money first. It was not an easy conversation, but Todd and I stood our ground. Dozens of other important companies headquartered in San Francisco signed the SF Gives pledge, and the initiative had a real impact on fighting poverty in the city. We were proud to be part of giving back to our community.

Running a startup is so difficult that it's easy to forget about the world around you. But tech companies, like all companies, are members of a community. In our sector and in our part of the world (Northern California), the gulf between the haves and have-nots is growing ever wider. At the beginning of this book, I explained that one of the reasons I want to share this insider knowledge is that the future of our economy depends on entrepreneurs. They are the ones who create more new jobs than any other sector. But creating jobs isn't the only way to help our communities. We can also share the wealth—the equity in our companies—so that when we do well, our neighbors do well, too.

You might be at the beginning of your journey, in bootstrapping mode, with barely enough to make rent, much less to hand out spare cash. But it's still worth creating a social impact plan for the years ahead. If you're lucky enough to do well, where do you want to have impact? What issues will your company care about? What causes will it get involved in? And then consider how to allocate some of your shares toward those goals.

It's not just the right thing to do. It's also smart. More and more employees want to work at companies that are committed to doing more than simply making a buck. Being a company that cares about social impact not only helps you give back to your communities. It helps you attract and keep the best talent.

Who You Promote *Is* Your Culture

"You can say whatever you want about your culture or your core values, but culture is actually based on the behavior you're rewarding," says Mariam Naficy, founder of Minted. In other words: who you hire and who you promote (as well as who you fire) will signal to your team what your company actually values.

Minted selects as its senior leaders people who have a comprehensive command of their functional areas. "It sends a signal to our workforce that we have a very high bar," Mariam says. They also place a premium on people who are very intelligent but not self-centered. "We are allergic to people who are very smart but egotistical," she says. At Minted, decisions get made through group discussion and hard data, "not based on who pounds the table the hardest."

Mariam's inspiration for this comes from Netflix's famous Culture Deck, a 125-slide PowerPoint, written in part by Patty McCord and first made public in 2009. It articulated many revolutionary ideas, including the practice of unlimited time off for employees. As Patty told me, one of the top corporate values at Enron, the energy giant that collapsed in the 2000s following the exposure of massive fraud, was "Integrity." Clearly, the people who rose to the top of that company did not live by that value. The rest of the company surely noticed—and followed suit.

Growth Mindsets Versus Fixed Mindsets

Hire the first early, the second later.

Stanford University psychology professor Carol Dweck's 2006 book, *Mindset: The New Psychology of Success*, is all about her groundbreaking research on "fixed mindsets" and "growth mindsets." People with fixed mindsets think talent and abilities are static. You either have them or you don't. People with growth mindsets believe they can improve and learn.

The mindset you have, Dweck discovered, directly impacts how well you can do in any particular area. People with fixed mindsets are more concerned with doing well and getting things right. They don't push themselves into uncomfortable areas for fear of failing. They tend to quit when they run into obstacles, and they prefer to avoid negative feedback. They can even feel threatened by other people's success.

People with growth mindsets, on the other hand, are more likely to try new things and view obstacles as challenges to be figured out and overcome. They're more likely to persist in the face of setbacks. They put in more effort, learn from critiques, and are inspired by others' success.

In your early days, you need to hire people who have growth mindsets. Develop hiring questions or exercises that test for this, so you can weed out people with fixed mindsets. Those types of employees won't thrive in the absence of rulebooks or established roadmaps. Worse, their discomfort can slow down or antagonize others. Later, when you've gotten bigger, figured out your product, and nailed down your operations, and now simply need people to run what you've set up, it's fine to hire employees with fixed mindsets, as long as they are in roles where consistency and execution are more important than innovation and imagination.

Call Out Bad Behavior Publicly

But don't shame anyone personally.

Culture isn't just what you say. It's how you—and your team—live every day. You know that quote that's often attributed to Aristotle: "We are what we repeatedly do. Excellence, then, is not an act but a habit."* That's what culture is: the stuff that happens and is reinforced every day.

When you see a member of your team behaving in a way that goes against your culture, you must nip it in the bud quickly—before it becomes a habit that spreads companywide. Rolling back negative cultures after they've taken root is almost impossible. I'm sure you can think of some famous tech companies with widely publicized toxic cultures that are now trying to get back on track. While they might have replaced the CEO or crafted new strategies, they're still facing long, bumpy journeys that will take years to complete.

Nipping bad behavior is a delicate task that requires subtlety because it's the behavior that you want to put on notice, not the individual. (At least not publicly. Individual performance issues should always be addressed in private.) Early on, when I would see something headed in the wrong direction, I got in the habit of talking about it in all-hands meetings. We once had a situation with a manager who yelled at his colleagues. So, during a company meeting, I talked about yelling and how it wasn't part of the Okta way. The team got the message. (I also talked to that person privately.)

In other cases, I'll even make myself the bad guy. We had a situation where two leaders from different organizations weren't communicating well, which caused our roadmap to slip precipitously. So I got up at a company meeting and started talking about the ways in which *I* was dropping the ball on communication, why it was a problem, and what *I* should be doing differently. Again, everyone got the message, but no one was embarrassed.

* For accuracy's sake, I should note that the phrase first appeared in a book written by American historian Will Durant, who paraphrased Aristotle's *actual* words, which are: "These virtues are formed in man by his doing the actions." (*The Story of Philosophy: The Lives and Opinions of the Greater Philosophers*, New York: Simon & Schuster, 1926.)

Be Aggressive (But Not Offensive)
Competitors will come for you. Get ready to fight.

You're going to have competition. Maybe not for a while. You might have gotten out of the gates before anyone else. But if you have a good idea, you won't be alone for long. Eventually, you're going to start battling for customers. And when that happens, you need to be prepared to fight.

Josh James is a Utah entrepreneur who founded the online marketing and web analytics company Omniture, which he took public and then sold to Adobe. Next, he founded Domo, a business intelligence software company currently valued at nearly $3 billion. Early on at Omniture, Josh had two main competitors: WebSideStory and Coremetrics. In 2007, Omniture acquired WebSideStory (by then called Visual Sciences). Josh was more interested in their customers than he was in their technology. The acquisition would give Omniture a bigger piece of the market pie.

So imagine his reaction when he found out that salespeople from Coremetrics, the other competitor, had started calling up all of WebSide-Story's customers and offering them a full year for free if they switched over, rather than staying with Omniture. Plus, they put up giant billboards on the highway near Omniture's headquarters, saying, "Just because the gorilla"—Omniture—"tells you what you have to eat, doesn't mean you have to eat it." Josh's phone started ringing. "We had so many calls from investors telling us our rationale for the acquisition—that we'd get all these new customers—was falling apart," he says.

Josh is a fighter. The next day he sent rolling billboards over to Coremetrics's parking lot with giant logos of all the companies that had switched from Coremetrics to Omniture. "The last one was a giant home improvement retailer that had just signed that day, and Coremetrics didn't even know it yet," Josh says. He also hired people to wear ape suits and hand out bags of banana chips to Coremetrics employees as they came to work. The bags said, "Come join the 800-pound gorilla just like these other companies have." Says Josh: "It's a little aggressive for some people's taste. But it's a dog-eat-dog world. I've got to survive."

Josh is right on two counts: His stunts are definitely aggressive. But he's also right that it's a very competitive world. It would be nice if business wasn't zero-sum, but sometimes it is. In Josh's case, either he was going to sign up that home improvement retailer and book that revenue—or the competitor would.

You don't necessarily have to adopt this kind of an in-your-face approach. It's best to remain authentic to who you are. But you do need to find the fight in you and be prepared to go to the wall to battle for customers. Do whatever it takes—legally and ethically, of course—to make sure you walk away with the win.

Doing Risk Right

The art and the science of encouraging risk-taking.

Startups are, by definition, risk-taking operations. They go up against giant corporations that are better funded and more firmly entrenched. They upend industries. None of that happens by following tried-and-true paths. It only happens by plunging into the unknown.

Founders aren't the only ones who need to be comfortable with ambiguity. In the early years, everyone in your company must be ready to shoulder risk. Not just in their initial decision to join your unproven startup. They also need to be comfortable taking risks in *the ways* they do their jobs, especially when you're still trying to figure out what the product is and how the business model should work. If your company's culture doesn't encourage taking calculated risks—trying out unproven features, or innovative marketing strategies, or unconventional pricing ideas—you'll never grow 10x in the short amount of time you have to work with. Here are six practices that will help you build a successful risk-taking culture:

1 **Hire for entrepreneurial mindsets** (at least among the first hundred employees). If the first 10 employees define a company's culture, the next 90 solidify it. Of course, the bigger you get, the more you'll start bringing in people who are psychologically more conservative. But the culture created by those first hundred hires will live on as your headcount grows to 500, 1,000, and beyond. The more entrepreneurial those first folks are, the more that ethos will be baked into your company's culture.

2 **Let your teams know that *you* know a project is risky.** One year, Minted launched a new business around personalized handbags. "I told the team, 'I don't know if this is going to succeed, but let's just go have fun with it,'" Mariam Naficy says. Her people tackled it with confidence, knowing that even the boss knew the project might not live up to her hopes. That gave them courage to run with it. "Nobody was saying, 'Oh, God, we have to be perfect, so I don't want to be on this team.'"

3 Make it fun. "Fun" as in playful, open-ended, and adventurous. Research has shown that the more playful a person's mindset is, the more creative breakthroughs they have. When you task people with trying something new, you emphasize exploration and discovery, rather than producing a specific result.

4 Don't "punish" employees whose projects fail. A culture where failure is penalized makes a founder's job harder. People will start hiding bad news out of a reasonable concern for self-preservation. If a team fails at something, "Don't come down on them too hard," Box's Aaron Levie says. And be mindful of what project you give them next. Putting "failed" teams on backwater projects sends a dangerous message. "People are going to start to think they should only work on high-profile, low-risk projects that are assured of success," Aaron says. Then, over time, "the company is going to stop doing really innovative, interesting things."

5 Set guardrails. The risks you and your teams take need to be proportionate. The size of a project should be appropriate to the experience of the person or team. Don't ask someone to climb Mount Everest before they've summited a hill in their backyard. Establish guardrails regarding the size of the project, the budget, and/or the timeline. Set milestones for reporting on the progress they've made and what they've discovered. And define parameters for the circumstances under which you should kill the project.

6 Do postmortems and celebrate learnings. A "failed" project isn't over until your team has studied what worked and what didn't—and they've extracted insights that the rest of the company can learn from. Then break out the champagne. That's what they used to do at Google X, which was launched by Sebastian Thrun before he went on to found Udacity and then Kittyhawk. "We always wanted to tell people that failure is about learning. When you learn something that gives you an important insight, that's great," he says.

seven

LEADERSHIP

In 2011, as we continued to miss our sales projections, we got a surprising lifeline: a Fortune 500 company offered to buy our software. It would be a multimillion-dollar deal, almost a hundred times bigger than any previous contract. And it was coming at a moment when bankruptcy seemed right around the corner. It couldn't have been better timing.

Or worse—depending on how you see it.

The prospect wanted us to fully customize our product to suit their very specific needs. We'd go from having a solution that could be used by anyone to one that worked only for a single company. That was counter to our business model. We wanted to build something that could be used by many customers.

On the other hand, Okta had about 30 employees. Their livelihoods were in our hands. If we couldn't find a way forward, everybody could lose their jobs.

What would you do? Take the deal to save the company, even though it meant giving up on the dream? Or stay true to the original vision and risk losing the company entirely?

Todd and I decided to stay true. It was one of the hardest decisions we've ever made. We had no interest in becoming a professional services company—in building bespoke software for individual clients. That business model is actually riskier in the long run. You always have to find new clients. A platform with a subscription model—which was our original idea—was more sustainable, if we could get there. Our board members agreed with us, even though they were as worried as we were about our prognosis. Still, they gave us the green light to turn down the offer.

Luckily, it worked. We ended up selling far more to a vast array of businesses than we ever could have to that one company. But, in that moment, we were tested.

Being a leader means *constantly* being thrown into the fire. You have to continually make decisions with only a fraction of the information you need. When conflicts are percolating inside your company, you have to tackle them quickly, so they don't get bigger. You have to learn to communicate with a wide range of people and do so in ways that work best for *them*, not for you.

The fate of your company rests on how you choose to lead. If you played sports in school, you know the difference a great coach makes—and the damage a terrible one can do. A great coach runs the team in ways that enable everyone to succeed. A bad one . . . well, a bad one comes in many forms. Some are scattered and disorganized. Others focus on skills or plays, but not on building confidence or cohesion. Some are loud-mouthed jerks who think more about covering their butts than pulling together. Even a coach who is really nice but unwilling to make tough calls can fail their team.

There are many great books on leadership out there. I personally like the ones that follow the career of a single leader, such as Disney chief Bob Iger's *The Ride of a Lifetime* or Bryce Hoffman's *American Icon*, which is about Alan Mullaly's attempts to turn Ford Motors around. (It won't surprise you I'm also a fan of Ben Horowitz's *The Hard Thing About Hard Things*, which is essentially required reading in Silicon Valley.) This chapter, however, contains the kind of rubber-meets-the-road tactical advice that other startup founders have found useful.

First, though, a thought: The irony of being a startup leader is that you have to believe two seemingly contradictory things. You need to have so much ego that you believe that the unlikeliest of events (a startup growing 10×) is within your grasp. But at the same time, you have to subsume that ego every minute of every day. You must give away power and responsibilities so the company can grow. You have to deprioritize your own needs in favor of those of your employees. And most importantly, you need to learn how to listen—to your colleagues, customers, investors, and mentors—so you can collect as much insight as possible to make those great calls. It's a tricky balance.

Being a leader means *constantly* being thrown into the fire. You have to continually make decisions with only a fraction of the information you need.

Prioritization 101

With a little help from Dwight D. Eisenhower.

The Eisenhower Decision Matrix

	URGENT	NOT URGENT
IMPORTANT	**DO** Do it now	**SCHEDULE** Do it later
NOT IMPORTANT	**DELEGATE** Give it to someone else	**DELETE** Scrap it

Tien Tzuo, my Salesforce colleague and the founder of Zuora, told me a story about a friend of his who moved to a startup after working at a large Fortune 500 company. There, he'd overseen an army of people and spent his days tracking 50 separate "top" priorities. "But now I'm in a startup," he'd told Tien, "and I know I can't get all 50 things done." So he'd narrowed down his list to the 10 most important things. Soon, he discovered that even making progress on just those 10 items was beyond his abilities. He realized he only had the bandwidth to focus on two—just two. "It was the hardest thing to let go of items 3–10," he said, "because I knew that things were going to fall apart." Systems would break. Customers would get mad. "But that's the nature of a startup," he said. "You have to focus on the things that are going to get you from Point A to Point B."

Tien's friend was right. There is so much coming at you in a startup that it's easy for you to get distracted. And if you get distracted, your people will get distracted. Then it's just a downward spiral. So you need to "keep the main thing the main thing." Be ruthless in your prioritization. Here are some principles and practices I use to keep my priorities clear:

- **Use the Eisenhower Decision Matrix.** This has different names, but it dates back to Dwight D. Eisenhower, the top US general in Europe during World War II (before becoming the twenty-fourth US president). Eisenhower knew what it meant to make decisions under pressure. His system is very simple:

  ○ Stuff that is neither important nor urgent? Scrap it.

  ○ Stuff that's not important but urgent? Give it to someone else.

  ○ Stuff that is important but not urgent? Schedule it for later.

  ○ Stuff that is both important and urgent? This is your area of focus. It's the "main thing." Make a decision, or at least start working on it.

- **Keep a running to-do list.** I use Evernote and Notion, and I keep them synced on all my devices: computer, phone, and tablet. I revise my list several times a day because everything is always changing. Other equally great tools include Box Notes, Dropbox's Paper, and Google Keep.

- **Be stingy with your calendar—very stingy.** Question every meeting request. Ask yourself: Does the meeting actually need to take place? If so, do *I* need to be involved? If so, does it really need to take 60 minutes, or can we tackle everything in 30? Be particularly wary of recurring meetings. You're probably not needed at most of them. (Every 30 or 45 days, I go through my calendar, and delete all *new* recurring meetings that other people have added me to. Then I wait to see how many people send me those invitations again, after they notice I'm not attending. Spoiler alert: very few.)

- **Control your email; don't let it control you.** Email is what *other* people want you to do. Ignore most of it. A lot are just FYIs. If you've hired great people, you don't need to follow the play-by-play. Maggie Wilderotter, the former CEO of Frontier Communications, told me that she deletes every email that has more than two people on the "To" line, as well as every one where she's cc'd. "Then what bubbles up to me are the really critical decisions or ones where I need to move something forward or course correct," she says. "Otherwise, I trust the people who work for me to get the job done." Another tactic: I block off two hour-long sessions on my calendar for email: one in the morning and one in the afternoon or evening. Usually, by the time I get around to whatever burning issue has been sitting in my inbox, it's already been resolved.

- **Keep your people focused.** Your team will come to you and start talking about five different things. Make them decide what *their* top two most important things are and then talk about those. When my team starts wandering, I bring them back and ask them: "What's the main thing?"

Ditch Your 1:1s

Most managers hold regular check-in meetings with their direct reports (often called one-on-one's or "1:1" for short). But Zuora's Tien Tzuo says he doesn't do them. Ever. Let me repeat that: the founder and CEO of a $3 billion company doesn't have regular 1:1 meetings with his senior executives.

Tien estimates that such meetings can quickly consume 80 percent of his week, which he doesn't think is the best use of anyone's time. "I just tell my executives, 'If you need me, call me. And if I need you, I'll call you,'" he says. Which makes sense. If you hired great people, why wouldn't you trust them to do a great job running their groups? Plus, Tien says his approach actually makes Zuora work more effectively. The 1:1 system ends up producing what he calls a "hub-and-spoke" approach to solving problems. "Everything is brought to you instead of your leaders working out issues among themselves," Tien says.

Tell Everyone to Keep It Short

The TL;DR approach to executive communications.

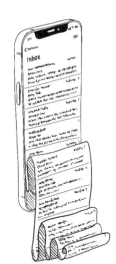

One of the most valuable things you can do is to coach your team to keep their communications short and focused. I never read long, meandering emails. I don't have the time. Instead, I flag them for my next cross-country flight, when I'll have hours of uninterrupted time—which, needless to say, usually comes weeks later. I'm not trying to be a jerk. But my days are overloaded. Every executive's are. I only look at email in brief, interstitial moments where I speed through subject headers looking for a clear Ask. When I find one, I act. Otherwise, the messages get buried.

Here's how I coach my team to communicate effectively:

EMAIL
Emails are modern-day memos. They should follow a standard structure:

- Subject line: Say *exactly* what you need from the executive. If it's just an FYI, label it as such ("FYI Only – Upshot of the XYZ meeting"). If this is the fifth in a chain of emails that now says something like "Re: Re: Re: Re: Thursday's meeting," rewrite the Subject line, so it will catch the executive's eye.

- First sentence of the email: Make your Ask so they know exactly what you need from them: "Please approve expenses for X." "Please comment on budget proposals for Y."

- List 2–4 bullets spelling out the main takeaways that the executive needs to know.

- Last: Write something to the effect of: "If you need to know more, I've included more detail below. And attached are ## documents."

- After that, write as long as you like.

PRESENTATIONS

Presentations to higher-ups usually take place because a staffer needs a decision on something, so that should be the focus of the meeting. Keep the main thing the main thing:

- Slide headers should be declarative summaries of the main points. The executive should be able to read nothing but the presenter's slide headers and understand what they are trying to communicate.

- The presenter should keep the meeting on track. Attendees can go down rabbit holes on nonessential points. The presenter should tell that person they'll get back to them on that item, and then pull the focus back to the main issue.

MEETINGS/PHONE CALLS

My team often asks me to hop into a meeting or onto a phone call for them. Account managers, for example, periodically need me to talk to their customers. Or someone from our Investor Relations team wants me to speak with an institutional shareholder. That person needs to prepare me properly for the meeting, or it'll be worse than if I never showed up.

At Okta, I have a stack of templates that my team uses to tee me up for different kinds of phone calls or meetings. The forms ask for relevant information, depending on the nature of the contact. For a customer call, the template will ask how Okta was introduced to the customer, how many employees they have, what their annual revenue is, what we need from the meeting, and the key points I need to get across. My team knows they need to fill out this document well in advance, so I can get up to speed. (Each executive at your company should draft their own templates and train their teams to use them.)

I bring these prep documents on customer visits. I even place them directly on the table in front of me, so I can quickly answer any question a customer might ask. Doing so also serves another purpose: Customers often notice the documents and ask what they are. I'll explain that the notes represent the summary of their company's needs and our understanding of what they're looking for. More often than not, the customer will actually ask to look at the documents. If our assessment ends up being off-target, the customer will let us know—which is a good thing, because now we can dive straight into the purpose of our meeting: figuring out what the customer wants and how we can get it to them.

Low-Information Decision-Making 101

Because you're always flying blind.

One of the hard realities of being a founder is that you consistently have to make important decisions with very little data. People always think that the people at the top have all the information. But they don't. They might have more information than most people (or, what I like to call "*less* imperfect" information). But it's usually only a sliver of what you'd prefer to have. And that's not just because your fast pace makes it difficult to collect all the necessary information. It's also because there is a lot of information people won't serve up to the top dog. (Especially when things are going sideways. No one wants to give the boss bad news.)

But you have to make those decisions. Remember: your money has a fuse on it—you can't wait. Worse, it never gets easier. Because if you make enough good calls, guess what happens? You stay in business! And the bigger you get, the more complex and high-stakes the decisions become. So how can you get good at making important decisions with imperfect information? Here are a few rules of thumb:

BEWARE OF FALLING FOR PATTERN RECOGNITION

This is often how companies get into trouble. You, the CEO, have just a handful of data points with which to make a decision, and you remember a similar situation from a ways back. You assume that, since the decision you made the last time worked, you'll make the same decision now. Right? Wrong. Your present context could be very different from the previous one. The company could be significantly larger (or smaller). The resources available now might be different from what you had then. The specific outcome you're looking to produce might be different. And so on. So, sure, take that last time into account. Use its lessons as one of many inputs. But don't rely on it alone.

STAY IN TOUCH WITH THE FRONT LINES

Your client reps or salespeople are closest to the customer. They best understand what the customer needs are and how they've changed. Use Maggie Wilderotter's "lion hunts," a practice detailed later in this chapter. Or develop your own. But make sure you keep a line open.

HIRE OTHER EXECUTIVES WHO ARE ABLE TO MAKE DECISIONS

Here's a litmus test I use to see if I'm on track with this practice: When I come back from a business trip and walk into my office, if there's a line of folks at my desk waiting for an answer or decision, I know things are breaking down. Either I'm doing a bad job of pushing information down (and therefore folks don't have the data they need), or I've hired the wrong people, ones who can't adequately make decisions. Either way, it's a clear indication that something needs to be fixed—pronto.

TRAIN YOUR TEAM TO WALK YOU THROUGH THE OPTIONS THEY DISCARD

I learned this one from Todd. Often, when one of your reports tells you they've decided to go in a particular direction or to work on a specific project, they just tell you about the decision itself. They don't walk you through the other options they considered and explain why they rejected them. But you need to train them to do just that, because you have more information than they do about the bigger picture. You know what other priorities are coming up, what partnerships or acquisitions are on deck, and what new hires or organizational changes are in the offing. Your more-complete set of information lets you assess all the possible directions more thoroughly and ensure that the one on the table is still the right one.

You Don't Need to Clone Yourself

But you do need to shed yourself.

I'm a big fan of letting my team members set their own goals. You have a roadmap for the company, right? So let your direct reports decide what their goals will be for the coming quarter. If you've hired the right people—smart, ambitious, motivated—they will usually set more aggressive goals than you would. And since they came up with those goals themselves, they'll usually be more committed to making them happen. Even if they come up short—if they only get 95 percent of the way there—they'll still be further ahead than if you'd given them their marching orders.

You'll review the goals, of course. They need to align directly with where the company's headed. But let them run with it. Get out of the way, except for periodic check-ins. For my team, that takes place every two to four weeks. I let my people lead these meetings and set the agenda. If there's anything I need to keep on top of (like headcount; we're always hiring, and I need to make sure my teams are on track), I'll give them a heads-up so they can prepare. Otherwise, they decide what we discuss.

This is ultimately how you share leadership without cloning yourself. The bigger your company gets, the more and higher-level stuff you, personally, have to take on. That means you need to constantly shed lower-level areas of responsibility. The more ownership I give my people, the more they grow and the more they can take on. In turn, that's less I have to do, which frees me up to focus on the company's most important strategic initiatives. Which is the ultimate goal.

Max Out on Mini Teams

To get big, you might have to start small.

Sebastian Thrun is a fan of autonomy. He cofounded Udacity and, more recently, is building flying cars at Kittyhawk. There, he sets up "mini-companies" organized around the principles of ownership, empowerment, trust, and accountability. "I'm not that smart," he says. "I can't make all the decisions." Each of Sebastian's mini-companies contains no more than the number of people who could fit in a van or a bus. He gives them a goal and sets milestones. "And then I basically walk away," he says. "My main job is to inspire people and remove roadblocks. Nothing else."

In 2019, Melanie Perkins took a similar approach at Canva. With 800 employees, the company had begun to feel unwieldy, so Melanie broke it into 17 groups that she dubbed "mini-startups." Each was responsible for one of Canva's target industries, and they were expected to function like actual startups. Each group drafted its own "pitch deck," outlining the group's vision and strategy. They received public relations support and managed the onboarding of their own people. "Rather than me having to hold the entire vision and all the details in my head, each group became the owner of their vision," Melanie explains. "I no longer have to be the person who figures out where every chess piece is and how to move it forward."

The approach also helps defuse some of the politics that often slow a company down. "Most companies act as if there's only a fixed amount of pie"—power and opportunities for advancement—"and everyone has to fight for their own little segment," Melanie says. But "at a startup that's rapidly growing, everyone's success comes from expanding that pie." She expects the number of these groups to grow as Canva does. "Instead of figuring out how to step on each other in order to move up, people focus on how to grow the company as a whole."

Always Measure the Stakes

If they're high, go slow. If they're low, go fast.

You'll have so much on your plate that you'll frequently feel the impulse to make quick, short-term decisions. In many cases, that's fine, because the stakes are low. Which office should you move into when you have just 10 people? Who cares? You'll be moving again in a year. Your brand logo? Unless you're a consumer product where brand identity drives adoption, it likely doesn't matter a whole lot, especially since you'll revise it a few times anyway.

But then there are short-term decisions that end up having huge downstream impacts. Hiring and promoting people are two such areas. Here's a classic example: You're two years into your company, and it's time to add a VP of engineering. The person who joined your company 18 months ago as your director of engineering expects to get the job. But in this case, you don't think the director is up to the task. You need someone who has robust experience as a director in a much larger company, with more complexity and bigger challenges than the director has had at yours. Meanwhile, however, your director has threatened to go elsewhere if they don't get the promotion, and you don't want to have that big of a leadership gap in your engineering group. So what do you do?

First, stop and breathe. It's going to be tempting to give the person the title. They're here. They're competent. Why not? Let me tell you why not. Every time you promote someone who's not qualified, the rest of your team notices. Other folks will expect to get similar promotions even when they too aren't ready for the new jobs. When you fail to hand out comparable promotions, they'll begin to question your culture. Are you really about excellence? Or are you actually about some kind of favoritism? Now, you're in a bind. You might end up promoting those people too, just so they also don't leave. Before you know it, you've got a team of mediocre senior executives.

These kinds of short-term decisions end up rippling outward. Having middling people in leadership slots impacts your ability to hire A players. Great people don't want to work for B players (much less C players). Once you've put a lackluster person in a leadership position, you can basically write off their entire organization.

It also hinders your ability to raise money. Your fundraising packet includes a list of your top executives. A mediocre player on that list is a red flag. Investors bet on teams. They might pass you over now.

So with every decision, take a moment to assess whether it's a low-stakes decision that you can make quickly or if it's a high-impact decision with long-range consequences. Specifically, ask yourself: Will this decision send the right or wrong message to my team? What other areas will this decision impact, and are those low- or high-stakes situations? In 18 to 24 months, how much will this decision matter? Then and only then, pull the trigger.

Hit the Clutch Shots

Recognize and focus on do-or-die moments.

As a founder, you'll be inundated with demands on your time: people who want meetings, decisions that need your sign-off, emails that need answers. You'll figure out how to navigate all of that. Still, among all those demands, there will be a handful of meetings and presentations—let's say 20 or so a year—that will really, *really* matter. Getting them right—or wrong—will have exponentially outsized impacts on your company. For example, a presentation to an enormous customer: nail it and your revenue could soar 50 percent. Or an investor pitch: knock it out of the park, and your startup has another two years of runway. These are life-changing events.

Your job as a founder is to recognize which items on your to-do list are clutch shots—and then optimize *everything* around them. For example, at Okta, now that we're a public company, I have to nail our quarterly earnings calls with Wall Street. If I flub even a tiny part of the question-and-answer session, our stock could roller-coaster through billions of dollars. So I optimize everything in the days leading up to those calls. I do tons of preparation, of course. But my assistant also knows to clear out entire chunks of my schedule, so I can get my head in the game. Anyone could bang on her door and insist they need to see me, but barring a life-threatening family emergency, they're going to have to wait. Even if the cost of making them wait is that we lose tens of thousands of dollars on a deal or we miss out on some great midlevel hire. The cost to Okta of that loss doesn't remotely compare to the cost if I mess up an earnings call.

When we were just starting out, I would worry over every dollar. Once, when I had to book a last-minute red-eye flight to get to a do-or-die sales meeting, I hesitated to pay the extra $150 for a business-class seat so I could get some sleep on the plane. When I called Todd to get a second opinion, he thought I was nuts. "Of course, you knucklehead," he told me. "Do whatever it takes to close the deal." You need to do the same. Money will be tight in those early days. But if flying out the day before and paying for an additional night at a hotel means you'll be well rested for a key sales pitch, do it. Need to pay extra to get a quiet hotel room? Go for it. Need time to prepare for an investor meeting? Tell your staff to wait until the following week to get your attention—even if it means lower-level mistakes are made in the meantime.

Get Up and Walk Around

The value of visiting the front line.

As Frontier Communications began to grow, Maggie Wilderotter used to take purposeful walks around her offices just to chat with employees. "I would make myself approachable," she says. "I'd get groups of employees together and answer questions or have a conversation about what's going on." Everything was informal. Maggie would ask people what they were working on and how they were doing. She'd inquire about their families and lives outside of work. She'd cheekily ask them what rumors they wanted her to start or, more sincerely, what rumors they were hearing. "You need to make it comfortable for people to interact with you as the CEO," she says.

The practice was so important that Maggie built it into her weekly schedule. She called these outings "lion hunts" because she—the lioness—would be "prowling around, seeing what's going on," she says. "The front line *is* your company. It's who the customer interacts with every single day. It was important for me to stay close to and build relationships with people who would tell me the truth about what's really happening."

The bonds she built created confidence that people could share bad news without worrying about blowback. "I always built cultures where frontline employees would tell me something before they'd let their bosses know," she says. That, in turn, would motivate midlevel managers. She'd take those issues to the bosses to find out what was going on. They weren't happy to be caught short, of course. "But they changed their stripes. They wanted to make sure there weren't any surprises that would be elevated to me," Maggie says.

Let Your Employees See You Make Mistakes

"I've done a bunch of embarrassing things," says Josh James, the Omniture and Domo founder. "For example, we printed up 1,000 books of 'Everything You Ever Wanted to Know About Online Marketing,' and we sent them out to 1,000 prospects." The books were all empty. The pages were all blank. Intentionally. The idea, says Josh, "was you'd open it up and be like, 'What the heck?' and then you'd call us, and we'd send the real one to you." It didn't work out as Josh had hoped. "A lot of people were pissed off. They asked us why we were killing trees. It was really embarrassing."

Still, Josh doesn't mind screwing up, even when he does it in a big way in front of his employees. "I think it's actually helpful," he says. "The team will see it's OK to make dumb mistakes. Because in the process of just trying stuff, you'll come up with great ideas."

Sebastian Thrun has taken this same approach at Google X, Udacity, and Kittyhawk. "You would be surprised by the amount of support that you will get from the team if you admit failure. You're instantly more personable. People will rally around you when you admit you made a mistake."

Be the 2008 Steelers, Not the 2006 Eagles
With apologies to Philly fans.

Jeremy Bloom founded his company Integrate, a marketing platform, in 2010. Before that, however, he played in the NFL as a punt and kick returner. (And before that, he was an Olympic freestyle skier.) Jeremy was drafted by the Philadelphia Eagles in 2006, and in 2007, he signed with the Pittsburgh Steelers.

The two teams operated in markedly different ways. "The Eagles were a very top-down, micromanaging organization that produced a fear-based culture," he remembers. "Coaches would consistently tell you that if you didn't do what you were told, you would be gone, 'because there are a hundred other guys waiting to replace you.'" This culture of fear meant that each player stayed in his own bubble rather than look for ways to support his teammates. "Guys were always just protecting their own job. It didn't feel like a lock-arms, one-heartbeat type of culture that you want to have as a football team."

The Steelers were a completely different story. It was a bottom-up culture where the players were the leaders. "The head coach was a great motivator. He never told you what you had to do, but he always provided ideas on how to achieve your goal," Jeremy says. "The locker room felt like a family."

The Steelers went on to win the Super Bowl in 2009 "with what I would describe as a less talented team than what I saw in Philadelphia." Jeremy took those lessons to heart when he founded Integrate. Here are three ways he baked the "Steeler Way" into his company:

- **Empower employees.** At Integrate every employee is considered "the CEO of their own job." "We always hire people who are smarter than us, and we ask them to tell us what they think they should do," Jeremy says. Employees are given latitude to run their areas, even if that means sometimes falling on their faces. "It's OK if you make mistakes," he says, because that's part of the path to building leaders.

- **Help your employees solve problems by asking questions.** Even if you know how to do a task that an employee is struggling with, you should start by asking questions. A person will be more committed to a course of action if they come up with it themselves. Plus, they'll sometimes figure out an approach that's better than the one the boss would have suggested.

- **Hire managers and executives who operate this way.** "It's a major hiring filter," Jeremy says. "If we get the sense that somebody might be too overbearing or a micromanager, we hire the other person."

They Are People, Not Machines

Flexibility is everything.

When I started at Salesforce, I was still very young, just 25, and I behaved like it: my weekend sometimes started on Thursday night. Roger Goulart had hired me as a business development manager. His core team gathered every Friday morning, and occasionally, I would show up "a little tired" or "under the weather."* I'm not proud of this, but facts are facts. Obviously, I was not at my best in those meetings. So how did Roger handle it? I'll tell you first what he *didn't* do. He didn't haul me into his office and chew me out. And he definitely didn't berate me in the meetings themselves. Instead, he just moved the meeting to Thursdays.

Roger explained this decision to me recently. It seemed a pretty amazing thing for a veteran executive to do for a wayward pup like me. Here's what he said: "I was there to make the team stronger, and this was something that was easy to do." A lot of managers would have come down on me with an iron fist. And, listen, I would have conformed. I liked Salesforce, and I wanted to keep my job. But would that have been the smartest choice for the whole group? Obviously, you can't have a free-for-all where everyone is doing whatever they want. But if the change is small and inconsequential?

Why not, Roger says. "As a manager, you make bets on people, and then you do everything you can to make them successful. You clear things out of the way, you give them resources, you give them help."

Many managers don't operate this way. They act as if they have a fiefdom, and everyone should bow to their will. But that doesn't always get the best out of people. In fact, it almost never does, especially in startups. "I want folks to be as attentive and involved as possible," Roger says. "Sometimes you just have to show a little flexibility, so that you get the maximum output from your team."

There's a little trick I learned from Dr. Gene Amdahl, the father of supercomputing. I get emotional just talking about it. One day, I'm working in this hugely successful company, and he comes into the computer room where I'm programming. He didn't know who I was, but he puts his hand on my shoulder and says, "What you're doing is super important. You're the only guy that can do this job. I'm so thankful you're here." I'm like, "Wow. This guy believes in me." If you instill that belief in your employees and let them know how important they are, they give back a thousandfold. It's not a disingenuous trick. For the vast majority of people, to know that they're appreciated by somebody that's seven layers above them, it's worth a billion bucks.

—Fred Luddy, ServiceNow

* OK, fine, I was hungover.

Leadership Two Ways

Different types of employees respond to different kinds of motivation.

When Jeremy Bloom started Integrate, he initially tried to motivate his staff the same way he, a former elite athlete, liked to get motivated. "I'm used to being around football players and Olympians, and that's how I initially led the company," he says. It worked great with the salespeople. "They have the same 'go get 'em' mentality. You can throw a big idea up on a whiteboard, and they're going to go charge it, right?" But the engineers? Not so much. "They hated me."

Tien Tzuo, of Zuora, knows why. "Engineers want to create," he says. "And they want to create things they are proud of." They aren't motivated by competition the way athletes and salespeople are. Instead, they want to understand how their work fits into the customer's life and makes it better. "They get energized by the idea that if they deliver certain features, they'll have a world-class product that's being used by thousands, if not millions of people," Tien says. "That gives them meaning, and it's where they get their motivation from."

To learn how to relate to and motivate a wide range of people, Jeremy became a Myers-Briggs Type Indicator (MBTI) Certified Practitioner. Not everybody has to take such a rigorous step. (He's got an Olympian's drive, after all.) But as a leader, you do need to understand that different individuals and groups are energized by different motivations. What works for one person or one set of employees won't necessarily work for another. Your job as a leader is to adapt your management style to each employee and group to help them succeed in the ways that work best for *them*—not you.

Sharpen the Contradictions

When there's trouble brewing, bring it out into the open.

Human beings prefer to avoid conflict. It's natural. Acrimony isn't good for business. As a leader, however, you don't have the luxury of avoiding conflict. When a problem is brewing, you need to get on top of it. Unaddressed problems only grow bigger. It becomes increasingly more costly—in energy, focus, resources, goodwill, and motivation—to ignore them.

Many founders find it tough to address conflicts among their people. Maybe you want to be liked. Or you don't want the combatants to turn their anger on you. Or you're just busy and stressed out, and you don't have the bandwidth for one more headache. So you hope the issue will resolve itself without your involvement. I feel you. I really do. All of this is hard. But bad news my friend: you still have to deal with it. And better sooner than later.

Our first investors, Ben Horowitz and Marc Andreessen, use a strategy they call "sharpening the contradictions."* It means bringing the conflicts out into the open. Sometimes even provoking them. Because once they're out in the open, you can start to identify what's really at the core and then figure out a resolution. "Get it out and then resolve it," Ben says. "You can't resolve it when it's low key. But when it's a crisis, you can resolve it." So provoke the crisis. Bring it to a head.

Here's an example: One year, we hired a senior executive into a C-level role. The executive was a highly respected leader with an amazing track record who'd held the same role at one of our much bigger competitors. We couldn't believe a person like that had agreed to come work at our little startup. The person could have commanded a position at any giant company and earned a lot more, but they said yes to us. It seemed like a score.

Within a few months, though, something seemed off. The executive's organization was at a critical juncture, and yet the person didn't seem to have much intensity around their work. Then the executive left for a three-week vacation in a remote location, with no connectivity—right when we were launching a key product.

If a junior person had performed this poorly, you can bet we would have sat their butt down and had a "difficult conversation." But with this person, we were scared. We had bet so much on them. The person was clearly gold on paper. Plus, we were terrified of having to start from scratch. C-level searches can take half a year or more.

We eventually accepted that we had to find out what was going on. When the executive got back from the trip, we talked to them about how they needed to put more into the job. A few days later, the executive came back and told us their heart just wasn't in it. We parted ways and began a new search. It wasn't fun, and it set us back. But if we hadn't had that blunt conversation, they might not have moved on until much later. Meanwhile, their whole organization would have been stuck in an eddy, setting us back even further.

* Full disclosure: Ben and Marc got this idea from Vladimir Lenin, who actually took it from Karl Marx.

Don't Be a Cowboy

I want to mention Roger Goulart's mantra, "You win as a team, so don't lose alone," again here because it's not just an important part of your company's culture. It's also an idea you have to internalize as a leader. You might be the founder, but you aren't all-knowing. You're not any smarter than the people you've hired. So when you're struggling with a problem, remember to ask for help. Ask your team. Ask your board members or investors. Ask other founders.

The more you model this behavior, the more comfortable the rest of your team will feel asking for help themselves. For example, every sale at Okta is led by an account executive. They're often competitive by nature—their "cowboy" qualities serve them well in the rough world of sales. But many other people participate in the closing of deals: presales engineers, professional services managers, and executive sponsors all play a role. So while we value our account executives' competitive fire, we also need them to be able to ask for help when they get stuck. We can't afford to lose a sale because someone was too proud to collaborate. Having executives at the top, like you, modeling this practice builds a culture that gives everyone permission to do the same. And that helps the whole company win.

Get Used to Giving Stuff Up
Especially, and most painfully, the stuff you like.

When we started Okta, I was the president and chief operating officer. Also the head of HR. And chief information officer. And chief security officer. And chief financial officer and General Counsel. As we grew, each of those functions also increased in size and complexity, and we needed to bring on people who were experts in those areas. That might seem obvious, but you'd be surprised by how much founders resist giving up the various jobs they have.

I was initially bummed when we hired our first vice president of sales in 2012. It was necessary, of course. This is one of the things Ben told me to do as he mentored us out of our death spiral. But I liked being out with customers. I liked explaining our story and trying to close deals. I worried that giving that up would leave me stuck in a back-office function. I got over it, of course. A year later, I already had a mountain of new responsibilities on my plate. There wouldn't have been enough time to lead sales anyway.

Over the years, I've gotten better at looking 12 months down the road and assessing which responsibilities I currently have that could be offloaded to better experts. For example, we've recently started buying other companies. Todd and I ran the first two acquisitions on our own. But it was clear from the beginning that an experienced corporate development executive would be key to doing more of these. We got one on board fairly quickly.

What trips up many founders is that they aren't willing to let go. In the beginning, you have to do everything yourself, and you enjoy many parts of it. Maybe you enjoy the intellectual challenge. Maybe you enjoy—or even need—the sense of control. But you rapidly become overwhelmed by the ballooning size of your company, and soon you're buried under the cumulative weight of all your work.

So here's my advice: Early on, develop the ability to anticipate when some part of your work is going to get so big that you'll need to peel it off and give it to someone else. Start the hunt for your replacement six to nine months ahead of that handoff. Resist the fear that if you give away "too many" parts of your job, you "won't have anything left to do." Trust me, you will. By the time your new person takes over that part of your work, your plate will be overflowing again.

eight

GROWTH

By 2018 we had long pulled ourselves out of the death spiral of 2011. In fact, Okta had gone public in 2017 and was expanding rapidly all over the world. The following September, I flew to Europe to meet with prospects and customers. As I boarded the plane in San Francisco, I thought about how different this trip was from my usual one- or two-night customer visits. I have family in France and was excited to see them. But I was also looking forward to what I was going to learn about doing business at a higher level in Europe. Growth unlocks those kinds of opportunities.

My packed schedule meant I had only brief moments to catch up with family. Even then, my time wasn't my own. I went to dinner at my cousin's home in Paris one evening and immediately had to step outside for a sales call. It was raining hard, so I had to press myself against the door to avoid getting soaked. Over eight days, I went to five countries and somehow passed through London's Heathrow Airport eight times. I remember thinking, *Well, isn't this glamorous.*

My point: Growth is going to put a lot of pressure on you as a leader. Even as it opens new opportunities, it's going to limit choices. Some people say leading a fast-growing startup is like winning a pie-eating contest: the grand prize is that you get to eat even more pie.

ServiceNow's Fred Luddy talks about how startups have three main phases. In the first, you're just working on getting a minimum viable product (MVP) into customers' hands. The second phase is where you learn what you *actually* should be building. Watching your customer use your MVP shows you what they really need. You go back and build that, probably going through multiple revisions until you finally nail it. This is when phase three kicks in. Fred calls it "scaling and operational excellence." I simply call it "growth." But the concept is the same. Says Fred, "Once you have a company that does something well and has a very large market to address, then you have to make sure that you have your internal processes and procedures in place." That is what this chapter is about.

Before now, you've mostly been focused on figuring out your product or service, as well as your distribution and marketing programs, and a pricing structure that will generate a decent margin. This gave you a foundation on which to grow. Now, your focus turns inward. Your operations up to this point have probably been scattered and inefficient. The "main thing," after all, was to get the product right. To scale, however—to grow really big—the internal machinery has to run smoothly and efficiently.

Of course, you're still racing at this point. You'll never stop racing. Even at Okta today, several years after going public, I'm often lurching from crisis to crisis. The challenges never stop—they just get bigger and more complicated. (Don't let the jovial demeanor of the founders you see on stage at conferences deceive you. They might look calm and relaxed, but offstage, five different fires are raging.)

My advice: Accept that you'll never do anything as well as you'd like. And know that's OK—as long as you stay focused on nailing the most important things.

You'll never stop racing. Even at Okta today, several years after going public, I'm often lurching from crisis to crisis. The challenges never stop— they just get bigger and more complicated.

First, Have a Growth Strategy

Then make sure you have a system, so everyone can execute it.

Founders are really good at getting stuff done. They're usually highly disciplined, super-resilient, and insanely hard-working. But getting a lot of stuff done doesn't mean much if it's not the *right* stuff that's getting done. Similarly, when your company grows to 200 or 500 or 1,000 people, their work won't matter if they're not all pulling in the same direction. Startups succeed when they're ruthlessly focused. They flounder when everyone's headed in different directions. To prevent that, you need a system.

Many companies use a tool called Objectives and Key Results (OKRs). At Okta, we use a system called Vision, Methods, and Targets (VMTs):*

- **Vision.** This is your starting point: your vision is a clear, concise phrase that explains what you're driving toward (and *why*) in a way that inspires you and your team.

- **Methods.** Next, decide on the four to six major objectives (Okta calls them "methods") for the next year. For each method, we identify the four to six activities or programs (which we call "sub-methods") that will drive results for that objective.

- **Targets.** These are quantifiable outcomes that will tell you if you've achieved your goals.

We start with a VMT exercise at the senior, companywide level. Then it cascades down through each division, which does its own VMT exercise, followed by each department, and then each group, all the way down to the employee level. We believe each person at Okta should have a VMT for their own job—a roadmap for where they should be spending their time and a list of outcomes they should be trying to produce.

* We based this on Salesforce's V2MOM framework ("Vision, Values, Methods, Obstacles, and Measures"), which was solid but (in our minds) a little too complex. Full credit goes to Angela Grady, an executive vice president at Okta and Todd's chief of staff, who architected Okta's version.

Even when you're small, this way of thinking is a good habit to develop. It will keep you and your team highly focused. Carve out time for these exercises. At Okta, we begin brainstorming at the company level in September, five months ahead of the start of our fiscal year in February. The smaller you are, the later you can begin, but as you grow, start ratcheting the process back earlier and earlier.

Why bother? We've found three main benefits:

- **It eliminates chaos and uncertainty.** Everyone is clear on what they're supposed to focus on.

- **It helps people understand what adjacent groups are working on.** This becomes increasingly critical as you get bigger, and groups grow farther apart physically. As they move to different floors, buildings, and then cities, you need increasingly structured ways for groups to stay in sync.

- **It creates the space for teams to be more independent and take greater initiative.** We can give them more leeway because we know they have the right roadmap.

VMTs also help with performance management because employees know what their leadership expects of them. At the end of the year, it's clear whether an employee has been contributing to the company's overall success—or if they've wandered off course.

Once drafted, VMTs can be used for practical purposes, like setting the quarterly and annual operational cadence. They can also help to frame the budget allocation process. Top-down, you can check whether all company-level methods are properly funded, and bottom-up, managers can use their VMTs to make sure that all cost allocations (like headcount and operating costs) are aligned with the company's overall goals.

The Smaller, the Faster

A startup's main competitive edge.

"Speed is everything," Zoom founder Eric Yuan says. "Don't worry about the big legacy players. They are very slow." Eric would know. He joined WebEx in the late 1990s when it was still a startup. In 2007, the company was acquired by Cisco, and three years later, Eric was miserable. And apparently he wasn't the only one. "I talked to customers every day, and not a single one of them was happy," he says. (Cisco has since redesigned the product.)

In 2011, Eric jumped ship and launched his own videoconferencing tool, which we all now know as Zoom. Although he was going up against giants in an extremely crowded market, he never doubted he could do better. By summer, he had about 20 engineers on staff, compared to the thousands working at the legacy players. "We knew that if we focused on the customer experience and their pain points, and if we innovated rapidly, we could grow quickly," he says. And he was right. The company doubled in size every year. By late 2021, it had 6,300 employees.

We all know what happened next. When the pandemic forced tens of millions around the globe into lockdown, Zoom became more than a company; it became a verb—and the top choice of many for remote communications. By fall 2021, the company was worth $78 billion.

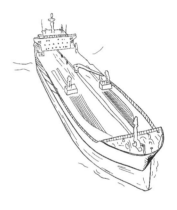

Legacy companies often seem fearsome. They have tons of money. They have deep relationships with their customers. They can out-hire smaller companies. But one area where they can rarely compete is on speed. Large companies are like oil tankers. Those ships need three whole miles to go from full speed to a complete stop, and the arc of their turns is usually miles wide. Your startup, by contrast, is a speedboat. You can stop, turn, and maneuver on a dime.

Even when large companies grasp how ecosystems are shifting, internal inertia often prevents them from changing in meaningful ways. Meanwhile, they often sideline customer delight in favor of maintaining margins and profits. Sometimes that's driven by a need to keep Wall Street happy. (Change usually involves investment in R&D, which drives down short-term profitability and often affects a company's stock price.) Sometimes it's because the company's preference for the status quo drives top innovators to leave for more creative arenas.

This is where you, the newcomer, have an advantage. If you can stay close to your customers and make their happiness your top priority (on LinkedIn, Eric still lists his primary job as "Delivering Happiness to Our Users"), you can often create something that supersedes what already exists and steal customers away. But you do have to move fast, because your money will only last so long. So you have to get to the point where you can overtake your legacy competitors before that money—and investors' willingness to keep bankrolling you—runs out.

Act Like a New Parent

"When I had my first child, I had no experience with babies," Medallia's Amy Pressman says. "I was in Europe when I gave birth, and I stayed in the hospital for five days. Finally, this very strict head nurse pulled me aside and said, 'Amy, I can't find any reason to keep you here.' She knew I was terrified, so she gave me the following advice: 'Listen to everybody. The stranger on the bus. Your aunt. Your friends. All the baby books, television shows, newspaper articles. Listen to all of it. Then make your own decisions.'" It's the same thing with entrepreneurs. "You're running something that you've never run before," she says. "We have to constantly be talking to people and learning."

Actively cultivate a network of founders who are just a year or two ahead of you. They don't necessarily have to be running the same kind of company as you. They just need to be dealing with the same types of problems. The list of challenges you'll be facing for the first time—whether it's in sales, supply chains, finance, legal, or human resources—will be extensive. Save yourself time by tapping your network for answers. You don't have time to reinvent the wheel or research solutions to every problem. Build that network, tap into it, and then pay it forward with the entrepreneurs who come after you.

Against Perfection
The case for good enough.

You've probably heard this saying before: "Done is better than perfect." It was posted on Facebook's walls in its feisty early years. You might prefer another commonly used motto: "The perfect is the enemy of the good." Either way, you need to internalize this mindset, especially in your early days. Momentum in that period is more important than perfection. If you wait until you perfect anything, you're going to run out of money. Plus, you never really know how good a thing is until you get it into customers' hands.

This is true both for the actual product or service you plan to sell and for your internal operations. For example, when you're still small, don't invest time in researching the best HR, supply chain, or finance software. (They're usually designed for large, public companies anyway.) Look for one that's good enough. Implement it, develop a process to track how well it's working (so you'll know when it's time to upgrade), and then move on.

"Done is better than perfect" doesn't mean you should create a shoddy product, of course. It just means to do your best within a specified time frame, and then send the thing out. Once it's out, you'll learn from how customers use it and figure out where refinements and fixes are needed. No matter what, however, keep moving. Sure, you might run into a wall, or something might blow up in your face. But no matter. Step back, look for a new way forward, and keep going.

... Except in Finance and Legal Matters
Don't "innovate" in these areas.

The two areas the previous advice does *not* apply to are finance and legal. Finance is governed by laws and regulations. Do not get creative. Do not get fancy. Follow standard practices. Either know them yourself or hire trusted professionals to look after this area. Get things right in legal as well. Make sure that contracts are drafted correctly. Listen to your counselors when they give you legal advice.

Because you know what *really* slows you down? Breaking laws. Breaking contracts. Visits from regulators and inspectors. Getting hit with lawsuits and legal fees. Or God forbid, ending up in jail.

Feel free to push the limits in all other areas. Just not in these two.

Beware of Bottlenecks

They signal something needs to be replaced.

Your company has four pillars that make it work: people, systems, processes, and data. No matter your size, no matter the challenges or opportunities you're facing, these are what you will need to upgrade as you grow. A system that supported your team when you had just a handful of customers probably won't be the same system you'll use when you have thousands. A process that worked fine when there were 30 of you—the way you managed expense reports, say, or kept track of paid time off—won't work when there are 1,000. Plus, as you get bigger, you need ever more granular and precise data to run the complex machinery.

The trick in all this is knowing *when* to make upgrades. There's no point in tackling things too early. Retooling a system or process brings everything to a halt while you switch things out. If everything is chugging along well enough, don't get in the way of that momentum. On the other hand, you can't wait too long after the company has outgrown something to deal with it. Just as a dirty, old air filter slows your car down, so will a system, process, or person who can't handle the new workload.

How do you know when it's time to make a change? When bottlenecks show up. A bottleneck is a clear sign that something is no longer working. When things start backing up, you need to press pause in order to switch out the old element for a new one. This is time and energy well spent. Many founders think scaling is just a matter of increasing customers and sales. But you have to scale your infrastructure as well.

The toughest of these four elements to deal with is the "people" one. Specifically, people who are no longer able to handle their jobs, usually because, as the company grows, the job becomes too big for them. Keep an eye out for these signs that a leader is starting to struggle:

- When the quality of a team's work starts to go down

- When a team loses people at a higher rate than other groups (which often happens when a leader doesn't know how to coach or groom employees for advancement or, worse, because they are too controlling or micromanaging)

- When other people start going around them

You don't have to fire a person who can no longer keep up. But you do need to start the difficult conversation about what their role should be going forward.

This kind of "topping out" is common, especially for early employees who joined the company when it was smaller and its demands were less complex. Some of those employees are happy to switch to a mid-level role where they continue to be very successful. But others will want to keep moving up the ladder, even though they're not ready or aren't a good fit. These people often decide to leave and go elsewhere when they don't get the jobs they want in your company. That's never fun, but your job as a leader is to keep an eye on the big picture—to make sure the whole company is functioning well—and sometimes that means letting people know they aren't the person to handle the responsibilities required for the next stage.

INSIGHT

Some of the most talented engineers I know are people who run 10-person organizations. When you put them at the head of a thousand people, they have to become a manager, and that doesn't let them exercise their genius as an engineer. It's true in sales and other functions as well. When that happens, our goal is to help that person realize what's required of them and that, if they're not going to enjoy it, we should find them a role where they're much better set up for success.

—Aneel Bhusri, Workday

Let the Customer Shape the Product

Within reason.

"Any successful startup that I've ever seen comes up with the initial idea, but then they let the customer shape the product," says Aneel Bhusri, Workday cofounder and CEO. Aneel launched the $73 billion cloud-based finance and HR software company in 2005 after a long run with PeopleSoft. Aneel started Workday with a good sense of what customers needed. But he still listened closely to his first 10 to 15 customers—mostly smaller companies—to figure out how Workday itself should work. As Workday acquired larger and more complex customers—first Chiquita, then Morgan Stanley, and then Thomson Reuters—it built close relationships that further shaped the products. "If I look at our roadmap over the years," Aneel says, "there's not a feature on it that wasn't tied to a specific customer."

We've done the same at Okta. We started with a hunch about what our customers would need, but the actual features we've built and the way we've organized the tools have all been directly influenced by what customers told us they needed. We don't think of our customers as people we sell *to* but rather as partners we work *with*. That partnership can ultimately become really valuable not just because it generates a lot of sales (hopefully, it will), but because if you become good at listening, and if you become seen as a trusted partner, executives will start asking *you* how the software should be built, and once that happens, you become a partner for life.

Once you help a client make their departments more efficient, or faster, or more insightful about their businesses, you end up saving them an incredible amount of money. And that's when you become really valuable. When that happens, most will never want to let you go. They'll trust that whatever you build will be smart, useful, and hugely cost-effective. As you develop more offerings, most of your existing customers will happily sign on to those too.

The Whale Fallacy

There is a caveat to the principle about letting your customers shape the product: In the early days, a big customer with a giant checkbook (aka a "whale") might ask you to build out features that don't make sense for anyone but them (like the Okta prospect I talked about in the previous chapter). These customers are effectively asking you to build custom software for them. Most will pay handsomely for it.

Don't do it.

Your listening expeditions should be in service of finding features and products that hundreds or thousands or hundreds of thousands of customers will need. That's how you grow fast—by creating products that you build once but sell to many. A custom set of features holds you back. If you want to win in the long run, stay the course and turn down the whales.

Bad News, You're Going to Fail Your Customers

Good news, it's usually not fatal.

You are going to mess up. Terribly. Look at what happened to us: When Okta was just a couple of years old, we had a multi-hour outage. Our customers, including some of our first household-name companies, couldn't use our services for an entire morning. They were locked out of some of their core tools, such as email.

It was horrible. The memory still turns my stomach. We had built a disaster recovery plan, of course, and we were scrambling to get it to work, but we just couldn't fix things fast enough. So Todd and I did the next-best thing: We picked up the phone and called each customer personally. Their first question was: Did you lose any of our data? We had not. One CIO didn't even seem particularly worried. In fact, he told us, "Better your problem than mine." That's because if an old, on-prem service had gone down (which they did, all the time), it would have been him who'd have to be scrambling. Now he could sit back while we solved the problem.

In the end, it was *the way* we handled the failure that made the difference. Our transparency built trust. Our customers thought, "Okta's not perfect, but I trust that team." That's worth a ton.

You will have days when everything blows up in your face. You can handle it because you're resilient. But it's still going to be mortifying. And potentially expensive. You may even worry that your business will collapse. But in those moments, remember that business is about *relationships* as much as it is about *transactions*. Just treat your customers the way you would want to be treated if your positions were reversed.

Stay Close to Your Customers

Yes, you, the founder.

Every morning, Amy Pressman reads 10 comments from Medallia customers. "Do you know how many light bulbs go off when you start to hear the customer's experience in their own words?" she says. The comments appear in an app that Medallia created, part of the platform they built to collect customer and employee feedback. Amy believes, as I do, that keeping a close tab on your customers is key to succeeding.

When you're small, you, the founder, can't help but be close to your customers. You're the one selling to them. You effectively man the customer support line. As you get bigger, founders start offloading these tasks to other people, and you risk losing touch with your customers. You might look at summaries from the frontline reps. Or you might rely on meetings with department heads. But you'll never get the full picture unless you speak directly to customers. Information always gets filtered—especially bad news.

Amy, who's spent the past two decades building tools to collect customer feedback, knows that some executives resist the idea of direct contact with customers. She told me about one executive she knows who used to think of customers as a "necessary evil." "He really disliked them because they complained," she says. But that's the irony: Hearing what customers complain about is actually incredibly useful. You'll discover what's not working or, better yet, you'll get ideas for new products and services.

As you get bigger and start to scale, don't forget to also scale your processes for having your top people—including yourself—stay in touch with customers. At Okta, we've put a couple of programs in place which work really well. Use them as inspiration for your own practices:

Making an Executive Sponsor Program Work

1 The Executive Sponsor Program*

Most of our VP level and above executives are paired with up to five of our top customer companies. They meet in person at least once a quarter, and they talk on the phone on a regular basis. The Okta executive (the "sponsor") keeps his or her counterpart abreast of our company's roadmap and any new features or products that might interest them. The sponsor also helps the counterpart remove any major roadblocks impeding their use of our tools.

The work done in these executive-to-executive meetings isn't something an account manager or a sales rep can do. The goal is to build our customers' trust and confidence by giving them one of our top people as their personal go-to "buddy." It shows them we're invested in their success. But it helps us too. It keeps our executives extremely close to what our customers need. It also creates a virtuous cycle: the executives give us great insights that lead to new products and features. Then the customers end up using more of what they buy from us, which leads to more sales.

2 Distribution of Meeting Recaps

I speak regularly with C-level executives at Fortune 500 companies. After each meeting, I send out a detailed recap to the top 100 leaders in our company. It includes primary takeaways but also a summary of what was discussed, why these things matter, and the original prep documents. This gives our leaders direct insight into what I'm seeing and hearing. The recaps help our executives make better decisions in their own domains. Even when the news is not good—or, maybe, especially when it's not—distributing this information allows a broader group of people to get involved in solving problems.

If you decide to implement a sponsor program, keep in mind that it's not "set and forget." At Okta, we have an executive whose sole function is to oversee the program and make sure it works well. Here are a few things we've learned:

Pair executives with common business interests or existing relationships. For example, if the IT department at our customer's company reports to their CFO, we might pair that customer with one of our finance executives. If the company is in the marketing industry, we'll pair them with one of our marketing executives.

Let account managers† drive the program. The person who owns the relationship with the customer is the one who drives and organizes the Executive Sponsor's activities. They tee up the meetings and phone calls. They provide the sponsor with any information to pass on to the customer. If a sponsor hears about a problem that needs looking into, he or she passes it back to the account manager for follow-up.

Limit each executive to a maximum of five customers. This work takes a lot of time and effort. Five is the maximum a sponsor can take on and provide the attention these relationships require.

---

* Full credit for this idea goes to Salesforce, where Todd and I first saw it in action.

† At some companies, this role is called a customer success manager.

Launching in a Down Market
There are silver linings to be found in a recession.

When a recession hits, would-be founders often ask whether they should wait to start a company until the economy gets better. The answer is no, absolutely not.

Many fantastic companies—General Electric, General Motors, IBM, and Disney, for example—were born in down markets. More recently, Microsoft, Electronic Arts, and everyone's beloved Trader Joe's also started in tough times. Okta started in late 2009, right in the middle of the financial melt-down, as did Airbnb (2008), Uber (2009), and Warby Parker (2010). Aneel Bhusri's Workday was founded three years before the recession hit, and he was just beginning to achieve some success when the economy bottomed out. "Our headcount stayed flat for the better part of two years, but we were very focused on not having to let anyone go," Aneel says. "We didn't know how long the crisis was going to last, but we were determined to grind it out." In the end, he told me, the recession helped make Workday stronger. Here's how:

- **It makes you more disciplined.** "You can learn a lot during a recession," Aneel says. "It makes you focus on what really matters. Every resource matters. Every person matters. Every dollar you spend matters." The experience made Workday a much more rigorous company than it was before the financial collapse.

- **It forces you to sharpen your sales pitch.** "Opportunity is born out of these challenging situations," Aneel says. "We had a very smart guy who had joined us a few years out of business school, and I told him, 'We've got to figure out a value proposition for companies during this downturn.' He built this really incredible model that showed that, over four or five years, we were half the cost of a legacy, on-premise system." Workday actually ended up *growing* 50 percent during that period.

- **It reduces your competition.** Workday was early out of the gate in bringing enterprise HR and finance operations to the cloud. But more companies would have emerged if not for the recession. Hard economic times scare people away. "It prevented a whole bunch of other startup competitors from getting into the space," Aneel says. "When you look at how our market evolved, there's only Workday today."

> **INSIGHT**
>
> You look at successful startups, and there's often just a revisionist history about what made their success. But after watching company after company, I'm a big fan of the last-man-standing rule. A lot of companies succeed just by toughing it out, working through all the difficult phases, and doing so over a long period of time. I tell would-be founders to pick a big market, show some resilience, and then lurch from crisis to crisis. You'll look back in 5, 10, 15 years and see that you built something special.
>
> —Tien Tzuo, Zuora

Ignore Competitors

They don't know more than you do.

You might have seen the wildly popular show *The Great British Baking Show*. It's a competition featuring a group of amateur bakers. Each episode has a segment called the "technical challenge," in which the bakers are given a recipe they've never seen before and told to whip it up.

There's always a point in this segment where you see a competitor trying to check out what the other bakers are doing, to figure out if they're on the right track. I never understand that. Everyone is in the same boat. They're all good bakers, and they're all equally perplexed. Why would you think someone else knows better than you? You could just as likely end up with the wrong answer as the right one.

It's the same with startups. You're going to have competitors. Maybe large, established companies mucking about in the same space as you. Maybe other startups racing for market share. It's incredibly tempting to get distracted by what the others are doing. Whether it's trying to keep tabs on their new features, studying their funding announcements, analyzing their advertising and marketing strategies, or tracking the types of employees they are hiring (are they taking on more sales reps? or laying some off?), you're naturally going to want to stay on top of how they're doing.

All of that is fine. You certainly want to keep an eye on your competitors—especially any who are beating you in sales opportunities or winning because of a certain set of features or functions. But here's what not to do: Do not change your strategy based on what you see others doing. Do not alter your feature set or, worse, pivot your company entirely. Stay the course.

Why? First, if you have a good product development process, it will tell you what *you* should be doing. You're getting your product or service into customers' hands, right? And then you're watching how they use it, correct? That will tell you what they need, what they're willing to buy, and how much they're willing to pay. These insights will let you hone your product-market fit. So why would you change course just because a competitor is doing something different? You don't know anything about how they're coming to their decisions. Maybe they're on course. Maybe they're completely offtrack. But for the most part, anything they're doing is a distraction and shouldn't impact what you do.

Do I Have to Relocate to a Tech Hub?

Not necessarily.

Tech founders who aren't already in a major hub like San Francisco, Berlin, or Hong Kong, often wonder whether they should relocate to one of those places. The arguments in favor of doing so are well known: These centers have concentrations of tech talent you won't find elsewhere. You'll also be closer to investors and get plugged into a network where you're more likely to meet people who can help you. For example, I personally met Marc Andreessen at a mutual friend's birthday party, long before Todd and I pitched him.

On the other hand, it's incredibly expensive to run a startup in the world's busiest hubs. The late Tony Hsieh, for example, moved Zappos to Nevada because he couldn't afford to staff his company in the Bay Area. And the competition for talent is fierce in the hubs. Employees are much more expensive and even demanding—for example, some programmers in hot markets have been known to submit their baseline requirements (like guaranteed window offices) before they'll even consider interviewing.

And, as the pandemic showed us, business goes on no matter where a workforce is located. Zoom and other remote-work tools have become powerful assets. Plenty of great companies have been founded outside of the hubs—or have moved away in order to grow. Grubhub, for example, was born in Chicago. Josh James built both Omniture and Domo in Utah. Fred Luddy's ServiceNow was started in San Diego. Jeremy Bloom's Integrate launched in Phoenix. Rachel Carlson moved Guild Education, a pre-IPO startup now valued at nearly $4 billion, from the Bay Area to Denver for the lower cost of living and better quality of life.

Shashank Saxena's VNDLY is based in Cincinnati. He's discovered several advantages to existing outside the fray:

CINCINNATI, OHIO

- **Lower cost of living.** Your money goes a lot further in the middle of the country than it does on the coasts. From hiring employees to renting office space, you get more bang for your buck.

- **Great talent.** "People underestimate the quality of talent available here," Shashank says. "In Cincinnati alone, we have a bunch of Fortune 500 headquarters. People who have built $100 billion companies have done a lot of things right." Plus, all these companies have sophisticated engineering teams. Before founding VNDLY, Shashank himself built an e-commerce platform for Kroger (the largest grocery company in the United States) and grew the organization from 9 engineers to nearly 400.

- **Proximity to customers.** "If you're living on the West Coast, how often do you get on a plane and fly to the Midwest?" Shashank asks. "Columbus, Indianapolis, Louisville, and Dayton are all within a 2.5-hour drive of me. Chicago and Nashville are 4.5 hours away." In a territory that large, it's a lot easier to find early users and build a customer base.

But there are also certain challenges:

- **The full range of specialists you need aren't necessarily available.** While there are tons of talented developers in the Cincinnati area—so much so that West Coast companies have established satellite offices there—"if you want people who have built a go-to-market SaaS engine before [meaning: a sophisticated sales process for identifying and selling to large corporate customers], you're not going to find that depth of experience here."

- **Developers tend to be more risk-averse.** The major hubs are filled with risk-takers willing to take pay cuts to work for exciting startups. Not so elsewhere. "My top-tier developer is a little older—he has a wife and two kids. He's bought a house in the suburbs and has a mortgage to pay," Shashank says. To lure this kind of talent to work for you, you have to be extremely transparent about the state of the company—which itself has to be robust (read: a lot of cash on hand)—to make these kinds of employees feel confident about giving up more stable jobs.

INSIGHT

You're going to hit problems with every one of your customers. Something's not going to work at some point, and you can't freak out and go, "We've failed!" You have to be able to take the blows. Your customers might need to be upset with you sometimes, and that's OK. Our customers are often IT departments, who have customers of their own. They are receiving the same tough feedback from their users, and sometimes they just need to pass along that frustration and anger. Usually, just listening, being honest and transparent, and letting them know how you plan to solve the problem will make you successful.

—Parker Harris, Salesforce

nine

CRASHING AND BURNING

In 2000, I was the first employee at a promising startup that wanted to help Fortune 500 companies deploy e-commerce platforms in Latin America. I moved to Buenos Aires, Argentina, to set up the office there. It was a dream job. I was 23 years old, and I'd been given an enormous opportunity. The entire world needed to move to digital sales, but most companies helping industries make this shift were focused on the United States. This job was a chance to get in early and have massive impact across an entire region.

But it soon became apparent the startup had serious problems. First, we had no strategic plan. There was no sales team, so instead of methodically building up a pipeline of business, we lurched from contract to contract. Internally, our culture was divided between "the Americans" and everyone else. One of the two cofounders, my good friend Benton Moyer, did his best to keep things afloat. But the other cofounder, the CEO, didn't communicate much. We always felt unsure of where the company stood.

Then things got worse. The dot-com collapse of 2000 followed by the attacks of 9/11 took the air out of Fortune 500 spending, the very companies we'd been targeting. Then in December 2001, Argentina exploded into riots. The government collapsed, and the financial sector imploded. After banks limited how much money any company could withdraw, I had to go to an ATM every morning to take out enough cash just to be able to pay our programmers for that day's work. I finally decided I couldn't run through the protest-filled streets every morning ferrying a backpack full of dollars. I hung my head in defeat, apologized to Ben, and gave my notice.

A stronger company with better leadership and a more robust culture might have survived.

Many new founders think building a startup is a straight line: You spend time in the "discovery phase," tinkering with your product and business model. Then, once you nail that, it's just a matter of growing, growing, growing.

The truth is that most companies have at least one near-death experience. Sometimes many. For example, you might get hit by external factors beyond your control: 9/11, a government collapse, a pandemic. Or perhaps you've based your strategy on a third-party platform (like Facebook or Google) that suddenly changes its algorithm to deprioritize businesses like yours. Or maybe you realize that you have the right product, but you've been targeting the wrong customers. (That's the story of Okta and of Udacity, both of which I'll tell you about in this chapter.) Or maybe you're on the verge of running out of money, and there's no way to get more. (That's Loudcloud's story, also in this chapter.) Or you realize that you've spent the last couple of years building something that customers love but that has no sustainable business model. (That's the Tiny Speck story, also told here.)

The industry often calls these existential crises "pivots." It's a gentle word that masks the chaos, terror, and frantic activity that takes place as a company tries to right its sinking ship. And there's an even worse experience to be had: one where you, as the founder, must face the fact that you're no longer the right person to helm your company. Fred Luddy, of ServiceNow, went through that, and I'll tell you his story as well.

Ironically, it's the very qualities that make someone a great entrepreneur that can lead them into the hole. Entrepreneurs' natural self-confidence and ruthless determination enable them to go up against odds that would terrify other people. They develop the habit of tuning out naysayers. As a result, they sometimes don't process that their company really is heading off course, until it's (almost) too late.

Couple that with the very human desire to avoid the extremely powerful emotions that come with acknowledging that you've made a terrible mistake: the shame of failure, the hurt you'll cause your employees and investors, and the pain of people being angry at you. To avoid this, many entrepreneurs keep barreling forward long after it becomes clear change is needed.

> The truth is that most companies have at least one near-death experience.

When you do end up in the middle of one of these crises (and the chances are good that you will), know that they're one of the most emotionally painful experiences you'll ever go through:

- **You're going to wonder if the company can make it to the other side.**
  Do you have enough money to carry you through the shift in direction? Will you be able to convince investors to give you more money after you've just admitted your previous "brilliant vision" was off base? Will you be able to build up enough revenue from your new direction before the bank account runs dry?

- **You'll worry that everyone is going to hate you.**
  Some probably will. Your employees will wonder why you made them work so hard on a product you're now telling them will never work. If they took a salary cut to join your startup in the hopes of an equity-powered upside, they're going to be furious when the company's value plummets. And your investors? If you chose the right ones, they'll stick with you and help you figure out a way through. But a lot of them will be pissed. Be prepared to be taken to the woodshed—a lot.*

- **You'll be terrified that you're going to look like an idiot.**
  And you probably will. Before he succeeded spectacularly with Slack, Stewart Butterfield failed equally spectacularly with Tiny Speck. "I made all these claims to the press that we were going to do all this stuff," he remembers—and then he had to admit to the world that he was wrong. Fun? Not at all.

It's during this period when your critical entrepreneurship qualities come into play. Anyone can be a great leader when the sun is shining. But the only way a founder can make it through these hundred-foot waves and gale-force winds is if they have those critical traits we talked about at the beginning of this book: resilience, innate drive, the ability to thrive in ambiguity, discipline, and self-confidence.

The best way to prepare for crashing and burning is to be psychologically prepared. First, by knowing that it's common and that it's not necessarily a referendum on you as an entrepreneur. Then, when the crisis hits, the best thing you can do is accept that this period in your startup's life is simply a part of the journey. Switch gears, stay focused, and keep going.

* This, by the way, is why it's so important to choose your investors wisely. Ending up in one of these situations is fairly probable, so choose backers who are going to work with you through this, not those who are going to pick up the phone and demand, "Where's my money?"

The Only Unforgivable Sin in Business

Hint: It's about the *#&%! money.

As a founder, you might think you have multiple jobs: Develop an amazing product. Find a great business model. Hire rock star employees. Build a well-run company.

In reality, however, you have one job above all. One job that, if you fail at it, nothing else matters. And that job is: *don't run out of money*. Harold Geneen, legendary CEO of ITT, who was one of the most significant business leaders of the 1960s and 1970s, and who some have compared to General George Patton and Napoleon, put it best: "The only unforgivable sin in business is to run out of cash."

Later in this chapter, I'll tell you about Ben Horowitz's stint as co-founder and CEO of Loudcloud in the early 2000s. You'll hear about how, as the company was running out of money and failing to find new investors, the only path to raising cash seemed to be to go public. Which seemed ridiculous to Ben. A company as riddled with holes as his shouldn't be positioning itself to Wall Street as a great investment. And Ben said that to his board. He told me what happened next:

"My friend Bill Campbell, who was on the board, says, 'Ben, it's not about the money.'"

"And I said, 'Oh, OK.'"

"And then he says, 'It's about the *f**king* money.'"

By which he meant: If you don't have money, you don't have anything. Who cares if you look like an ass for trying to go public? If there aren't any other options, play the cards you have. What's the worst that could happen?

I'm not advising you to drive yourself into the ground and then take crazy shots in the hopes they'll work. The point is this: Your number-one job, as the founder and CEO, is to make sure you *never* run out of money. Prioritize and make decisions accordingly. Just don't run out of money.

The Udacity Pivot

Going after the wrong customer.

In 2019, Udacity decided to dramatically change directions. For eight years, it had been known as a pioneer in democratizing high-quality education and making it available to the masses. Founder Sebastian Thrun had been inspired by Khan Academy, and after getting a resounding response to putting his Stanford University artificial intelligence course online, he decided to create a startup that would give people a top-shelf education at a fraction of the Stanford price.

But his original vision didn't pan out. "I was so idealistic," Sebastian says. A year in, Udacity had to switch to an on-demand vocational-training model after universities and faculty balked at giving students college credit practically for free. The new approach got traction among early adopters, but eventually consumer interest plateaued. Meanwhile, interest was picking up from companies that paid Udacity to develop training for their workforces. "It took us a while to realize that the enterprise space made for a much better business," says Sebastian, who, while remaining at Udacity as executive chairman, eventually ceded the CEO slot to focus on his flying car company, Kittyhawk.

Udacity began a massive project to retool the company so they could go after that enterprise business. The move made headlines, especially since Udacity had to lay off 20 percent of its workforce as part of the shift. But it turned out to be the right choice. By 2020, the company was finally profitable. Five out of the seven telecom giants use Udacity. Half of the top 200 US companies are customers. Governments like Egypt's pay Udacity to train tens of thousands of students in tech skills. Among consumers, Udacity saw graduation rates of around 35 percent. But among enterprise customers, it's 80 percent. "I wanted to help people be able to get better jobs," Sebastian says. "It's easier to get students' commitment when we reach them inside corporations."

Pivots are common among startups, simply because you're never going to know where your opportunities lie until you get out into the market. In the business world and at conferences, pivots are discussed clinically, as if they were just a matter of tweaking this and rejiggering that. But they actually cause massive upheaval and heartache. You have to reengineer your entire company and often must let go of numerous employees so you can reposition the company for the new direction. There's no roadmap for making a pivot, but here are seven things Sebastian learned in doing his:

- **The market isn't logical, so listen to your customers.** "It's very easy to talk yourself into believing that the market will want the perfect product you build," Sebastian says. But that's not the case. "Udacity cost about $1,000—significantly less than community college. Our data showed you had an 88 percent chance of finding a new job, and you'd be making an average $24,000 more," Sebastian adds. And yet, most students still chose to go to community college. "Math doesn't dictate consumer behavior," he explains. So you need to stay obsessively focused on your customers. They'll steer you to the path you need to take.

- **It usually takes longer than you think to recognize the need to pivot.** "In hindsight, the switch became obvious," Sebastian says. "But in the middle of it, it's like being in the stock market. It's hard to decide which stock to pick." Udacity's new CEO had been discussing a switch to enterprise with the company's board for about a year before they finally pulled the trigger. "Every company will say they could have been faster at pivoting."

- **Hiring more people won't fix a market problem.** "When we saw consumer interest drop, we tried hiring more salespeople," Sebastian says. "But our problem wasn't an execution problem. It was a market response. More salespeople weren't going to fix that."

- **The need to fundraise can be a forcing function.** In 2017, Udacity was getting ready to take another swing at the capital markets. "When you fundraise, you have to explain yourself to investors, and the best way to explain yourself is to have a rapidly growing, profitable business," Sebastian says. That forced the leadership team to take a hard look at where future growth would really come from.

- **You will probably have to revamp your entire organization.** Pivoting doesn't mean just rejiggering your product or service. Big chunks of your company will have to reset as well. Your marketing strategy will change, as will your approach to selling. Be prepared to do a massive overhaul.

- **You should be transparent with your employees.** Lawyers who advise startups on layoffs usually tell CEOs to keep everything secret until the changes are announced. That's what Sebastian did at Udacity, and he regrets it. "It created a lot of bitterness. People came to work one day and learned they'd lost their jobs," he says. Later, when Sebastian had to do layoffs at Kittyhawk, he took the opposite approach. "I looped in the entire staff from day one. I told them, 'The board made this decision, and I want you to know because it might affect your life,'" he says. "If people trust *you*, you need to trust *them*. If you treat them like partners, they'll act like partners."

- **Many people will leave—even of their own volition.** People who might be a good fit for the company's new direction might still decide to leave. Two years after the changes at Udacity, only a single member of the executive team remained. "It's rough on people," Sebastian says. "When you tell people that the thing they've poured their passion, time, and sometimes identity into is actually the wrong thing, and this new thing is the right thing, it's very hard for some people."

"If people trust *you*, you need to trust *them*. If you treat them like partners, they'll act like partners."

The Okta Pivot

Targeting the wrong-sized businesses.

There's a pretty simple reason why Todd and I ended up targeting the wrong customers at the beginning—a mistake that almost cratered the company and left us needing to overhaul our entire business in that terrible year of 2011: those "wrong customers" were the only people taking our calls.

The first product we wanted to build was a way for companies to manage access to online apps for their employees. As I've mentioned before, the experience Todd and I had working at Salesforce told us there was demand for such a product. But we had to find customers who would give us guidance on how they needed it to work. When you're a tiny startup that no one has heard of, the head of IT at a small or midsize business (know as "SMBs") is more likely to take your call than the CTO of a Fortune 500. So we went where we were welcome, figuring we'd build from there.

We had a good reason to do things this way: it's what we'd seen work at Salesforce. Ten years earlier, when Salesforce was launched, it planned to replace on-prem software (sold by giants like Siebel Systems) with its new, cloud-based systems. But CEO Marc Benioff was smart enough to know that he would have to bring hard proof to enterprise-sized clients that showed Salesforce could actually improve the functioning of their sales teams and save them a lot of money. The only way to do that was by starting small—with SMBs—and working up.

Todd and I figured the same approach would work for Okta. But there were a few critical differences between Salesforce and us. Salesforce was a customer relationship management (CRM) product that allowed sales teams to manage leads and prospects. Many of the products that existed before Salesforce were terrible; sales executives hated them. So Salesforce would first approach various sales managers, who had the authority and budget to buy simple products. Once a critical mass of teams at a particular company had signed on, Salesforce would go to the

organization's CIO and ask if they wanted to roll everything up into a single contract, emphasizing that doing so would give the company a better overall price and a standardized approach to using the system. More often than not they said yes.

We couldn't take that approach at Okta. Identity management isn't managed by individual teams. It's overseen by the IT department. And that's where we faced a Catch-22. The IT directors who agreed to take our calls were the ones who worked for smaller companies. But they weren't the ones experiencing the pain around this issue. It was the CIOs at much larger companies, the ones who *wouldn't* take our calls.

Our brilliant idea to follow in Salesforce's footsteps nearly killed us. The entire way you structure and staff a company is different when you're going after SMB customers than when you're going after large enterprise customers. You need different kinds of people with different sets of expertise, especially in marketing and sales. You offer different products. You set up different internal processes. You develop different brand messages. So when Todd and I finally came to terms with the fact we'd been chasing the wrong customers, we had to rip apart the organization we'd built and start building an entirely new one.

But it took Todd and me a while to even realize that that was what we needed to do. Like other founders, we were "extremely confident" in our vision. One of the first signs something was deeply wrong was when a couple of our most senior programmers left the company. We knew we were struggling with sales, but when senior staff with strong track records lose faith in you, it's a clanging alarm bell that you might have much deeper problems.

It wasn't until fall 2011, after that painful board meeting, that Todd and I accepted we needed to change directions. We started working on contacting enterprise-sized customers and began the search for an experienced vice president of sales. When that person finally came on board in 2012, he was able to architect a game plan and build a sales machine that allowed us to gain traction and grow.

Today, when I advise founders going through the same experience, here's what I tell them:

- **Be honest with everyone, especially yourself.** Todd and I didn't really let our team know how bad things were until fall 2011. If we had shared the situation with them earlier, they could have helped us pinpoint the source of our problems and identify possible fixes much sooner. You'll be surprised how much people will rally around you when you give them the actual information and the opportunity to really impact the business.

- **Do an analysis and create a plan.** Insanity, as you know, is doing the same thing over and over again and expecting different results. (Todd and I should have clued in a lot faster that our plan wasn't working.) Next, when you do the analysis, do it quickly. You don't have time to do a 30-data-point regression analysis. You need to make your best guess as to where the problem is and then create a plan to fix it.

- **Commit to the new plan and only the new plan.** Once you've figured out what you need to do—in our case, move away from SMBs toward large enterprises—commit to that. You don't have the time and money to continue on both paths. The faster you ditch the first boat and jump into the second, the better your chances of not sinking.

- **Be ultra-clear with your team**. It's human nature to resist change, so when you, the leader, give mixed signals about what the company needs to do, your people will default to what they have been doing. It's more familiar and comfortable, after all. So you need to be absolutely clear that the company is changing directions, and that everyone needs to start heading down the new path.

- **Beware of bad pattern matching.** What got us into this mess was the assumption that we could follow Salesforce's approach. Pattern matching is seductive. Often, it can help you make faster decisions—and ones that are good enough. But when the stakes are high, you need to make it a practice to stress-test any patterns you're thinking of relying on.

Our brilliant idea to follow in Salesforce's footsteps nearly killed us.

The Loudcloud Story

Almost running out of money.

In 2001, the bottom fell out of Loudcloud, the SaaS company Ben Horowitz had cofounded two years before. Until then, the company, which offered infrastructure to support business-to-business e-commerce, was humming along nicely. "We booked $27 million in sales in our third quarter—nine months after we started," Ben recalls. Then in the spring of 2000, the dot-com bubble burst. Ben had been planning on raising more money—their burn rate was through the roof—but suddenly the venture capital industry was battening down its hatches. "It was Armageddon everywhere," he says. By late 2000, Loudcloud only had about five months' worth of cash left.

The only way to raise money was to go public. The idea didn't come out of nowhere. Given its stellar performance, Loudcloud had already started making plans to IPO. But now, the idea seemed preposterous. "We couldn't forecast our sales. We couldn't forecast what we had booked already. A lot of our customers were going bankrupt. And we probably needed to change out a bunch of the executives," Ben says. A conversation with his board, however, made him realize there were no other choices. It was go public or declare bankruptcy.

Loudcloud priced the stock at $10—the lowest it possibly could without heading into territory where the financial institutions Ben was hoping to attract simply would steer clear. Even then, Loudcloud had to reverse-split the stock (create fewer shares) just to get there, which horrified Loudcloud's employees. "They weren't aware of how bad things were," Ben says. "They felt like I hadn't been telling them the truth." Then, on the roadshow,* investors weren't particularly welcoming. The NASDAQ was crashing. Tech stocks were the anchor dragging it down. During Ben's three weeks on the road, the value of Loudcloud's "comparables"—the companies it was being compared to—were cut in half. One of the bankers who worked on

Loudcloud's deal later told Ben it was "the worst f**king thing I ever experienced in my life." *Businessweek* called it "the IPO from hell."

Against all odds, Loudcloud managed to go public. The fresh infusion of cash would allow them to live to fight another day. But the company's problems weren't over. In some ways, the worst was yet to come.

Even with the new money, Loudcloud's business was spiraling downward. Potential customers started balking as waves of internet companies went belly-up. "It became too dangerous [for corporations] to outsource [their] infrastructure to one of these new-type Silicon Valley companies," Ben says. When Loudcloud announced they were going to miss their forecast, their stock price sank to $2. Some Wall Street analysts simply stopped covering them. Then 9/11 happened, sending the economy into a deeper tailspin. Two weeks later, Loudcloud's biggest competitor—once worth $50 billion—went bankrupt.

Ben couldn't sleep. He couldn't see how Loudcloud was going to get out alive. He was wracked by the thought of losing everyone's money, putting his employees on the street in an economy where there were no jobs, and watching his reputation evaporate. It's a situation many founders eventually find themselves in. The moment when a founder realizes that their beautiful vision is turning into a multicar pileup leaves them curled up in a ball, desperately looking for a way out.

In the face of imminent ruin, however, Ben did something radical. He asked himself: What if Loudcloud was *already* bankrupt? What if the train wreck had already taken place? What would his next step be?

The answer was simple: he would ditch the part of the company that hosted software for clients—the part that no one was interested in (but that was currently its primary business) and instead buy the software Loudcloud had developed and build a new company that would sell that product directly to customers to manage themselves. Corporations that resisted hiring Loudcloud to manage their infrastructure would nevertheless want great software to

---

* The "roadshow" takes place in the period right before the actual IPO. It's when a startup's executives visit investors to drum up interest in buying the stock.

do it themselves. So he kicked off a project to separate the software from the rest of Loudcloud.

The only problem: Loudcloud was again running out of money. Ben knew how much he needed until he could spin off the software, and he cobbled together a plan to get it. The day before he was supposed to meet with prospective lenders, however, his largest customer informed him they were going bankrupt. The resulting loss in revenue blew up any possibility of securing outside money.

Ben scrambled to put a new plan in motion—to find a buyer for the hosted part of the business as fast as possible. By summer, a deal was done. The sale gave Opsware—as Ben's spinoff was now called—enough money to launch the new software-only business. For the first time since late 1999, he was able to breathe.

But not for long. Wall Street couldn't understand why he had sold off the revenue-generating part of the company. Opsware's stock price fell to $0.35, and there were more layoffs. It would be another five years of slogging before Ben's gamble paid off. In 2007, HP bought Opsware for $1.65 billion.

Shortly after that sale, Ben got a call from a private equity firm wanting to hire him. He didn't understand why. They said, "We do turnarounds, and we've studied every tech turnaround in the last 30 years, and the greatest one was Loudcloud to Opsware." Ben turned them down. "You're aware that I'm the one who f**ked it up in the first place, right?" he said. Give Ben credit for his honesty. But he did learn a lot from the experience. Here are six main takeaways:

- **One day you have a great product. The next day you don't.** "Product-market fit is ephemeral," Ben says. "But no one ever talks about it that way." Barring the dot-com crash, Loudcloud might have succeeded. The same goes for the pandemic or for the financial crash of 2008. Plenty of startups were doing great until they were hit by external forces. Never assume that because everything's going well now, it will necessarily stay that way.

- **Loudcloud's spending made it vulnerable.** Companies usually hash out spending plans based on projections of future revenue. But those future projections are usually based on past performance. After the dot-com crash, Ben continued to plan as if that $27 million quarter was predictive of the future. "That's how we got caught with our pants down," he says. Had Loudcloud revised its spending plan sooner, it might not have ended up in as big a hole.

> Had Loudcloud revised its spending plan sooner, it might not have ended up in as big a hole.

- **Once you're in the hole, you must become ruthlessly focused on getting out.** Loudcloud's hundreds of employees became furious when they realized how dire things were. Ben could empathize, but he couldn't get distracted. "You have to keep focusing on your next move. Because all you have is that one move," he says.

- **You're going to have to choose between a bad option and a terrible one.** Business school case studies often make it seem like the choices leaders face include a good option and a less-great one. "That's bulls**t," Ben says. Once you're in the hole, the choices are usually all bad. It's incredibly difficult psychologically. "Making a big change is really traumatic for everyone," he says. But if that change has better odds of success, you have to find the courage to pull that trigger.

- **You should be candid with your team about what's failing.** When you stand up in front of the company and tell them that the current path is no longer viable, you need to acknowledge, unequivocally, that your original vision failed—even as, in your next breath, you try to convince them to believe in the new vision that you now want the company to rally around. "It's one of the hardest leadership problems there is," Ben says. "Most people won't do it." Your integrity, though, is all you have at this point. It's what will make at least some of your employees give you a second shot. But if you fudge the truth, they'll know. "That's when a founder loses the company," Ben says.

- **When in doubt, turn the question around.** The part of Ben's story I like best is when he stopped and asked himself: What if everything had already blown up? Putting yourself in that frame of mind liberates you to see things clearly. If there's nothing more to save, what would you do then?

Tiny Speck's Real-Death Experience

Knowing when it's time to throw in the towel.

No founder ever wants to give up. Most are psychologically programmed to be Energizer Bunnies: they just keep going no matter what. It's an important quality for a founder to have—until it's not.

Most of the time, when startups shut down, it's because they've run out of money. The founders simply don't have any other way forward. They've looked for funding, as Ben Horowitz did, but it wasn't forthcoming. When there's nothing left in the bank, they have to call it quits.

So it takes an extraordinary person to recognize that there's no point in continuing, even while there's still plenty of cash on hand. Stewart Butterfield is one of those unusual founders who pulled the plug on his own startup. As one of the founders of Flickr back in the early 2000s, Stewart did well for himself when the image-hosting company was sold to Yahoo. He left Yahoo a few years after that and founded a gaming company called Tiny Speck.

Tiny Speck's game Glitch launched in 2011. It was an ambitious multiplayer that pushed the boundaries of how people imagined a game could work. But it took massive amounts of resources to support, and by 2012, Stewart could see it wasn't attracting enough paying customers to become profitable.

At this point, many founders would have tried to keep going anyway. After all, Tiny Speck still had plenty of money in the bank, and the pull of inertia is strong. "There are a bunch of forces aligned against throwing in the towel," Stewart says. "First, it's humiliating. I had made all these claims to the press that we were going to do all this stuff. I got the players excited, and I took money from investors." And then there were the company's employees.

"I had convinced them, in some cases, to turn their lives upside down." There was one employee Stewart remembers having persuaded to move to Vancouver, where Tiny Speck had an office. "He had a young daughter, and three months earlier, I had convinced him to move away from the support of his in-laws who were helping with his kid, and he'd bought a house. Now I have to tell him he doesn't have a job anymore," Stewart says. "When I caught his eye, I started crying."

Most founders in Stewart's situation would have tried any number of things to avoid shutting Tiny Speck down. Maybe they would have hired more people. Or ramped up their advertising. Or worse, tried to raise more money (likely on very onerous terms).

For Stewart, however, the realization that it was time to stop came down to a single thing: He just didn't believe in it anymore. "Founders always have doubts and fears," he says. "But they do believe that their vision is possible." One sleepless night, as he was tossing and turning at 2 a.m., he accepted that his belief was gone. "I realized that if I, the CEO, didn't believe it, then it wasn't going to work. Success doesn't just spontaneously happen," he says. "The board can't make it work. The employees can't. Leadership has to believe. It's a necessary condition for success." The next day, he gathered his cofounders and his board and told them his decision.

One of the upsides of making the decision while there was still money on hand was that Stewart could wind the company down gently. "We gave every employee a pretty generous severance," he says. They also built a page on their website called "Hire a Genius," where they posted the résumés and portfolios of the artists, animators, musicians, and others who were now looking for work. They gave their users the option to get their money back, let Tiny Speck keep it, or donate it to one of three charities. It was a silver lining to an otherwise crushing experience. "We had to clean it up in the most elegant way we could," Stewart says.

Although Tiny Speck didn't succeed, Stewart realized that a communication tool the company had built for its teams might be something that could become its own business. At the time, many people were using chat services like Google Chat or tools like Basecamp to coordinate with colleagues. Stewart's team had built their own in-house tool, based on an old (and very basic) technology called Internet Relay Chat, or IRC. "It lacked most of the features that people would expect from a modern messaging app, so we just kept adding stuff," he says.

After they shut down Tiny Speck, Stewart and his co-founders started building a new company around this tool, which had been such an afterthought that they hadn't even given it a name. It was an uphill battle to identify a market for it, though. Glitch had been a game for consumers. This new thing was an enterprise tool they now wanted to sell into companies—a completely different ball game. "When we said it was a 'channel-based messaging platform,' people had no idea what that meant," Stewart says. It was hard to convince people to give it a shot. "Even at friends' companies, it took us five meetings of explaining and showing it to them."

But eventually, they broke through. By 2017, the tool was fairly widely known. It went public on the New York Stock Exchange. The pandemic, which forced companies to operate remotely, accelerated its adoption. And in 2020, it was bought by Salesforce for nearly $28 billion.

The name of that company? Slack.

"I realized that if I, the CEO, didn't believe it, then it wasn't going to work."

Stepping Down

When it's time to stop being CEO.

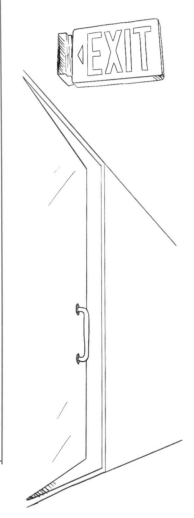

Few founders willingly give up the CEO title. Their company is their baby. They want to see it through. Ego, of course, plays a role. Why should you give up the top slot when the company was your idea and you put in the sweat and sleepless nights to get it off the ground?

CEOs do get replaced, however—usually when their board loses faith in them. Travis Kalanick at Uber and Adam Neumann at WeWork are examples of CEOs getting the boot, albeit for some pretty troubling reasons. But it's not uncommon for boards to replace leaders under less dramatic circumstances.

A few enlightened founders can even tell when they are no longer the right person for the job. Seven years after Fred Luddy founded ServiceNow, the company was cash-flow positive and enjoying about $100 million in annual revenue. (A decade later, it's raking in over $4 billion annually.) But the company had moved out of the tinkering-with-the-product phase and into the develop-operational-excellence phase. The focus now was on fine-tuning internal systems so the company could really grow.

"One of my investors asked me, 'Do you want to be the product guy or the CEO?'" Fred recalls. They're fundamentally different jobs, especially once the company gets big. The investor told him: "We'll support you either way, but we don't think you can do both." An engineer by training, Fred had always enjoyed building products. He was now in his fifties, and this was his first CEO gig. He wasn't sure what the next few years would involve. His investor took him to meet the CEOs of companies his size and bigger. "I saw what these guys were doing every day, and I told my investor, 'I don't think I have those skills. And more importantly, I have no interest in acquiring them,'" Fred says.

Soon after that, ServiceNow brought on a new CEO, Frank Slootman, the former head of a data storage company, and Fred moved into a product role. A comment he later made to *Forbes* confirmed he'd made the right choice: "Frank made us into a very large, well-oiled machine, scaling out the organization in a way I never could have."

Some founders will choose to helm their companies for a long time—Bill Gates, Mark Zuckerberg, Jeff Bezos, and my old boss Marc Benioff come to mind. Todd will do the same at Okta. But for many, there will come a time to consider passing the baton. There are two primary signs that time may have come:

- **You don't have the drive and determination needed for the next stage.**
  You might be feeling sluggish or finding it difficult to focus on the challenges and opportunities in front of you. It's increasingly harder to get "in the zone." You've stopped waking up in the morning feeling energized. All of these are signs that you've lost interest—in your role, at least, if not in the company as a whole. Ego becomes your primary obstacle at this point. Recognize that staying in your role might eventually undermine the company. Employees can tell when the person at the top is drifting, and it can impact their own motivation. Work with your board to carve out a new function, one that will let you apply your unique strengths and interests to the company.

- **You're experiencing serious operational challenges.**
  Despite a huge market opportunity, growth has stalled or, worse, is in decline. Barring an obvious exogenous factor (like a pandemic), or an internal one (like a pivot requiring a reset), growth should continue upward, especially in a big, growing market. Slowing growth can mean that you're not making the right decisions, including hiring the right people or pulling the right operational levers. All of that adds up to the same thing: the job has become too big for you. If you're no longer in your wheelhouse, work with the board to carve out a smaller role that's a better fit.

Don't Let the Terror Win

"We had a saying: if your guts aren't boiling, you aren't even trying."

That's how Ben Horowitz described the two-and-a-half years from the end of 1999 to the middle of 2002 when he finally unloaded the hosted part of Loudcloud. In those terrible days, Marc Andreessen, who was Ben's cofounder at Loudcloud before they joined forces to create their eponymous VC firm, told him that, as a startup founder, you only ever experience two emotions: euphoria and terror.

During his nadir, Ben regretted having taken the CEO job: "I hadn't wanted to be CEO. A couple of my friends had started the company, and when I asked who would be the CEO, they said, 'You.'"

At one point, as Ben and Marc were driving away from a meeting with an investor who had proposed a deal so dilutive there was no point considering it, Ben hit his breaking point. "I turned to Marc and said, 'Look, if you want any f**king person to run this company other than me, please do it now. Let me out. I have no problem with that.'"

Marc just looked at him. "I could tell by the look on his face that there was nobody else," Ben says. "I knew I was stuck."

Stuck is a concept Ben has used before to describe what it feels like to be a founder. He likens the entire Loudcloud experience—from the day they launched to the day they finally sold themselves to HP—to a nightmare of claustrophobia and terror: "You get in that car, and you can't get out."

It's true. In the worst, most crushing, most unbearable times, you feel like a prisoner of your own ambition and success. If you're lucky, you make it through and eventually find some measure of stability where you're pretty sure (knock wood) you're going to be fine. Despite how gray my hair has become, Todd and I did ultimately prevail. And no matter how many years we lost to stress, I wouldn't trade those terror-filled days for anything.

ten

MANAGING YOURSELF

I **'ve heard a lot of people** talk about work-life balance, and I think the sentiment is well intentioned, but it overlooks a key opportunity. Running a company is hard as hell. Even in good times, it can be a grind. It's definitely critical to carve out personal time, but you should also think about ways to bring more of your life into your work. I like to think of it as work-life *integration*.

Let me give you an example. I love ice hockey and play late every Tuesday evening and early most Sunday mornings as part of a Bay Area league. It's something I've done the whole time I've been building Okta. Getting on the ice is my way of clearing my head and blowing off steam. For a couple of hours, I get to leave my stress and responsibilities behind.

But I also try to fold hockey into my workday where it makes sense. For example, when I travel for sales meetings, I regularly invite prospects, customers, and investors to come to a game with me. I've gone so far as to plan trips around the NHL calendar. It has a lot of upsides. I get to spend time with customers in a fun way. It distinguishes Okta from competitors. And it often leads to more business.

I also carefully guard my family time. I am home for dinner with my wife and children every night (unless I'm out of town). I put my phone on our foyer table when I arrive home, and it stays there until the kids go to sleep. I don't take work calls on weekends unless it's an absolute emergency. And I attend every parent-teacher conference (even if I have to do so by phone when I'm in another city).

It's easy to take family for granted and allow yourself to get pulled into never-ending work demands. It takes discipline to switch gears and focus on your partner and children. But the work demands will never ever stop. And your family time is both precious and fleeting. My children will never again be the ages they are now. I love spending time with them, and I want to be involved in helping them grow. So I invest time in the upstream work—hiring really great people, establishing clear goals, and giving the team the autonomy to execute as they see fit. That way, when I come home, I don't have to worry that the company will collapse if I step away for a few hours.

People in business and tech talk endlessly about fundraising, product-market fit, design thinking, the latest tech, management techniques, consumer trends—everything except the need to keep yourself in fighting shape. That's crazy. Building and running a startup is exhausting. All founders need to create strategies to stay fit—mentally, emotionally, and physically. You don't want your company to implode simply because you never carved out time to exercise or sleep.

The rigors of startup life are certainly difficult in the beginning. Unfortunately, they're also difficult in the middle, and even after you've gone public. My company brings in more than $1 billion dollars a year in revenue, and yet I still wake up in the middle of the night obsessing over work. In this chapter, I share advice on how to take care of yourself. What's most important is simply to be aware that you need to. Here are practices that have worked for me:

- **Find founder peers at the same stage as you, or slightly ahead.**
  Develop relationships with other entrepreneurs who'll understand what you're going through and the problems you need help with. Your friends and family can offer general moral support, but none of them will really *get it* the way a fellow founder will.

- **Follow the "oxygen mask" rule.**
  You know the old flight-safety advisory: "Place your mask over your own mouth and nose before assisting others." You can't help your company if you're not able to perform at your best. Create routines to stay physically, emotionally, and mentally fit.

- **Take vacations.**
  You're going to feel like you can't. But remember how we talked earlier about needing to pause in order to upgrade a system or process? Sometimes you will need to upgrade yourself, even if it means stepping away from the company (which won't slow down because you've built a well-oiled machine that runs well without you, right?) so you can recharge your batteries and get energized for the next leg.

People in business and tech talk endlessly about everything except the need to keep yourself in fighting shape.

Don't Keep Up with the Joneses

Every business is different.

In the early days at Okta, Todd and I kept a spreadsheet where we'd track other startups' performance. The sheet included: year started, money raised, number of employees, revenue, and next-year forecast. At lunches with friends or industry gatherings, people would often mention other companies' numbers for various of these variables. As soon as I'd get back to the office, I'd dump the new intel into our sheet. We wanted to assess how Okta was doing as compared with other companies.

It was a silly thing to do.

Startup founders tend to be competitive. Of course they want to know how they stack up. But there's no single roadmap to success. Every company is different. Consumer companies are different from enterprise ones. Startups selling to small businesses will grow differently than those selling into the Fortune 100. It's useless to compile the information we were tracking. It might give you the illusion you're assembling some kind of useful insight. But you're not. It's a waste of time—time that you don't have to waste.

In competitive auto racing, they teach drivers to "focus on the road, not the wall." Look at the wall and you'll crash. To win, you need to keep your eye where you want the car to go. I share the same principle with new founders: Don't worry about what anyone else is doing or how they're performing.* Just focus on your own road, your own race.

* The only exception to this is if you are an enterprise company, and you keep losing deals to competitors because they have specific features or functions that you don't. Pay attention to that because it might tell you what you need to do to become competitive.

Take a Microbreak

In the early days, you're going to feel like you need to give all your time to your business. When given the choice between taking a moment to call a friend or churning out another 10 lines of code, the pull of the code will be strong. But taking 20 minutes to reach out to an old pal is a far better use of your time, in part because it actually restores your energy, rather than sapping it.

"Take the night off," Saul Kato, one of my best friends, always tells me. He's a successful serial entrepreneur, a professor at the University of California, San Francisco, and my cofounder at a second company I recently helped launch, Herophilus, which helps discover new neurotherapeutics. "Waste some time," Saul will say. "Watch your NHL game. Go out to a bar. You've earned it!" Research shows that you can't work nonstop without seeing your output progressively decline. Reaching out to friends and family members—even casual acquaintances who make you laugh or raise your spirits—can help ground you, refresh you, and give you an all-around reset before you plunge into your next work jag.

How to Get Your Head
Back in the Game
Lessons from an Olympic athlete
turned startup founder.

"One of the hardest things to do as a founder is to manage our own psychology," says Jeremy Bloom, who was an Olympic skier *and* professional football player before founding Integrate. The kinds of highs and lows he experiences as a startup founder aren't much different from those he went through as an athlete. "You'll wake up thinking you're going to take over the world, and by noon, you'll be wondering if you can make payroll," he says.

He's right. That's exactly what it's like: emotional roller coaster after emotional roller coaster—often in the same day.

Jeremy is a remarkable guy. He won three world championships as a freestyle skier, which combines moguls, aerials, and half-pipes. And he's been to the Winter Olympics twice. In 2002, he placed ninth overall, and when he returned in 2006, he was gunning for the podium. He ended up placing sixth. It was a crushing disappointment. So how did he handle it? "I gave myself two days to sulk, and then I headed for the NFL combine," he says. And wouldn't you know it, he got drafted by the Philadelphia Eagles and ended up playing professionally for two years.

Giving yourself time to absorb a loss is important. For Jeremy, after the Olympics, it meant holing up on his own for 48 hours and replaying everything that had happened during the Games, as well as the four years leading up to them. "I tried to distill everything down to its simplest form, so I could extract learnings from that experience," he says. Jeremy applies that principle as a founder today. "Sometimes it's just 10 minutes," he says, but it's time he needs to recalibrate and return his focus to the main thing.

Failure can weigh people down. They can get stuck in it. As a founder, you have to keep moving. "When we can extract learnings from an experience," says Jeremy, "we're going to be so much stronger moving on to the next goal."

Depression Among Founders

It's more common than you think.

Founders have been shown to have higher rates of depression than the average person. That doesn't mean that a founder will definitely become depressed. But when it does happen, a founder should know it's not particularly unusual. According to a study conducted by the University of California, San Francisco's Dr. Michael Freeman, approximately a third of entrepreneurs reported that they suffered from depression, about twice the rate as the study's comparison group.* Other studies have also looked at this question. Their findings vary on whether entrepreneurs have meaningfully more depression than the general public—but, Dr. Freeman says, none has found that they have *less*.

There's no single reason for this phenomenon, says Dr. Freeman. While many people, no matter their occupation, may have a genetic disposition for depression, it never becomes an issue because they never find themselves in the kinds of situations that might flip the depression switch. It's similar to how some people may have a genetic propensity toward diabetes, but as long as they eat well and maintain a healthy weight, the diabetes may never appear. So if you put someone with a preexisting vulnerability to depression in the pressure cooker that is startup life, it could be triggered. "A lot of people get overextended," Dr. Freeman says. "They don't get enough sleep. They eat junk food. They get socially isolated because they're spending so much time at work. They might have conflicts with their cofounders. They might get slapped with a lawsuit or get pushed out by their board. At a certain point, you cross over the tipping point."

Some of this is simply the expected result of the unique blows you suffer in the entrepreneurial life. "When you're trying to disrupt the status quo, there are a lot of forces that don't want to be disrupted. So you run into pushback, and the frustrations involved can be demoralizing," Dr. Freeman explains. There's also the constant rejection, especially in the beginning. "Many entrepreneurs make the mistake of believing that their identity and their value as a person are the same as the success of their business," he adds.

* Michael A. Freeman et al., "The Prevalence and Co-occurrence of Psychiatric Conditions Among Entrepreneurs and Their Families," *Small Business Economics*, 53:323–342, 2019, https://link.springer.com/article/10.1007/s11187-018-0059-8.

When they pitch venture capitalists and get rejected over and over, it's devastating. "If you can't see that the investors are rejecting the concept or the technology, and you personalize it, that can lead to demoralization, low self-esteem, and, ultimately, depression."

I'm not bringing this up to alarm you. Just the opposite. This might never affect you, except possibly in discrete episodes in response to specific blows. If so, you'll probably recover with no lasting effects. But if this does sound like you, know that you're not alone. Take a look at the successful founders you see at conferences, on TV, or in magazine profiles. You can bet that a chunk of them deal with mental health challenges. It still isn't widely discussed in the industry, unfortunately, but it is par for the course. As such, it's not an impediment. Just something to manage.

Lifetime Prevalence of Mental Health Conditions Among Entrepreneurs Versus Comparison Group

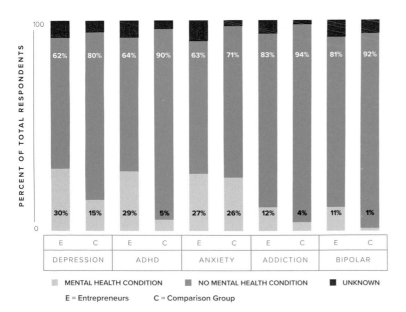

Source: Michael A. Freeman et al., "The Prevalence and Co-occurrence of Psychiatric Conditions Among Entrepreneurs and Their Families," *Small Business Economics*, 2, August 2019, https://link.springer.com/article/10.1007/s11187-018-0059-8.

> **INSIGHT**
>
> I think about building a startup like climbing Mount Everest. We know the prize is at the top. You've got to get there. But that doesn't change the fact that, if you're at Camp 3 or Camp 4, you're still an insanely good climber. You have to take stock of that because it'll give you the extra boost you need to get to the top. Take that time to appreciate the difficulty of what you're doing and how well you're doing, in spite of the trials and tribulations. Otherwise, it's too easy to beat yourself up.
>
> —Alex Asseily, Jawbone

How Entrepreneurs Stay in Fighting Shape

Step away. Zone out. Regain perspective.

SHASHANK SAXENA, VNDLY

I play cricket on Sunday mornings. When I'm on the field, my focus is on the field, and I'm just there in the moment. Founders need very clearly defined timeouts where they can zone out. Cricket gives me a break from thinking about work because you think about it all the time. Even when you're showering, you're thinking about work. On the cricket field, my phone is 50 feet away, on a bench. That's my time when I disconnect.

MARIAM NAFICY, MINTED

You need reminders that, for the most part, this is just a business. We're not saving people's lives. You need to get away sometimes and focus on what's really important in life. My children help me to remember what's really important. They put things in perspective.

JASMINE CROWE, GOODR

We have bikes in the office, and Goodr is off of the BeltLine in Atlanta, which is a really long outdoor trail. I'll go out there and ride my bike.

JEREMY BLOOM, INTEGRATE

Sleep can heal the body emotionally and physically. I do three things to ensure I get a good night's sleep. As soon as the sun goes down, I put on orange glasses. Research shows that blue light [from devices] suppresses the secretion of melatonin, which helps us fall asleep. I make sure my bedroom is cool, dark, and quiet. I keep a consistent bedtime, and I don't eat for three hours before that. If I do, my fitness tracker shows that my heart rate goes way up because my body is spending energy digesting that food instead of restoring the cells that need to be restored.

Miss a Deadline
Every Now and Then

The case for (sometimes) letting things slide.

You'll constantly feel like you need to run all out. You're going to set deadlines and milestones that you'll convince yourself you *must* hit. Because your money has a fuse on it . . . because nothing happens until someone sells something . . . because you have to keep the main thing the main thing, and the main thing is growing this business—*fast*.

But sometimes, it's OK to slow down. Let's say a release is scheduled to go out *tomorrow*. But it can't really get done without everyone working crazy hours (after weeks of already working crazy hours). Will it really matter if you postpone it to next week? If it means you (and your team) get a mini break, and you can take your head (and body) out of the game briefly to recharge elsewhere, then why not? If the release date was arbitrary, and it's not going to make a huge difference to change it, go ahead and push it back.

Building a startup really is a marathon. A trade-off now in favor of everyone's physical and mental health will pay dividends down the road. Don't do this on the big stuff: the numbers you have to hit for the year, the money you have to raise in the next round, the international office you have to open in three months. But the smaller stuff? Every now and then, give yourself permission to let things slide.

eleven

BOARDS

B

ack at the beginning of this book, I told you how Ben Horowitz gave me two tactical pieces of advice that ended up saving our company. The first, which I talked about in Chapter 3, was that I couldn't do multiple important jobs at the same time and still do them well. Now, I'll talk about the second piece of advice. In 2011, as I discussed earlier, our sales were cratering. The small and medium-sized businesses we were targeting didn't need what we had built. We had started with them because we thought we needed to create a healthy foundation with those customers before we could go after big enterprise companies, which were our real target. Ben was the one who told us that our approach was flat wrong.

This is the power and importance of a startup's board of directors. They should be able to see what you don't and, in cases like this, let you know when you're headed off course.

The Okta platform has a wide range of functionality today, but when Todd and I started, we only had a couple of products, one of which helped companies onboard and offboard employees. This process gets more complicated—and therefore more painful—the bigger a company gets. Ben pointed out that smaller companies didn't really feel this pain, so they weren't biting. Big companies, however, experienced this problem, and they would leap at our solution—if we could figure out how to reach their decision makers.

Ben was right. But we didn't have any experience pitching those big companies. With their thousands of employees, we didn't know how to identify which executives to target and how to approach them.

That's when he reminded me of the first piece of advice: you need to hire people who can do what you can't. So we quickly recruited a new sales team and shifted our attention to these larger companies. Within a few months, our sales ticked up, and within the year, we were seeing exponential sales growth. We had survived because of our board.

Founders sometimes think of boards of directors as committees to whom they make periodic presentations. You show up and run through your slide deck. The directors ask some questions, and then you all recess for coffee.

That's not it at all. Board members are strategic partners who, at their most valuable, lend their expertise so you can make the best possible decisions.

In Chapter 4, we talked about how you should be thoughtful about whose money you take because you're not just taking their money. You're also bringing them on as a board member, and thus as a key advisor. In this chapter, we'll discuss what makes for a strong board and what kinds of people you should seek to serve on yours. Many board members will end up being with you for 10 years or more. You need people who are raring to go the distance—and will be effective in helping you succeed.

For help with this topic, I turned to three of Okta's board members, all of whom have extensive experience serving on startup and corporate boards: Michelle Wilson, a former senior vice president and general counsel at Amazon; Shellye Archambeau, the former CEO of MetricStream, which creates corporate compliance and governance tools, and a director at Verizon and Nordstrom; and Pat Grady, a partner at Sequoia Capital, who has served on over 20 startup boards, including those of Zoom, HubSpot, and Qualtrics.

Board members are strategic partners who, at their most valuable, lend their expertise so you can make the best possible decisions.

Boards 101

The basics you need to know.

A board's primary responsibility is what's called "governance and oversight." Board members represent shareholders*—the collective owners of the company. When the company is still private, these responsibilities are mostly focused on making sure its executives are making the best possible strategic decisions that will enable it to grow. "The board's job is to enhance shareholder value and make sure the company is thinking about all its constituencies in a holistic way," says Michelle Wilson.

It's also a way for venture capital investors to keep an eye on their investments. They want to know which companies in their portfolio are doing well—and therefore should be discussed at partner meetings so that money is reserved to invest in follow-on rounds—and which ones are in trouble.

Later, after a company goes public, there are rules companies must follow, which are enforced in the United States by the Securities and Exchange Commission (SEC). The board helps ensure the company adheres to those.

Who's on the Board?

The composition of the board will evolve as you grow.

WHEN YOU FIRST LAUNCH In your company's infancy, the board is composed of just you and your cofounders. It's less of a board and more of a technical mechanism through which a number of activities must take place, including the awarding of shares and decisions about executive compensation.

WHEN YOU FIRST TAKE INVESTOR MONEY The board consists of the CEO (who usually serves as the chairman) and possibly a second cofounder (if it makes sense), along with partners from one or two of the firms that invested in you.

WHEN YOU GET BIGGER (POST–SERIES B) You will start adding independent directors—people who aren't investors (hence: "independent")—who have skills and experience that will be particularly useful as you grow.

* At least this is true in the United States. In other countries, boards have responsibilities to other stakeholders as well. This chapter focuses specifically on US boards.

What Boards Do

PRIMARY	• Review company strategy • Give the CEO advice • Bring in the perspective of the outside world
FORMAL	• Hire and fire the CEO • Approve stock allocations • Approve executive compensation plans • Approve annual budgets • Approve decisions to raise additional funds • Approve mergers and acquisitions
INFORMAL	• Make introductions to potential customers and partners • Interview candidates for senior executive positions

What Boards Don't Do

• Force the CEO to follow any particular strategy
• Do any of the day-to-day work or management

How to Build a Strong Board

Think Marvel's Avengers.

Who's on your board is as important as who's on your executive team. My friend Alex Asseily, formerly of Jawbone and now cofounder and chairman of Elvie, a London-based femtech startup, compares them to Marvel's Avengers. Each board member, he says, should have their own superpower. Together, the team should be able to tackle any problem. So give a lot of thought to the investors you take money from (they'll usually put someone on your board) and the independent directors you add separately. "You want people who are there for the right reasons—who want to help build the company—not so they can add to their résumé," says Michelle Wilson.

LOOK FOR PEOPLE WHO HAVE PASSION FOR YOUR VENTURE

You want people who are constantly thinking about your company, sending you links to articles, talking you up to other investors, and putting in that extra effort in finding solutions to your problems.

BRING ON DIRECTORS WHO UNDERSTAND THE "OLD" WORLD

Founders sometimes steer clear of veterans in the space they're trying to disrupt, for fear that their old-school mindset will hold back the company's thinking. But these folks know where the constraints and obstacles are. You don't have to take their advice about the future, but you do need their insights about the present.

HAVE AT LEAST ONE PERSON WHO'S RUN A COMPANY SIMILAR TO YOURS

Your board can only offer you really good advice if they actually understand the space you're in. If you are building an enterprise company, have someone on the board who's built an enterprise company before. If you're building a consumer company, bring on someone who's steeped in consumer products.

BRING ON DIRECTORS FROM DIFFERENT BACKGROUNDS

Inclusive boards are stronger at problem-solving because they bring a wider range of experiences and insights to the issues you face. They can tap a wider range of networks when it comes to hiring, and candidates will be able to see from your board demographics that your company values a wide variety of people.

BRING ON PEOPLE WITH FUNCTIONAL EXPERTISE

"You probably want one person who knows 'go-to-market' so your sales and marketing team have somebody they can bounce ideas off of," says Pat Grady. "You also want somebody who knows about product development and technology, so your product and engineering teams have somebody to run ideas by. And then you want someone who's been a CEO to help you as CEO."

DON'T HIRE YOUR FRIENDS

You need people who will ask hard questions and give tough feedback.

DON'T BRING ON PEOPLE WHO CAN'T STAND EACH OTHER

Vet potential board members to find out if they have any issues with your existing directors. Tension between directors is a net negative.

AVOID PEOPLE WHO AREN'T WILLING TO HAVE DIFFICULT DISCUSSIONS

You can have the smartest people on your board, but if they won't level with you, they're not much use. There are any number of reasons why a director might hold back. Sometimes they're just spread too thin in other areas of their life. Sometimes they're more interested in preserving a relationship with a more senior person on the board (to maintain access to other good deals, for example). Either way, do your due diligence to make sure that your directors will bring their full energy and voices to your table.

DO DUE DILIGENCE ON EACH PERSON

For every potential director— including investors you're considering taking money from—find three founders who had that person on their board *and* whose startup ran into serious challenges. Then ask those founders how useful the director was. They will let you know whether a director has the drive, focus, and seriousness to help you through your most challenging times.

How to Work with Your Board

It all starts with the meeting agenda.

There are two main ways you'll interact with your board: during your periodic board meetings (perhaps monthly at first, but eventually quarterly) and in discrete situations in which you tap them offline for advice or help. What follows are ideas for how to get the most out of both cases.

DURING BOARD MEETINGS

Board meetings aren't about show-and-tell. They're about getting help on your most important and pressing issues. These practices will help:

- **Send out the agenda a week in advance.**
  It's your responsibility, as chairman, to set the agenda. Send it out far enough ahead that the board has time to get up to speed. Remember: Information that is old hat to you will be new to them. They need time to absorb it.

- **Focus the meeting on your most important strategic issues.**
  A mistake new founders make is to use the board meeting to provide a general status update. That doesn't help you, and it's not particularly interesting to your directors. What they want most is to tackle problems or figure out strategy. So think of your board meetings as working sessions where you're going to hash out one to three (but no more—there won't be time) issues your company is currently struggling with. Use the first part of the meeting to quickly run through the big picture, then dedicate about 45 minutes for each issue with which you need help.

- **Don't bring in a stream of executives to present updates.**
  Founders sometimes let their executives present to the board—both as
  a reward for great work or as an opportunity to get experience working
  with boards. Don't do this. It sucks up time and hampers your ability to
  focus on the most strategic challenges.

- **As the company gets bigger, cull the slide deck.**
  Founders often get in the habit of filling out the same templates for
  each meeting. As the company grows, they add new slides for new parts
  of the business. Before you know it, you have a 50-slide deck. Cull
  it! "Curating the deck is as important as curating the conversation,"
  Pat Grady says. Make it a habit to cut slides that have receded in
  importance. "Unless you make a deliberate choice to stop talking about
  something, you'll fall prey to inertia," he adds.

- **(Optional) Write a narrative about each of the strategic issues.**
  The primary document for most board meetings is a slide deck. But
  isolated pieces of data or short bullet points don't communicate
  nuance and complexity. If you feel so inspired, sit down and write a
  three- to five-page summary of at least one (if not all) of the issues
  you're struggling with, and send it to the directors along with the
  deck. I've seen this work very well for Todd. It gives the board a clear
  sense of the most important things on his mind. "A written narrative
  really crystallizes what you thought of those data points and what is
  concerning you as the person running the business," explains Pat. "It's
  also a way for you to make sure you actually understand the issue and
  that you're prepared to discuss it."

OUTSIDE OF BOARD MEETINGS

You can contact board members outside of formal meetings. Most directors
are fine getting calls from founders who need help with something in
the director's wheelhouse. In the early days, when it's just you and your
cofounders, you might find yourself contacting an investor daily. "I don't
think it's unreasonable to want to be on the phone every single day," Pat
says. "The board member is like a cofounder at that point." In other situations, when a board member is very busy, you have to be more strategic
about when you hit that person up. In all cases, make sure your conversations are tightly focused and that you're asking for help with something
specific. You want to use their time effectively.

* Now, as a public company, we're
required by the SEC to hold votes.
But even so, it's mostly a formality
because we're able to reach
consensus through discussion.

Board Majority Doesn't Matter

Until it does.

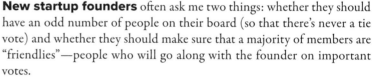

New startup founders often ask me two things: whether they should have an odd number of people on their board (so that there's never a tie vote) and whether they should make sure that a majority of members are "friendlies"—people who will go along with the founder on important votes.

Here's what I tell them: Don't worry about it.

In theory, boards use votes to make decisions. In practice, however, the vote should just be a formality. If you've chosen good people and you work well with them, you should all be on the same page. I don't think that the Okta board ever voted on anything when we were a private company, other than maybe officially confirming financing plans and equity grants.* We generally made decisions through discussion, which is common for start-ups. If you find yourself with such a deeply divided board that you need to take votes to settle matters, then you have a more foundational problem than the mere number of members on your board.

The only times I've heard about startup boards holding votes is when they've decided to remove the founder from the CEO slot—and the founder is not going willingly. (Votes also sometimes take place on financing plans that have gotten contentious.) But even voting to oust the founder is rare. Not because boards don't sometimes need the founder to step down. That happens. But boards usually are able to get CEOs to leave willingly through a mutual (if not always amicable) agreement regarding separation terms. A board vote to oust a CEO is such an extreme move that it often damages the value of the company (especially if litigation ensues), which is something both the board members and the CEO, who still has shares, want to avoid.

Remember, Your Board Isn't Your Boss

As the CEO, you don't have a boss. The buck stops with you. You make all the decisions about how to run your company. (Although if you're a cofounder but not the CEO, then you do have a boss—the CEO.)

A board will never give orders. That's not their job. Sure, some directors might *very strongly* suggest that a certain course of action would be a *really good idea*. But it still remains advice. They don't have the right to actually tell you what to do. "It's up to the CEO to internalize feedback and choose which parts of it they want to act on," says Pat Grady. "After all, the board could be wrong."

The only way in which the board *is* like your boss is that they hold the power to fire you and hire another CEO. They represent the shareholders. It's their responsibility to ensure the company is being run well. If they lose confidence in the choices you're making, they might decide to cut you loose. "If you're the kind of person who is motivated by feeling like you need to deliver for someone else, then go ahead and think of them as your boss," Pat adds. But otherwise, simply think of them as strategic partners who are highly motivated to ensure you get things right.

A Cautionary Tale
The right board for the wrong mission.

Jawbone was one of the most exciting consumer electronics companies on the scene in the late 2000s when it released one of the first high-quality Bluetooth headsets. Wireless earbuds are commonplace today, but back then, they represented newfound freedom from the tangled cords of wired headsets.

Alex Asseily is the first to admit that Jawbone had a lot of challenges. Despite their first-mover advantage, they had to shut down in the late 2010s. One of the mistakes Alex talks about was the composition of his company's board. It was full of very experienced investors and operators—but most came from the software or enterprise sectors, not the world of consumer technology, much less consumer hardware. "They couldn't see around those corners," Alex says. "And that's ultimately what you want—someone who can see around corners."

Alex compares building a startup to climbing Mount Everest. "You need someone to tell you how much rope you need or whether you take the crevasse route or the ice sheet route," he says. "Consumer products are just very different from enterprise products. You have inventory. You have hardware development. It's much less forgiving if you make mistakes because you ship a whole bunch of products, and you can't easily get them back" if they're faulty—the way you can fix bugs with software updates if your product sits in the cloud.

Looking back, Alex wishes he'd brought a few people on to the board who had direct experience with the issues Jawbone faced: brand-marketing experience for consumer products, consumer-product finance and operations, or hardware experience. "It's really important for founders to understand the kind of business they're in and then bring on people who have climbed that particular mountain," he says. "Those are the people who are going to help the most."

How to Build Credibility with Your Board
And how to lose it.

In the beginning, your board is going to think you're amazing. They wouldn't back you if they didn't. But that can change once they start working with you up close. You need to maintain your credibility with your directors because they have the ability to go to bat for you when you go through rough patches. They won't do that if they lose faith in you. And faith, once lost, is very difficult to regain.

Credibility with your board comes down to two things:

1 **Honesty.** Be candid with the board about the state of the company—where you're doing well and where the challenges are. It's natural to want to deliver a rosy picture, but a picture that's too rosy won't allow you to get the help you need from your directors. Worse, they'll see right through it. They've been to this rodeo. "If I've got to ask a lot of questions to uncover the issues, it makes me wonder what else I don't know," says Shellye Archambeau.

2 **Execution.** If you say you're going to do something, *do it*. The board's role is to make sure the company can grow. The most basic way to believe in the CEO's ability to scale the company is to see that he or she can follow through. If you fail to deliver on what you've promised, the board will question your ability to tackle the even bigger issues coming your way.

On the other hand, one thing that won't impact your credibility with the board is whether you take *all* their advice. In fact, doing so might be a red flag. "Nobody knows the company better than you do," Shellye says. "If a CEO always does everything a board says, I'd be concerned." Instead, listen to their advice and then process it as you would any other person's whose experience and insight you value. Integrate their wisdom with what you already know about your business, and then make the best decision for the company.

When Issues Arise

Your directors are members of your team, and when issues arise with a director's performance, address it the way you would an employee's (while remembering, of course, that this person is not an employee):

When a director doesn't seem engaged, but you want to keep them.
If you know a director can be valuable, but they don't seem engaged—for example, they don't show up prepared, or they don't participate in discussions—reach out to let them know you value their participation and ask if there's anything you can do to ramp up their involvement.

When a director doesn't seem engaged, and you *don't* want to keep them.
Sometimes you realize someone's not a great fit, or they don't have as much to offer as you'd hoped. In this case, broach their lack of engagement respectfully but directly. "You can just go to them and say, 'It doesn't seem like you want to be here. If I'm reading

Seriously, Skip the Board of Advisors

They're not worth the time and money.

A board of advisors is simply a group of people you can call on for their expertise. They have no role in oversight or governance, as the board of directors does. Instead, in return for some equity, they're "on retainer" so you can get insights or help on specific issues you're struggling with. Plus, if they're particularly famous, their names on your website can help wow potential investors, potential hires, or customers.

On paper, a board of advisors sounds great. My take is controversial: I don't think such a board is a great idea. Here's why:

- **Advisors aren't engaged enough to be able to really help.** Sure, they're on speed-dial. But they don't have the depth of knowledge about what's going on with your product or company to be able to offer highly useful insights—not without you spending hours on the phone just to get them caught up. Plus, they aren't always accessible the way your board members are. They squeeze you into their limited downtime, and they sometimes act like they're doing you a favor. Some even forget that they're an advisor, and when you call for help, you have to remind them of their commitment. Crazy, but true.

- **You pay them a lot for not much return.** Advisor arrangements are often just for a single year. Need to talk to Advisor Bob three months after that year runs out? Technically, you're out of luck—or will have to draft a whole new advisor agreement (often for more equity), which is grating when they still have the old equity that you're working your butt off to make ever more valuable.

- **Advisor shares can complicate your cap table—*if they start piling up.*** The capitalization table ("cap table") is a document that lists everyone who has shares in your company, along with the many assorted rights they have. Every time you raise a new round, the cap table is updated, based on the agreements with the new set of investors. There's a lot of complexity in managing a cap table, and advisor shares quickly become vestigial remains of something that once might have been useful but isn't anymore.

Bottom line: There's a lot of complexity—and cost—involved in setting up a board of advisors. You're much better off turning to a network of peers or hiring a particular expert as a consultant. If nothing else, you can always try seeing if someone will talk to you in an isolated case as a favor. Some people are receptive, especially if they can learn from you too. (They might want your front-row insights into customers or industry dynamics, for example.) Just don't forget to send them a nice bottle of wine afterward.

---

that correctly, would you like to be excused?'" advises Pat Grady. Things may have shifted in their lives, or they simply might not have the time they thought they would. They might actually welcome the opportunity to bow out.

When you want to replace a director with someone else at their firm.

This is tricky. If a board director from a VC firm isn't cutting it, you might decide that someone else at their firm would do a better job. Whether you're in a position to ask the firm to make a switch depends on how well your company is doing. If you are one of their top-performing startups, the firm will be motivated to keep you happy and may accommodate you. But if your performance sits in the middle of their portfolio or, worse, down toward the bottom, the firm probably won't be receptive. (Making a change is a disruptive move for them—egos and all that.) Instead, you might try to find ways to help the board member be more productive.

twelve

IPOS

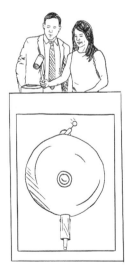

Okta went public on Friday, April 7, 2017. We sold 11 million shares at $17 apiece. As we rang the NASDAQ opening bell that morning, it probably looked pretty good on TV. While it took eight years to get there, by outside metrics, we had succeeded.

Neither Todd nor I saw it that way, however. The IPO wasn't a finish line. It was just the beginning—more like a graduation from high school. Now it was time to *really* get cracking.

There's a lot of mythology around IPOs, so much so that it's easy to think that going public is the whole point of launching a startup: cash out, retire to a beach, and start drawing up plans for rockets to Mars.

But that would be wrong. The IPO is just a way station on the road to getting *really* big. Microsoft was a $600 million company when it IPO'd. Today it's worth more than $2.5 *trillion*. Stitch Fix IPO'd at $1.6 billion in 2017. Four years later, it's worth more than twice that.

No one tracks what percentage of startups make it from zero to IPO, but if you look at the drop-off rate at each round of funding, it's clear that the number is minuscule. A ballpark estimate would be that only one-tenth of the companies that make it to a Series A actually ever get acquired or go public. So if your motive is to get rich quick, take my advice: do something else.

In fact, if you had to take just a single lesson from this book, I'd want it to be this: *Find something you love to do, and focus on that*. If that happens to be building a company, then the IPO shouldn't change much. You'll be working on your company before the IPO, and you'll be working on it after.

Here's what happened with me after Okta's IPO. After the opening bell ceremony, Todd and I flew back to San Francisco and threw a party for all our employees and their families. Then I slept through most of the weekend. On Monday morning, I got up early and was back in the office by 7 a.m. for a sales call with a large European bank. That's what it looked like to transform into a public company. No resting on our laurels. No jetting off to tropical islands. We'd won the pie-eating contest. Now it was time to eat more pie.

To Offer or Not to Offer
Upsides and downsides of going public.

While much of the fanfare around an IPO focuses on which players are suddenly drowning in wealth, for the company itself, going public is an inflection point. Many newly public companies are still technically only in their infancy. Going public is often a step the company takes so it can get much bigger. Being public brings a slew of advantages that you don't have when you're private. (As I like to remind entrepreneurs, IPOs aren't about *going* public, they're about *being* public!)

FIVE IPO UPSIDES

1 **It raises your profile.** An IPO is a once-in-a-lifetime media opportunity. Many publications will want to write about you, some for the first time. Plus, the overall excitement generates enthusiasm among prospective customers.

2 **You get new customers.** When you're a small private company, there are whole swaths of larger organizations and government agencies who won't buy from you. To them, private companies are too risky. What if a company they depended on went bankrupt? Being public puts your financials out in the open. Those larger prospects can now reassure themselves you're a legitimate and thriving concern.

3 **International customers become more interested.** The NASDAQ and the New York Stock Exchange are, alongside London, Hong Kong, and Tokyo, the biggest exchanges in the world. When you list with exchanges like these, it ups your standing overseas and opens up new markets.

4 **A new tranche of employees and executives are now interested in working for you.** Startups aren't for everyone. If you've got a mortgage or kids headed to college, you can't take a pay cut to roll the dice on a company that could very well fail. Many experts in the things you need to grow really big require more stability than you could previously offer. Now, however, they'll be willing to come on board.

5 **It becomes a more efficient way to raise money.** Fundraising from venture capitalists takes a huge amount of time: meetings after meetings to get small piles of cash that you have to pay for with big chunks of shares. Once you're on the public exchanges, you can raise a billion dollars in a morning simply by issuing debt or selling shares on the open market.

But it's not all sunshine and rainbows. Being public also creates complications.

THREE IPO DOWNSIDES

1 **You are now on the quarterly treadmill.** Once you go public, you're required to file quarterly reports about how you're doing. Suddenly, you have to start thinking in 90-day cycles. It's a big shift. And it makes it harder to innovate. Innovation requires investment—short-term increases in costs—which Wall Street doesn't like. Making decisions about how to grow your company becomes a lot harder.

2 **You can't be as transparent with your employees.** At Okta, transparency is one of our corporate values, but SEC rules regarding the "quiet periods" before and after the end of a quarter mean that there are a lot of things we can't discuss publicly for about half the year. In fact, Todd and I now have to send all presentations to the legal department to make sure we're not inadvertently breaking the law. "No comment" becomes your go-to phrase.

3 **You're subject to the vagaries of the stock market.** You might be doing fine, but if you're a tech company, and Wall Street suddenly goes sour on tech stocks, you could see your price tank through no fault of your own.

INSIGHT

We wanted to build a special company where employees were happy, and customers were happy, and we had fun, and we innovated. The IPO was just a step along the way. I think we were slightly over $200 million in revenues when we went public, and now we're supposed to do $2.7 billion in revenue. So the IPO is a rite of passage. It's not the end. It's a place that helps you continue to accelerate the business.

—Aneel Bhusri, Workday

It's Your Coming-Out Party, Not Theirs

Most CEOs dread the tedious, expensive process of putting together an IPO. "I could not find one person who said they enjoyed going public," says Eventbrite cofounder Julia Hartz. Most CEOs accept it as a necessary evil, and many outsource as much as possible to their CFO. Not Julia. "If you have a clear intention, it can be a very positive moment and momentum-builder for the company," she says. Here's how she handled it:

SHE TOOK CONTROL

"What normally happens is a bunch of bankers and lawyers who've done this a million times run you through this gamut," Julia says. It creates a lot of churn and disruption for the startup's executives. "I thought, 'If we're going to do this, we're going to do it our way and try to get the maximum value out of it.'" Julia invited all those outsiders to a kickoff meeting at her home (which she shares with her husband and cofounder, Kevin). "The kids served them drinks, and I handed out Eventbrite jerseys," she says. It was a rite of initiation: "I told them, 'We're now all the same team. We're going to create a dynamic of mutual respect and accountability.'"

SHE TURNED THE S-1 DRAFTING INTO A STRATEGIC EXERCISE

The S-1 is the official SEC document a company must file to register its shares with the exchange they're joining. It's a beast. Julia decided to use the drafting process as an opportunity to review Eventbrite's 12-year history. "It allowed us to get crystal clear about what we had built and where we were going," she recalls. "We were codifying our strategy and really defining our market for the world for the first time."

SHE USED IT AS A BRANDING EVENT

Eventbrite has historically been confused with Ticketmaster and other ticketing services. But it actually operates in a different space, giving individuals and small to midsized organizations everything they need to set up, promote, and sell tickets for an event. The best way to communicate that was through their users' stories, which Eventbrite folded into their S-1 and investor presentations. "We used the story of our customers as the vehicle to explain how we're different and why people buy what we do," Julia says. When it came time to ring the bell on the floor of the New York Stock Exchange, some of those users came with them. In September 2018, Eventbrite went public at $23 a share, raising $230 million. "We came out of it a stronger company," she says. The money helped accelerate the creation of new features and services for customers.

The IPO Roadshow

Not for the faint of heart.

The two weeks before your IPO, you'll make a whirlwind trip around the country—the "roadshow"—to talk about your company with institutional investors, the people who decide whether to buy your shares. It's an exhausting expedition. Todd and I met with 330 people at 262 institutions over the course of two weeks in New York, Los Angeles, Boston, Philadelphia, Baltimore, and Kansas City, as well as in our hometown of San Francisco.

There's a long-term goal as well. You want these investors to develop confidence in you and the company, so that, in the years ahead when you hit the inevitable potholes, they won't race for the exits. The best way to do that is by meeting them and making your case in person.

Your underwriters* will walk you through the process of pitching the investors, but here are a few tips the bankers won't tell you.

DO

- **Pace yourself.** You might have as many as 10 to 15 meetings a day. You have to bring your A game to each one of them. Take a lot of deep breaths, eat well, sleep when you're able, stay hydrated, and check in with your family regularly.

- **Listen.** This is as much an opportunity for you to learn about the investors as it is for them to learn about you. Some of these organizations will become major shareholders. They'll play as important a role in your company going forward as your VCs did in the past.

- **Take notes on who should get first dibs on shares—and who shouldn't.** After your meetings, the investors will let your underwriter know whether they want in and, if so, how many shares they want to purchase and at what price. This is called "book building." If you're lucky enough to get oversubscribed—meaning, there's more demand for your shares than the number of shares being offered—you, the founder (along with your advisors, board members, and bankers), get to decide who gets what.[†]

  During our roadshow, I had someone on my team discreetly take photos of every person we met so that, later, when we were building the book, we could remember who they were. This might sound trivial, but we were oversubscribed, so in some cases, our decisions about who got into the book simply came down to who had come across as a decent person and who had acted like a jerk.

- **Bring enough clothes, so that you have a clean outfit every day.** You won't have time for hotel laundry.

* Your underwriter is the investment bank (or banks) that do the logistical work of putting the IPO together.

† Okta's IPO ended up being heavily oversubscribed. We received almost 27 times more requests for shares than we were offering. You might read a lot about oversubscriptions in the media. It's a metric they get excited about, but it's often overhyped. Its biggest significance is just that it means we were successful in convincing Wall Street that we were a company worth betting on.

DON'T

- **Get too cocky or too bummed.** If a meeting goes poorly, move on. You've got another 20, 40, or 60 ahead of you. And if you do great, don't let it get to your head. Every new meeting sets the scoreboard back to zero. Play accordingly.

- **Stay out late, or make plans to see friends.** Keep the main thing the main thing: You're here to wow investors. Every minute you're not doing that should be spent sleeping, eating, or preparing.

- **Let the process overwhelm you.** Easier said than done. I certainly hit a wall at times. But if you can, take a minute or two when you're shuttling between meetings or flying from one city to the next. Pause, take a breather, and smile. It'll all be over soon!

The Alt-IPOs

There are other ways to go public.

Doing an IPO is a lengthy and expensive proposition. Underwriters charge a lot of money—typically 3–7 percent of the total proceeds that the company generates from this initial public sale. Startups can end up leaving a lot of money on the table if their stock price "pops" on the first day (goes up significantly). That's great for investors, but not so great for the company, which loses out on that extra money they could have reaped if the stock had been priced higher out of the gate. In recent years, some startups have looked to two other vehicles for getting onto public exchanges. Each has advantages and disadvantages:

1 **Direct listing**. In an IPO, the underwriter facilitates the whole process. They help investors get to know the company, which builds confidence in the stock and interest in buying it. In a direct listing, a company puts *themselves* on the exchange. It's a much less involved process and significantly less expensive. Plus, there's no lock-up period.* In a direct listing, any shareholder can start selling immediately.

Unlike in an IPO, however, no new shares are created, so no money is raised for the company. Companies that choose this route are already healthily funded. But getting onto the exchange enables their original investors to cash out. Still, because there's a less involved process of investor education, a company that is not well known can suffer if buyers don't show up.

Companies that have done direct listings: Slack, Spotify, Asana.

COMPANIES THAT HAVE DONE DIRECT LISTINGS:

Slack

Spotify

Asana

* The Securities and Exchange Commission, which regulates the stock market, usually bars shareholders from selling their stock for 90 or 180 days after a company goes public, during what's called the "lock-up period." This prevents the market from being flooded with stock on the actual day the company goes public.

DraftKings

2 **SPACs (Special Purpose Acquisition Companies).** These are somewhat convoluted, so bear with me. A SPAC is a shell company that raises money in an IPO on a public exchange in order to buy an *as-yet unnamed company*. Investors are willing to put money in SPACs because they have faith in the people behind them— the same way limited partners are willing to invest in VC funds because of their belief in the VCs. A startup can later go public through the backdoor by getting acquired by that SPAC. The chief reason for going this route is often just speed. The IPO process takes a long time. Being acquired by a SPAC involves negotiating directly with the SPAC itself. Once a company is acquired, the SPAC's shareholders now have public shares and can cash out through the exchange.

Companies that have done SPACs: DraftKings, Virgin Galactic, Vivint Smart Home.

Virgin Galactic

Vivint Smart Home

Not Ready? Don't Get Ahead of Yourself

An almost fatal mistake is to go public before you're actually ready. You need to be a company Wall Street can depend on. Otherwise, you'll get creamed. Your stock price will tank because investors lack confidence in your ability to perform.

How do you know you're ready? A key rule of thumb is that you should have a track record of "operating like a public company" for at least four quarters prior to your IPO. (Eight quarters is better.) This boils down to being able to accurately forecast key metrics (starting with revenue, margins, cash flow, and profitability) several quarters ahead. You need to master this because once you're public, most companies give Wall

Street guidance on where they expect their numbers to land in the coming quarter and the year ahead—and you need to be able to deliver what you say you will.

It usually takes 16 quarters (four years!) of consistently accurate forecasts before Wall Street has confidence in a company. Why does that matter? Because no matter how well you do, you'll inevitably hit bumps in the road and miss a forecast. Investors who believe in your company are more likely to forgive the hiccups—to chalk them up to one-off situations that don't signal any foundational problem with the company. Lack of such confidence means those bumps will send investors running for the hills.

thirteen

WHAT COMES NEXT

A

s I said in the previous chapter, Todd and I viewed Okta's IPO as a high school graduation. During the previous eight years, we had mastered the basics of creating and running a great company. We'd figured out a product that large enterprises wanted to buy. We'd refined it into a powerful offering. We'd put all the pieces in place to execute on a large scale. And we'd proven that we could generate continuing and meaningful profits. But we still planned to get bigger than we were when we filed our S-1 and rang the bell on the NASDAQ. Much bigger. Going public just meant we were ready to *really* start scaling.

The IPO was a strategic choice. It wasn't about cashing out and retiring, as the popular mythology would sometimes have you believe. It was about *becoming* a public company—and gaining all the advantages that being public would give us, so we could become so much bigger than we were. Being public meant there were many more companies and organizations that would be willing to do business with Okta, businesses that were too big to roll the dice on a startup but that would now be open to talking to us. We'd also be able to hire a whole range of new executives and professionals who had the expertise to help us perform at this much larger scale but who also tended to avoid startups in favor of the stability of larger public companies. And then there were the many potential client companies overseas for whom a listing on the NASDAQ was an important signifier—of both stability and capabilities.

To achieve this growth, however, to keep cranking, we had to make sure our employees didn't bonk at the IPO. "Bonking" is a term runners use to describe what happens when their bodies run out of gas. They go from 60 to 0 in a split second. One minute, they're flying. The next, they're struggling for every step. At Okta, we had to make sure the team wasn't so laser-focused on the IPO that the second we crossed the line, they'd lose steam and deflate. So we did what any leader would do: we moved the goalposts.

About nine months before the IPO, Todd and I started talking to our employees about our vision of building Okta into an iconic technology company. We talked about emulating companies like Salesforce, Oracle, and Intel. We didn't just want to become successful in number terms. We wanted to be the leaders in our field. Todd and I explained that this is something that takes *years* to achieve, far beyond the go-public date. We talked about what was involved in achieving such a status—how organizations like these had a certain number of customers, this much revenue, and these kinds of growth models. The IPO, we explained, was just the beginning of a much bigger dream. The more we talked about it, the more excited our team became.

We did something else around that time that might seem counterintuitive but that was consistent with moving the goalposts: we stopped talking about the IPO. It had, of course, been an endless source of discussion the previous seven years, as was natural for a company where employees stood to watch their bank accounts grow once their stock options became liquid. But that summer of 2016, when Todd and I announced that the IPO would take place within the next year, we let the company know we wouldn't be talking about it anymore. We were required to do so anyway due to the SEC-mandated "quiet period," which effectively bars executives from speaking publicly about their company. But strategically, we wanted to start directing the team's attention to the new goalposts.

We also wanted to stave off a potential exodus of employees, as sometimes happens once startups go public. After all, once they could cash in their shares, many people would make tidy fortunes. If people started thinking about leaving, they could lose focus on the work that remained. (The stories about Silicon Valley office parking lots filling up with Porsches and Teslas following an IPO are more or less true.) We didn't want our talented and highly valued people walking out because they'd been infected with never-have-to-work-again fever. The best way to prevent that was to give them big new exciting goals.

This idea of moving a team's goalposts *before* you reach a target is one we've used throughout Okta's history. Of course, it's important to give people a chance to celebrate their big wins. For the Okta IPO, we rented out AT&T Park (now called Oracle Park, home of the San Francisco Giants) and invited everyone to bring their families to a big party. But by the time you celebrate, everyone should already be cranking away on the next goal. For example, if you get everyone excited to hit $10 million in revenue, then as soon as you start getting near $6 or $8 million, you need to move the goalposts to $25 million. Celebrate the $10 million when it arrives, and then when you get to $20 million, move the goalposts again, this time to $50 million. Celebrate the $25 million when you hit it . . . and so on.

I'm telling you this because I hope it will help inspire you. As I said in the beginning of this book, our future depends on *you*. The vast majority of new jobs will come from the companies created by entrepreneurs. The more of you who succeed, the stronger our economy will be.

I hope by now I've convinced you of two things: Taking this route will send you down one of the most difficult paths you've ever walked. But it will also be one of the most rewarding. I wish you the best of luck in navigating the shoals and storms that await you. But if you do, then like me, you may well discover there's nothing else you'd rather do.

> The IPO was a strategic choice. It wasn't about cashing out and retiring. . . . We wanted to be the leaders in our field.

ACKNOWLEDGMENTS

Though only my name appears on the cover, this book was the ultimate team effort. (As I always say, "You win as a team!") Thank you to everyone on the immediate and extended team for all your help, support, and guidance every step of the way.

Thank you first to my amazing wife, Sara, for encouraging me throughout my entrepreneurial journey, especially during the darker days and months. To my three wonderful children, Nico, Zoe, and Charlie, for keeping me grounded and honest. To my sister, Juliana, and brother, Marc, for putting up with my entrepreneurial antics from a young age. And to my parents, Sandra and Jacques, the best role models any child could want, who gave me endless opportunities and without whom none of this would have been possible.

Thank you to the personal and professional mentors who nurtured me along the way. Doug Flanzer and Saul Kato, two of my oldest and dearest friends, took me under their wings when I was a wayward undergraduate and taught me about self-determination, responsibility, and hard work. My cousin Adrien Laugier-Werth always models the importance of a positive outlook, a growth mindset, and a deep sense of family and humanity. Roger Goulart is the best manager I ever had, and he showed me what true leadership looks like.

The dozen-plus professional years that preceded the creation of Okta helped me grow as a leader and laid the groundwork for what we've been able to achieve since. Thank you to Benton Moyer, who introduced me (with the necessary dose of humor) to the school of hard knocks in South America. Eric Eyken-Sluyters, Jim Steele, and Frank van Veenendaal showed me what excellent corporate leadership looks like during rapid growth, and at scale. The entire MIT ecosystem—led by President Emerita Susan Hockfield, MIT Sloan School of Management Dean David Schmittlein, MIT Sloan Associate Dean Kathy Hawkes, MIT Sloan Assistant Dean of Admissions Rod Garcia, Professor Ed Roberts, Managing Director of the

Martin Trust Center for MIT Entrepreneurship Bill Aulet, MIT Sloan Associate Dean for Innovation and Inclusion Fiona Murray, Professor Antoinette Schoar, Ken Morse, Jennifer Burke Barba, Howard Anderson, Shari Loessberg, Peter Kurzina, and Scott Alessandro—welcomed me with open arms and professionalized my entrepreneurial inclinations. Lars Leckie, Mark Gorenberg, John Hummer, Ann Winblad, Mitchell Kertzman, and the HWVP (now Aspenwood Ventures) team gave me my first peek behind the VC curtain.

I'll never be able to adequately express my gratitude to Todd McKinnon for taking a flyer on me when he was looking for a cofounder back in 2009. Thank you, Todd, for teaching me so much about leadership, partnership, and building for the long term. To say that Okta has had a major impact on both my personal and professional lives would be an understatement! Thank you also to my friend Charlie Dietrich, who served as a strong mutual reference while Todd and I were "founder dating," and to my friend Alex Asseily, who set off down the entrepreneurial path ahead of me and who always had time to lend an ear while also, with his Jawbone cofounder Hosain Rahman, providing a literal roof over our heads when Todd and I were first starting out.

Ben Horowitz, Marc Andreessen, and Scott Kupor at Andreessen Horowitz took a bet on us when we were just two guys with an idea and a really bad pitch deck. They not only stuck with us when the going got really rough but readily called in experts like Margit Wennmachers, John O'Farrell, Mark Cranney, and Jeff Stump to help us solve some of our biggest challenges. Pat Grady, Doug Leone, Jim Goetz, Carl Eschenbach, Roelof Botha, Matt Miller, and Sequoia Capital—the most well-prepared venture firm I've ever met—brought endless expertise and perspective to help us accelerate our vision. Aneel Bhusri, Asheem Chandna, Reid Hoffman, Sarah Guo, Jeff Markowitz, Tom Frangione, and Greylock Partners generously shared their experience and network. Ron Conway, Scott Jordon, Vinod Khosla, Mike Maples, Steve Marcus, Ann Miura-Ko, Maynard Webb, and David Weiden are foremost among the early-stage investors who channeled their hard-earned wisdom our way.

Thanks to Ed Haddon, Hassan Shabber, and Dr. Bruce Victor for helping me keep my mental, physical, and emotional health in balance over the past decade, and for helping me grow, both as a person and a leader. Thanks also to my amazing executive assistant and longtime business partner, Jessica Martinez, who is the key to my getting anything done.

Thank you to the generation of entrepreneurs ahead of us, who always had time to share advice and feedback, including Brian Halligan and Dharmesh Shah of HubSpot, David Schneider of ServiceNow, and Tien Tzuo of Zuora. Thanks to the members of Okta's board of directors, both past and present, for the guidance and direction over the years: Shellye Archambeau, Aneel Bhusri, Robert Dixon, Jeff Epstein, Pat Grady, Ben Horowitz, Mike Kourey, Becky Saeger, Mike Stankey, and Michelle Wilson. I've been lucky to count on invaluable advisors, including Byron Deeter of Bessemer Venture Partners, Saar Gur of CRV, Enrique Salem of Bain Capital Ventures, former Frontier Communications CEO Maggie

"Magic" Wilderotter, Rich Wong at Accel, and our longtime counsels from incorporation to this day—Anthony McCusker of Goodwin Procter and Sarah Axtell and Rick Kline of Latham Watkins.

Thanks to everyone who helped make this book a reality: my dear friend and partner in crime Josh Davis of Epic; Liza Boyd, who time and again took my jumbled thoughts and somehow made them sound cogent; the tireless Epic team, including Clark Miller, Kiana Moore, Josh Levine, Jon Steinberg, and Will Staehle; my literary agent, Jim Levine; my editor, Casey Ebro, and the team at McGraw Hill Professional; my friends and colleagues who took the time to read rough drafts and provide thoughtful feedback, including Ryan Carlson, Emily Chang, Charlie Dietrich, Avid Larizadeh Duggan, Mark Gorenberg, Lindsay Life, Mike Kourey, Dharmesh Shah, and Maynard Webb.

Many of the insights and stories in this book come from the entrepreneurs and investors who were kind enough to participate in the *Zero to IPO* podcast that preceded it: Marc Andreessen, Alex Asseily, Aneel Bhusri, Jeremy Bloom, Stewart Butterfield, Beth Comstock, Jasmine Crowe, Charlie Dietrich, Carl Eschenbach, Parker Harris, Julia Hartz, Ben Horowitz, Frederick Hutson, Andre Iguodala, Josh James, Aaron Levie, Fred Luddy, Patty McCord, Ann Miura-Ko, Melanie Perkins, Amy Pressman, Sebastian Thrun, Therese Tucker, Tien Tzuo, Maggie Wilderotter, and Eric Yuan. Thank you as well to Shellye Archambeau, Paul Arnold, Ilya Levtov, Mariam Naficy, Shashank Saxena, Alfredo Vaamonde, and Michelle Wilson who generously shared what they've learned from their many years in the trenches.

Thank you to everyone at The Operator Network (TheOperator Network.com), an angel investment group of public company executives I founded to help the next generation of entrepreneurs with operating advice alongside our personal capital. You inspire me, and I learn from you every day: Bradley Armstrong, Kristin Baker, Ryan Carlson, Charlie Dietrich, Mike Dinsdale, Avid Larizadeh Duggan, Stacey Epstein, Viviana Faga, Todd Ford, Tom Gonser, Roger Goulart, Alex Huff, Aaron Katz, Jacques Kerrest, Clark Lindsey, Bill Losch, Olivia Nottebohm, Jonathan Runyan, David Schellhase, David Schneider, Marty Vanderploeg, Dan Wright, and Kelly Wright.

Finally, thank you to every seasoned entrepreneur who takes the time to field calls from new founders. You are helping the next generation build a better tomorrow for all of us.

INDEX

ABOUT THE AUTHOR

Frederic Kerrest is the executive vice chairman, COO, and cofounder of Okta, an enterprise software company that IPO'd in 2017 at a $2 billion valuation and now has a market cap of over $40 billion. Frederic is responsible for establishing and driving Okta's corporate priorities; accelerating innovation across the company; working closely with customers, partners, and prospects; and serving as a key liaison with the investor community.

A software entrepreneur at heart, Frederic cohosts the *Zero to IPO* podcast, featuring founders, entrepreneurs, and investors who share insights from their experiences building innovative technology companies. He serves on the Executive Advisory Board of the Martin Trust Center for MIT Entrepreneurship and advises early-stage software company founders. Frederic is also the chairman and cofounder of Herophilus, a platform drug discovery company.

Frederic earned a BS in computer science from Stanford University and an MBA in entrepreneurship and innovation from the MIT Sloan School of Management. Outside of work, he enjoys spending time with his family, reading, skiing, and playing ice hockey.

Please visit ZeroToIPObook.com.

FROM ZERO TO IPO— AND BEYOND

Continue the journey and visit ZeroToIPOpodcast.com for episodes of the *Zero to IPO* podcast series, featuring conversations with:

Marc Andreessen

Fred Luddy

Melanie Perkins

Ben Horowitz

Patty McCord

Aneel Bhusri

Sebastian Thrun

Andre Iguodala

Beth Comstock

and more

For more insight and opportunities to engage with Frederic, follow him on Twitter and LinkedIn at: fkerrest